THE
COUNSELING
PROCESS

SECOND EDITION

THE COUNSELING PROCESS

SECOND EDITION

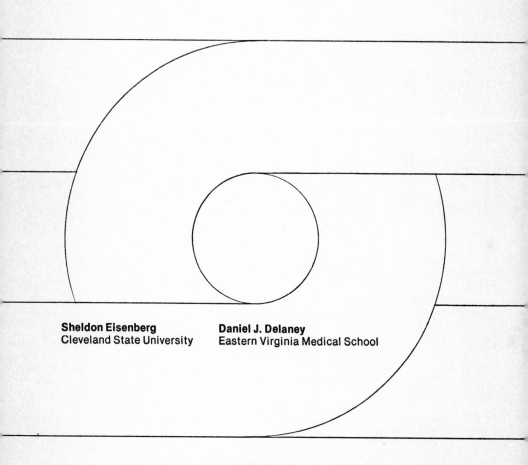

Sheldon Eisenberg
Cleveland State University

Daniel J. Delaney
Eastern Virginia Medical School

Rand McNally College Publishing Company, Chicago

Rand McNally Education Series

B. Othanel Smith, Advisory Editor

77 78 79 10 9 8 7 6 5 4 3 2

To Our Children
Jerry and Danny Eisenberg
Ann-Mary, Joe, Ed, Tom, Dan, and
Maureen Delaney
With Love

Preface to the second edition

The essential goal of this edition of *The Counseling Process* is the same as that of the first edition: to develop concepts and principles of effective interpersonal helping that counselors can use to critically assess and improve their helping efforts. Many changes have been made to improve this edition.

Six of the eleven chapters are completely new. Chapter 1 was developed to provide the reader with an overview of the essential qualities and attributes of effective helpers. While the goals of counseling were considered in the first edition, Chapter 2 in this text was developed to give the reader an expanded view of the different kinds of goals that are the work of the counselor. The purpose of Chapter 4 is to present a new and deeper insight into the important dimensions of counseling as a process. Chapter 6 provides extensive treatment of the confrontation process, a crucial part of the insight approaches to helping. Our understandings of the reluctant client have expanded considerably since the first edition. Chapter 7, therefore, deals with understanding and working with clients who are reluctant, a major concern of counselors in all settings. Chapter 10, "The Process of Marriage Counseling," is also new for this edition.

Much of the content of the first edition has also been reworked, specifically to clarify and present coverage of greater depth. For example, the different levels of empathy and self-exploration have been analyzed in greater detail. The Johari Window is used to describe the development of trust and open communication as ongoing processes. Different forms of defensiveness are discussed and types of counselor responses that facilitate and block communication are described more fully. The material on human emotions and self-concept has been reworked and now has much greater depth and clarity.

Another important change is that a new format has been used to present the major case studies. In the first edition verbatim typescripts were presented, but with limited analyses. In this edition an overview of the total helping process for each client is presented, along with information about the client as an individual. Sections of typescripts have been selected from a total interview to highlight how the important ideas in the chapter were actually incorporated into the counselor's work. Each case presentation is followed by an in-depth analysis, with an emphasis on using the concepts of the chapter as the basis for the analysis. The authors believe this new format will be much more effective in helping the reader relate theory and principle to actual situations.

Three new appendixes have also been added. The first has been designed to help the counselor write case notes in such a way as to clarify his or her thinking about the client and future sessions. The second appendix contains a survey instrument to help the client provide feedback about his or her counseling experience. The third is a presentation of a typescript for desensitization.

These changes occurred as a result of feedback from two sources: our own views about what changes would represent improvements and comments offered us by users of the first edition. We would especially like to thank those colleagues and students who took the time to share in-depth feedback with us.

We also wish to thank those whom we love for their understanding when we were not as available to them as they wanted us to be. Dr. Lewis E. Patterson, Chairperson of the Department of Educational Specialists at Cleveland State University and deeply valued friend, gave lots of help at a variety of levels. Through his personhood he has taught the senior author much about effective helping. Donna Magri and Marilyn Larcher are two very nice people who also happen to be fine secretaries.

Sheldon Eisenberg
Daniel J. Delaney

September, 1976

Contents

Chapter 3.

Chapter 4.

1. Some perspectives on effective helping

Consider the different occupational fields that use the term "counseling" in their titles. A long list comes to mind quickly: school counselors, employment counselors, marriage counselors, drug counselors, legal counselors, investment counselors, college counselors, and pastoral counselors. It is not by accident that these apparently diverse occupational fields all use the term "counselor" in their titles; they all have much in common. Exploring the areas of commonality helps to understand the essence of counseling.

Professionals in all these fields view themselves as helpers. They see themselves existing to provide helping services for people who want or need help. Indeed, because this is so, counseling is often described as a people-helping profession.

Although there are obvious differences in the specific focus of their helping efforts, the process of helping is much the same for these different counselors. All are approached by people who feel some level of stress and uneasiness about a concern or problem they need help in working through. At some point in the helping process, all see themselves as helping their clientele develop plans, clarify options, and make important decisions about future courses of action. All see themselves as providing information that their clients will find useful in coming to a decision, making plans, or working through a problem. All see themselves as helping their clients to identify options and to explore what is involved in implementing the different options available. High school counselors find themselves helping students develop post-high school plans. To do this, counselors may help students explore and clarify what they would like to do after high school as well as what they consider themselves capable of doing. The counselor may very well help the student find information about different career fields, and may also use a variety of self-assessment procedures to help the student acquire relevant and useful information about self (talents, interests, personality characteristics, etc.).

Similarly, a marriage and family counselor may help a couple concerned about the health of their marriage to analyze the dynamics of their family interaction patterns. The information that comes from this analysis can help the members of the family to develop more effective ways of relating to each other.

Frequently, counseling has a crisis orientation where the client experiences stress, agitation, disappointment, doubt, and confusion. An unemployed worker who needs help finding a new job, a family encountering marital unhappiness, an adolescent girl who is pregnant, a student who is an isolate and has no friends are a few examples. Ohlsen (1974) offers examples a high school counselor may expect to encounter as a part of his or her professional life:

———a student who has been let down or hurt by a loved and trusted one

———a student who is questioning the love and affection from someone he or she loves very much

———a student who feels guilty about hurting or letting down another

———a student who is grieving and depressed over the loss of a loved one

———a student who does something he believes is wrong and cannot cope adequately with feelings of guilt

———a student who recognizes a problem, but does not know how to solve or resolve it

————a student who is experiencing intense conflict and who is in a dilemma about what kind of action would be sensible and effective

————a student who intensely dislikes self

————a student who is unhappy about some important circumstance in her or his life, but does not know how to change these circumstances for the better

————a student who is capable of doing well in school, but who experiences debilitating anxiety about taking tests and performing well on classroom assignments

————a student who feels insecure about his or her ability to bring about a highly desired goal

At other times, counseling takes on a decision-making and developmental orientation, as, for example, the high school student who wishes to learn more about specific careers and who wishes to improve his job-seeking and interviewing skills; couples who perceive themselves as having a healthy marriage, but who wish to enrich it; people who desire to improve their interpersonal effectiveness; parents who wish to improve their parenting effectiveness; and people who wish to understand more fully themselves and others. Often, developmental counseling goals are pursued in group, rather than individual settings.

The essence of all counseling relationships, independent of their specific focus, is to help a person cope effectively with an important problem or concern, to develop plans and make important decisions to bring about a desired future, to acquire information about self and relevant aspects of the environment, and to explore and consider options available. Often the helping process also includes an exploration of the client's feelings and perceptions about self, significant others, and important aspects of his or her environment.

All counseling efforts, whether crisis based or developmental, have a clear focus on the client's future   The unemployed worker wants a job for his or her future. The family experiencing marital crisis want to work out the stress in their relationship so that they can look forward to a more enriched marriage relationship in their future. The choice the pregnant girl makes concerning what to do about her child will have a profound influence on her future life. Thus, an essential aspect of all counseling relationships is to help the client focus on his or her personal future and to explore what is desirable and what is possible, and to develop plans that can lead to a desirable future. Helping people focus on their personal futures is both a difficult and exciting process, which will be explored in Chapters 2 and 9.

Personal learning activities

Personal learning activities are provided in several chapters of this book. All have been designed from a discovery learning model. The intent of each is to help you, the reader, draw from important personal life experiences and to help you expand and enrich basic understandings of some aspect of effective helping. While most can be done in private, all will have more meaning if shared with others participating in the same learning experience. The purpose of the first personal learning activity is to help you identify the important qualities and characteristics of effective helpers.

Personal learning activity I

During your life you have encountered experiences where you were a receiver of help; you have also participated in other experiences where you were the provider of help. Whether or not these experiences were labeled as counseling, at important points in your life you have both given and received help. For this first exercise, think of two different occasions when you received help from another. The first occasion should be one in which the help you received was valuable to you, that is, the helper was effective in offering help to you. The second occasion should be one that did not result in success: you did not receive the help you needed; the helper somehow was not able to provide you with whatever you needed or wanted. In both instances, the helper might be a friend, spouse, parent, teacher, counselor, or someone who had administrative authority over you. However, the two experiences should involve two different helping people.

Using a paper and pen, think of the first experience and respond to the following questions:

———What kind of help were you seeking? (What were you concerned about? What did you hope to accomplish as a result of your discussion?)

———How did the helping person treat you? What were his or her basic attitudes toward you and your concerns?

———What response patterns did you notice about the person who offered help to you?

———What were the most memorable characteristics of the person who offered help to you?

When you have completed this activity with the first helping experience, respond to these questions again with the second (less successful) helping experience in mind. Do not proceed until you have completed this step.

Having completed both rounds, now compare and contrast the two helping experiences and the helpers who were involved. What factors were present during the first helping experience that were missing during the second? How did the two helpers differ from each other? Write down the comparisons you observed. Again, please do not proceed until you have completed this step.

Once you have completed your comparisons, see if you can verify from your own experiences the observations that follow.

Characteristics of effective helpers

What are some of the characteristics of effective helpers? While there are many problems in conducting conclusive research on this question, from the research that has been done, it is believed effective helping includes the following abilities and characteristics:

Effective helpers are skillful at reaching out   By their demeanor and underlying views about others they are able to help others communicate openly and honestly with them. They avoid responding in ways that create defensiveness and blocks to communication.

These helpers do this by participating in active and involved listening. They are able to concentrate fully on what is being communicated to them and not only to understand the content of what is being said, but also to appreciate the significance of what another is saying for his or her present and future well-being. They listen actively for the feelings, beliefs, perspectives, and assumptions about self, significant others, and life space circumstances. They are able to control their own feelings of anxiety while hearing of another person's concerns and anxieties.

Effective helpers inspire feelings of trust, credibility, and confidence from people they help   In the presence of effective helpers, clients quickly sense that it is all right to risk sharing their concerns and feelings openly. They will not be ridiculed, embarrassed, made to feel ashamed, or criticized for the thoughts, feelings, and perceptions they share. Nothing "bad" will happen as a consequence of sharing, and there is a very real chance that something gainful can come of it.

Effective helpers are also credible. What they say is perceived as believable and honest communication. Still further, effective helpers do not have hidden agendas or ulterior motives. They are viewed as honest, straightforward, and non-manipulative, again supporting the general perspective that they can be trusted.

Effective helpers are able to reach in as well as to reach out   They do a lot of thinking about their actions, feelings, value commitments, and motivations for their actions. They show a commitment to non-defensive, continuous self-understanding and self-examination. They are aware of feelings they experience and the sources of those feelings. They are able to manage anxiety by being aware of it and its sources rather than blotting it from awareness. They are able to respond with depth to the question, "Who am I?" They can help others think openly and non-defensively about themselves and their own concerns, because they are not afraid to participate in these experiences for themselves.

Effective helpers communicate caring and respect for the persons they are trying to help   They are able to communicate by their demeanor: "It matters to me that you will be able to work out the concerns and problems you are facing in the present. What happens to you in your future also matters to me. If things work out well for you and you achieve success, I shall be happy about it. If you encounter frustration and failure, I shall be saddened." The opposite of caring is not anger, but indifference. Effective helpers are not indifferent to the present and future of the people they try to help. To the contrary, effective helpers agree to offer time and energy to another because the future well-being of the person to whom they are reaching out matters to them.

To respect another person means to hold that person in regard and esteem. It means to have a favorable view toward that person—to acknowledge his or her talents and not think less of that person because of his or her limitations. Applied to effective helping, it means to believe that he or she is capable of learning, of overcoming obstacles to growth, and of maturing into a responsible, self-reliant individual. With this perspective, effective helpers communicate regard for others by offering their time and energy and by active, attentive listening which shows involvement. They also show respect by not treating the individual as if he or she were stupid or ridiculous, incapable of sensible thinking and reasoning. Effective helpers also like and respect themselves, but they are neither arrogant nor conceited and, thus, do not show arrogance toward the people they are helping.

Effective helpers like and respect themselves and do not use the people they are trying to help to satisfy their own needs   Every human being wants to be accepted, respected, and recognized by significant others and to be acknowledged for his or her special talents and achievements. However, some people are especially dependent on others for recognition and acknowledgment. They purposively respond to "You're OK and likeable" feedback messages from others ("strokes" in Transactional Analysis terminology). They are responding in these situations to satisfy their own needs. People who do this excessively eventually "turn other people off" and make them afraid. This interpersonal pattern blocks honest communication and, instead, leads to game playing. Truly effective helpers feel secure about themselves, like themselves, and thus are not dependent on the people they are trying to help for respect, recognition, and acknowledgment.

Effective helpers have special knowledge in some area of expertise that will be of special value to the person being helped   Investment counselors have special knowledge about different forms of investment and resulting payoffs and risks. Employment counselors have some special knowledge of jobs available in their local community. Pregnancy counselors have special knowledge about the different clinics available, about the functioning of the human body, about the laws and philosophical and religious beliefs pertaining to abortion, and about human sexuality. When people need help, they turn to the significant other whom they can identify in their life space as having the most knowledge and expertise about the problem of concern to them. When faced with a personal problem, they will turn to whomever they can identify as having an especially strong knowledge of human behavior.

Effective helpers attempt to understand, rather than to judge, the behavior of the people they try to help   There appears to be a very human tendency for people to judge the quality and sensibility of each other's actions. While appropriate when casting a vote, this judging tendency seriously interferes with the processes of effective helping. Effective helpers work hard to control the tendency to be judgmental. Instead, they accept a given behavior pattern as part of a person's way of coping with life and try to understand how a given pattern developed, and why the person they are trying to help behaves the way he or she does. With continued efforts to understand why, a given behavior pattern almost inevitably becomes progressively more understandable.

As a consequence, effective helpers have developed an in-depth understanding of human behavior. They understand that behavior does not simply occur. Their approach is that all behavior is purposeful and goal directed, that there are reasons and explanations for human behavior, and that to really help another, the reasons and explanations for that person's behavior must be understood rather than judged.

Effective helpers are able to reason systematically and to think in systems terms   A system is an organizational entity where each of the components relates to each other and to the system as a whole. Examples of systems include the human body, the organizational setting in which a person works, family units. In "high entropy" systems, components work cooperatively with each other and contribute favorably to the goals of the total system. In "low entropy" systems, components do not work cooperatively and sometimes work against each other. Applied to helping, effective counselors are aware of the different social systems a client is a part of, how he or she is affected by those systems, and how he or she, in turn, influences those systems. In other terminology, effective helpers are aware of the forces and factors in a client's life space and the mutual interaction between the client's behavior and these environmental factors. Effective helpers realize that a client's concerns and problems are influenced by many complex factors that must be identified and understood as an inherent part of the helping effort.

Effective counselors are contemporary and have a world view of human events   Counselors are aware of important present-day events in all the systems affecting their lives. They are aware of the significance and possible future implications of these events. For a school counselor to be contemporary means he must have an in-depth understanding of contemporary social concerns and an awareness of how these events are affecting the views of adolescents—especially their views about the future. The converse of being contemporary is to be encapsulated—to be unaware of what is happening in the systems and environments that comprise one's life space (Wrenn, 1973).

Effective helpers are able to identify behavior patterns that are self-defeating and help others change the self-defeating behaviors to more personally rewarding behavior patterns   People frequently do things that are counter-productive and goal disruptive, rather than goal enhancing. Some communicate ridicule and hostility when they want respect and friendship. Others run away from frightening situations rather than confront the aspects of a situation that cause anxiety. Still others do things to betray trust and cannot understand why others do not trust them. There are others who are afraid to respond assertively when people make unreasonable demands on them. Effective helpers are able to distinguish between healthy and unhealthy behavior patterns and to aid others in working toward the development of healthy, personally rewarding patterns. Effective helpers have a model or in-depth image of the qualities and behavior patterns of a healthy, effective, or fully functioning individual. Included in this model is an elaborate image of effective and ineffective ways to cope with the stressful situations of life.

Truly effective helpers are skillful at helping others look at themselves, and to respond non-defensively to the question, "Who am I?"   It is easy to describe aspects of self that are likeable and admirable. It is difficult and painful to look at aspects of self that are not admirable. Yet, self-improvement and growth require an honest, open awareness of those aspects of oneself that a person would like to change. Effective counselors are able to help others look at themselves, at both their likeable and less admirable aspects without debilitating fear, and to identify personal changes that would represent personal growth and improvement, and to develop approaches to bring those improvements about.

A personal reaction

In the previous section, eleven characteristics of effective helpers were generated. How did they compare to the characteristics you identified in the first personal learning activity? Did you identify some characteristics not discussed in the section you just read? The observations you made through this experience will contribute to your personal image of effective helping. Were there characteristics discussed in the previous section you did not identify? Reading about the ones you did not see should cause you to think about whether and how those qualities might have fit your personal helping situation.

While some of the characteristics discussed in the previous section may have seemed obvious to you, others will be controversial. You probably observed, for example, that concepts such as empathy, genuineness, positive regard, concreteness, and self-disclosure were not used anywhere in the previous section. Consideration was given to the qualities behind these concepts; the concepts were used, but not those labels. The choice was based on the observation that while many trainees learn to use the labels, it is not so easy to help trainees understand at an operational level what it means to implement them. Experience as practicum supervisors has led to the observation that it is difficult for many trainees to use these concepts to evaluate their own counseling. It has been observed that many counseling professionals cling to these terms with a religious zeal considered excessive. What is important is to understand the processes and interpersonal dynamics behind those terms, and these can be better communicated by avoiding the terms altogether.

Perhaps there are some qualities you have trouble accepting. Why not discuss those you have doubts about with your colleagues? As you discuss, perhaps each will help the other clarify and elaborate further. You will be acting as helpers for each other.

References

Ohlsen, M. M. *Guidance services in modern school settings.* (2nd ed.) New York: Harcourt Brace Jovanovich, 1974.

Wrenn, C. G. *World of the contemporary counselor.* Boston: Houghton Mifflin, 1973.

2. The goals of counseling

In any human endeavor, before thinking about *how* to accomplish something, it is essential to clarify *what* is to be accomplished. So it is with counseling. The primary purpose of this chapter is to clarify the outcome goals of counseling—what it is that counselors try to accomplish as a result of their efforts.

To do this, it is important to first clarify the meaning of the word "goal." The authors prefer the following definition: a goal is a *future event that a person wants to make happen*. There are three elements of a goal statement implied by this definition: it is rooted in the future, it is a description of an event, and it implies a valuing position.

The valuing component of a goal statement is especially important to understand. A valuing statement is a statement about the desirability of an action or a future event. Any statement that can be initiated with the expression "It is good and desirable that . . ." is a valuing statement. Phrases such as "should," "ought," "want," or "hope" indicate valuing positions. So, for example, if you were to say, "A goal for me is to respond more assertively on occasions in which I believe unreasonable demands are being imposed on me," you would also be expressing a valuing position for yourself. You could also say, "It is good and desirable for me to respond more assertively when I believe unreasonable demands are being imposed on me." The observation that goals statements are also valuing statements will become especially important in the discussion concerning the setting of specific goals with clients.

All the literature on the process of counseling affirms that the essence of counseling is to provide help or assistance to others. Indeed, counseling is often described as a "people-helping profession." As such, the outcome goals of counseling must be defined not by what counselors do, but rather in terms that describe what they try to bring about for their clients as a result of their efforts.

Counseling is a human transaction process to help individuals achieve goals, such as the following:

——understand self

——acquire information about present and possible future environments

——make important personal decisions

——set personal goals that are achievable and growth enhancing

——develop plans in the present to bring about possible and desired futures

——develop effective solutions to personal and interpersonal problems

——change ineffective behavior to more effective behavior

——cope with difficult environmental and life space circumstances

——gain control over negative and self-defeating emotions, such as debilitating anxiety, guilt, self-pity, loneliness, alienation, hopelessness, and basic insecurity

——acquire, and learn to use, effective interpersonal transaction skills

——acquire and use the essential elements of the decision-making process for making important personal decisions

————acquire a sense of basic liking and respect for self and a sense of optimism about one's ability to satisfy one's basic needs

————engage continuously in self-examination

Counseling literature has suggested four orientations to the counselor's efforts: (1) to help people make important personal decisions, (2) to help people deal and cope with crisis situations, (3) to help people reduce counter-productive behaviors, and (4) to stimulate healthy individual growth. The counselor as a helper for personal decision making has been an essential dimension of the counselor's identity, at least since 1909, when Frank Parsons recognized that in a complex, industrialized society people needed help in making vocational choices.

Making wise vocational choices was just one kind of human problem for which people needed help. Often problems that related to vocational decision making were reflections of deeper underlying problems. The role of the counselor as a person who helped people overcome other kinds of personal and interpersonal problems seemed to evolve naturally as an extension of the vocational choice involvement and was accelerated rapidly with the work of Carl Rogers, who provided a model for helping people to cope with crisis and to work through difficult personal and interpersonal problems they faced. An essential assumption of Rogers's model was that self-awareness and knowledge about self were keys to overcoming problems, coping with difficult life space situations, behaving in new ways which would be more rewarding than previous ways and, beyond that, stimulating personal growth. While they disagreed with Rogers about the nature of people, about the critical principles that account for growth and change, and about approaches for effective intervention, the writings of behaviorists added to the view of the counselor as a person who helped others to reduce undesirable or counter-productive behavior and to acquire behavior that would be rewarding and, thus, growth enhancing.

Both these perspectives recognized that helping people overcome problems, cope effectively with critical points in their lives, and make wise personal decisions would also be growth enhancing experiences. For any given individual, a counseling experience could be at once crisis intervention, decision making oriented, and growth enhancing. While for any specific client there may be more emphasis in one area over another, in all counseling situations all orientations apply and help to understand what the participants are trying to accomplish in each other's presence.

This recognition has led to an emerging trend to cast the goals of counseling into a developmental framework and to see the counselor as a stimulator of the favorable growth of individuals. Often groups are used as the basis of this activity.

The fully functioning individual

Since all the present orientations to counseling emphasize growth enhancement as an important goal of the counselor's efforts, it is essential that counselors have some basis for distinguishing between growth that is healthy and growth that is not. The criteria for making such judgments emerge from a vast array of surprisingly congruent literature on the emotionally healthy, fully functioning, self-actualizing, powerful, and productive individual. The model proposed by Ellis (1967) from a Rational-Emotive framework is entirely congruent with the models of Erikson (1968), who emphasizes identity development, Jourard (1974), Maslow (1968), and Rogers (1961), whose ideas come from a humanistic orientation, and White (1973), who stresses the importance of personal and interpersonal competence. In describing his Effective Personality, Blocher (1966) identifies six qualities that all these models have in common:

1.   *Consistency* describes the tendency to behave and make decisions that are reasonably consistent "both within social roles through time and across social roles. The element of consistency is based upon a well-integrated sense of personal identity that gives direction and unity to behavior."

2.   *Commitment.* The effective person is able to commit self to goals and purposes that are enhancing and helpful to self, others, and the various groups and organizations of which one is an integral part. Such a person can differentiate between reasonable and unreasonable risks and take reasonable, calculated risks to move toward desired goals. On occasion, such a person can commit self to "self-transcending" values that give meaning and purpose to life and thus protect from hopelessness, obsessive fear of death, and "existential despair."

3.   *Self-Control.* The effective individual experiences emotions, such as joy, fear, and anger. But the level of intensity of

those emotions is reasonable in proportion to the situation related to them. Emotions do not get in the individual's way of appraising the situation rationally and responding effectively to it.

4. *Competence.* The effective individual recognizes that there are three orientations to coping with a problem situation: to operate on the environment and relate with the people involved so as to reduce the problem identified, to accept the problem as unresolvable and cope with its continued existence, or to move away from the problem situation. The effective individual tends to explore the first orientation first and has the ability to relate effectively to people, to appraise rationally the elements of the situation, to generate several possible intervention approaches for dealing with the situation and to anticipate accurately different outcomes of these possible solutions. He or she operates pro-actively rather than re-actively on the environment and never feels entrapped or enslaved by it. Such an individual tends to be oriented more toward "anticipatory problem solving" than a "crisis coping" base.

5. *Creativity.* Definitions of creativity include the ability to produce something new; the ability to think divergently; the ability to generate a variety of ideas, and the ability to develop unusual and effective solutions to difficult problems. By any of these definitions, effective individuals possess creativity. They tend to regard an effort that has not succeeded as a mistake, rather than a failure.

6. *Self-Awareness.* In addition to being aware of talents, abilities, and limitations, the effective individual is "tuned in" to his or her affective world. He or she is aware of the motivations, beliefs, values, feelings, and assumptions that affect personal behavior and decisions. Actions tend to be spontaneous and congruent with highly prized values. Feelings, when experiences are drawn upon, contribute to, rather than interfere with, healthy problem resolutions.

The qualities described by Ellis (1967) include the above and several others. As is true of creativity, there are several definitions of tolerance, including the recognition of the right of others to take a viewpoint different from one's own, the right of others to be wrong, and the respect for others who have different backgrounds from one's own. By any of these definitions, the effective individual communicates tolerance for others. Ellis also recognizes the ironic statement of the ancient Chinese: "It is very difficult to prophesy, especially about the future." The healthy individual thus has the ability to accept uncertainty and to tolerate ambiguity. The healthy individual accepts the fact that "we all live in a world of probability and chance where there are not, nor probably ever will be, any absolute certainties," and that it is not at all horrible to live in such a probabilistic, uncertain world. Indeed, he or she recognizes that in many ways that is what gives life fascination and excitement.

Commentary on the fully functioning individual

The qualities described in this model of the effective individual must be thought of as ways of being and behaving, rather than as a set of discrete skills. While they may be analyzed more fully into component parts, it is difficult to define them as terminal objectives. They represent qualities for continuing ongoing development for the growing individual. They are value-laden, but it is difficult to refute their importance for people living in an evolving and rapidly changing society.

These qualities are important to counselors for three reasons. First, they represent important dimensions for personal self-assessment and growth. If stimulating the favorable growth of others is an important goal for counseling, then stimulating his or her own personal growth is an important goal for the individual counselor. The dimensions described above can help the developing counselor assess his or her present level of growth and, subsequently, to set specific growth goals for self. Second, these qualities represent criteria the counselor can use to assess the present level of development of clients as a base for identifying areas in which further client growth may be especially important. They offer the counselor criteria to decide whether or not the more specific goals stated earlier will be helpful for an individual client. Finally, these qualities affirm a basic but difficult-to-accept proposition about counseling: counselors do make judgments about the growth and behavior patterns of their clients. There must be some standard for determining the worth of a given goal for a given client. That standard is how the goal, once achieved, contributed to the client's future growth.

Krumboltz (1966) provides a description of some behavioral goals of counseling that can contribute to a person's growth and future well-being. These include:

—making effective socially assertive responses

—increasing social skills necessary to meeting new people

—increasing skills instrumental to maintaining relationships with others

—increasing the ability to concentrate for longer periods of time on schoolwork

—accepting responsibility for a task and carrying it through to completion

—learning to respond calmly to hostile and critical remarks

—learning to manage interpersonal conflicts in such ways as to reduce them

—increasing patterns of cooperation

—learning to discriminate between insults and friendly teasing

—improving the ability to communicate accurately and clearly

Preparation for the future as a perspective for understanding counseling goals

Helping people focus on their personal futures is clearly an important part of the counseling process. The counselor's activities in the present are designed to help the client bring about a more desirable future for self. From a developmental perspective, an ultimate goal of the counseling process is for each individual to acquire those skills and abilities involved in being able to shape his or her destiny. Each of these skills can be seen as a potential goal of counseling. A synthesis of the literature indicates the following to be essential qualities:

—the ability to focus attention on the long-range, as well as short-range, future, and to include in one's thinking ideas about what is possible and what is desirable (Toffler, 1972)

————the ability to verbalize both long-range and short-range personal goals with sufficient clarity that one can clearly evaluate when and if those goal events have occurred

————the skills and reasoning processes involved in making important life decisions, including the abilities to: generate different approaches to goal achievement, seek information that will be useful in making decisions, clarify preferences and give priorities to different available alternatives, estimate likelihoods of success of different options, and develop an action strategy for goal achievement and a basis for evaluating whether goal achievement has occurred (Bergland, 1974; Gelatt et al., 1973; Krumboltz, 1966)

————a sense of basic optimism in one's ability to bring about important life goals, that is, personal security, confidence in self, a self-focused attitude of "I'm OK" (Erikson, 1968; Hamachek, 1971; Harris, 1967; White, 1973)

————tolerance for new and unusual events and openness versus defensiveness toward new ideas (Maslow, 1968)

————effective human relationship skills, including the capacity to understand other people's feelings, beliefs, desires, and motivations, and the ability to respond with empathy to those affective experiences (Carkhuff, 1972; Johnson, 1972; Mosher & Sprinthall, 1971)

————an effective, rational thinking process for dealing effectively with interpersonal conflicts (Ellis, 1967; Gordon, 1970)

————an approach for reasoning through moral dilemmas (Mosher & Sullivan, 1974)

————the courage for continuous self-examination about one's feelings, assumptions, beliefs, and values about one's self, significant others, current social problems, and the future (Eisenberg, 1974a,b)

People who seek a counselor's help frequently do not come with future goals clearly defined; often they come with concerns or problems that are focused in the present. An essential part of the counseling process is to help clients clarify and specify the goals they would like to attain as a result of their transactions with the counselor. For clients who come with statements of concern, this means that at some point the discussion must include a conversion of present concerns to future goals. The cases of Mike and Janice which follow will illustrate this dimension of the counseling process.

Case study 1:
Mike—career choice

Career education activities were a very important part of the curriculum at John F. Kennedy High School, where Mike was a junior. All the counselors were actively involved in planning, coordinating, and implementing career education programs. As a result of these activities, Mike had been thinking a good deal about his post-high school future. He had come to the conclusion that he did not want to go to college, at least for a while, after he graduated. He had received some exposure to a number of career fields, but felt he still did not have enough information about them.

In the group guidance courses, the counselors had often mentioned that they would be pleased to talk to anyone who wanted to follow up on some of the learning activities done in the group guidance sessions on careers. So Mike sought out his counselor, and, after the usual amenities, the counselor asked, "Mike, how can I help you?" Mike's reply was that he had been doing a lot of thinking about the kind of job he wanted to get after high school and was feeling confused. Some occupations looked interesting, but were not available to a high school graduate; others were available, but uninteresting. To this the counselor responded by saying, "I can see that you have done a good deal of thinking about the things we have discussed in our group. Share with me some of the ideas and questions you have been thinking about."

This invitation led to a good deal of exploration of the various issues that Mike had been thinking about. The counselor said little, but listened actively to Mike's discussion of the different occupations he had been considering and his assessment of the various points about each occupation he considered favorable or unfavorable. During this session, the counselor made three different kinds of responses. She frequently reflected, summarized, and synthesized Mike's thinking ("So while selling in a department store does not appeal to you, working as an electrician in that store might"). Sometimes she used the phrase "tell me more about the thinking you have done . . .". Occasionally, she responded to help Mike clarify his views, values, and feelings ("As you describe this to me, Mike, it sounds as though you prefer outdoor work to indoor work. Am I hearing that correctly?").

Later in the session, Mike began to assess his knowledge about himself. But the counseling time was beginning to run out, so the counselor asked Mike if he thought another meeting would be useful. Mike answered affirmatively, so they scheduled a meeting for the following week.

At the beginning of the second meeting, the counselor summarized the discussion of the first meeting. But before continuing, she said, "Mike, we have talked a lot about careers and the things you felt confused about. I think it would be useful if we could talk about your goals for our meetings. Let's try to clarify what you hope to accomplish from our discussions."

Mike:	Well, as I said, I was really confused and I thought you could help me.
Counselor:	Right. Would that mean that your goal would be to become less confused about the kind of career you want to pursue?
Mike:	Yeah, but somehow that doesn't say it quite right. Maybe it sounds too weak or something.
Counselor:	OK. How about if we said that your goal is to become clearer about which careers seem attractive to you and which seem unattractive.
Mike:	Yeah, that sounds better.
Counselor:	Good. But to help us both clarify still further, how would we determine when we have reached that goal?
Mike:	[long pause in which it was clear that Mike was thinking about the counselor's question] Well, I don't think I have to make a definite choice right now. So I wouldn't say that making a final choice would be a goal. . . . I guess I would say we would be successful if we found three or four careers that seemed interesting enough for me to learn a lot more about. Then maybe you could help me figure out

	some ways to learn more about those careers.
Counselor:	Good, Mike. Now we both have a clearer idea of what we are aiming for. And once we have discussed the various careers you have been considering, I'll be glad to help you follow up.

With goals established and clarified, Mike and the counselor continued their discussions, which went two more sessions. They discussed other careers, Mike's views about himself, his appraisal of his skills and interests, and his parents' thinking about his future. Finally, Mike focused on electrical repair work, machine shop work, and plumbing. The counselor helped Mike arrange some after-school visits with workers in these fields and Mike was able to spend some after-school time shadowing these workers.

Eventually, during his senior year Mike chose to seek a job with the local power company as a lineman. The counselor then did some role playing with Mike to help him learn how to handle a job-seeking interview effectively. Mike was able to obtain a job with the power company at the end of his senior year. At this writing, Mike has been with the company for a year, has been doing very well, and is being considered for a training program as a supervisor.

Analysis

The case of Mike will be considered later in Chapter 9 to explore further how the counselor helped Mike through the exploration-focusing stages of his search. The reason for presenting the case at this point was to illustrate the importance of setting goals and how that can be done as an essential part of the counseling process.

The case illustrates much that has been said so far. Mike was feeling confused and his goal was to clarify his confusing perceptions, views, values, and feelings about his future as a participant in the world of work. To do this, he needed, among other things, accurate information.

Note that the counselor did not tell Mike what the goals of counseling should be. Nor did she press him right away to specify his goals. She waited until she understood him and his concerns deeply enough so that the goals which were subsequently established were a natural extension of his concerns. Her involvement in the goal-setting process was to: determine when, during the counseling process, it was appropriate to discuss goals; help Mike describe and clarify the goals as he saw them; help Mike determine what criteria he would use to evaluate the effectiveness of counseling; and to judge whether Mike's goals seemed sensible and reasonable. These steps in the process of goal setting will be considered in more depth in Chapter 8.

The counselor handled the initial contact well. By responding with a simple "How can I help you?" she was communicating her perceptions of herself and her profession. Her next response was also important. By observing, acknowledging, and supporting the thinking Mike had been doing she communicated a great deal of regard and respect for him. Clearly, she did not view Mike as stupid or immature. With this response, she also offered Mike an "invitation" to communicate and share his feelings with her. Both are important components of effective reaching out. The session took thirty-five minutes—a long time to commit to one individual and another obvious expression of caring.

During the session, the counselor did more listening than talking. She neither gave advice nor blocked communication. The clear intent of her responses was to facilitate still more relevant communication that would aid in later focusing and clarification.

To set up job visits, the counselor had to have contacts in the community. This illustrates the counselor's role of being knowledgeable about the community and its resources. Finally, the entire counseling process was initiated as a result of Mike's exposure to his counselor through a career guidance project. It was through this form of outreach that Mike came to understand the role his school counselor played.

Analysis of outcome goals

One of the major questions in counseling has been over the issue: How specifically must outcome goals be stated? People with a behavioral orientation have argued that to be well-stated, goals must meet the following criteria:

1.   They must be stated in terms of specific changes of behaviors that are observable
2.   The stimulus conditions under which the new behaviors are to occur must be identified

The advantages stated to this approach are that clarifying goals to this degree of specificity helps both client and counselor have a clear focus on what they are trying to accomplish together. Clarifying goals enhance the chances for success; vague goals lessen the chances for success. Specifically, stated goals provide an opportunity to monitor and get feedback about whether what is happening in the counseling process is being helpful. If what is happening during counseling is leading toward the acquisition of the specified new behaviors, then the process is being effective. If the events of the process are not leading toward such changes, then the process is not being effective, and reexamination must take place. With goal statements meeting the above criteria, it is also possible to evaluate when and if counseling has achieved a successful completion. In an era of accountability, being able to provide evidence of success is important, and, perhaps, even essential to future survival.

Those who disagree with this orientation say that overt, observable behavior changes are only the surface manifestations of the counselor's effort. Most of the counselor's work involves subjective states: thoughts, feelings, beliefs, values, perceptions, assumptions, and motivations. By themselves these phenomena are not observable. Insistence that goals be stated in terms of overt behavior seems to exclude these subjective phenomena from the area of counseling; yet, such phenomena are the very essence of counseling. The tendency to reduce goals to such specificity may blind both client and counselor to other things they need to attend to. Specifying too soon may cause anxiety for the client.

The major problem in this debate seems to be how does one put into overt behavior terms, events and phenomena that are not directly observable. The work of the counselor includes helping people improve their self-image, reduce anxiety, examine and change their views toward self and significant others, and clarify hopes and expectations about one's future. Yet self-concept, emotional states, views, assumptions, and hopes and expectations are not observable per se. Should they, therefore, be excluded from statements of outcome goals? Since these phenomena often comprise the essence of counseling, this approach would not seem to make sense.

There is a resolution. Although self-concept, emotional states, and underlying attitudes are not observable per se, observable *indicators* or signs are available of their presence and strength. Indicators are observable signs of the occurrence of a nonobservable event. They are often consequences of the occurrence of the events they signify.

Just as falling objects are indicators of gravity, and smoldering ashes in an ashtray in an empty room is an indicator to a television detective that someone has been smoking recently in that room, so are there indicators of a person's sense of personal security, feelings of happiness and anger, and views toward self and significant others. Indeed, we infer the very existence of these nonobservable events by their observable signs.

Thus, indicators of self-concept include a person's interpersonal relationship patterns, his or her risk-taking tendencies, speech fluencies or dis-fluencies and open versus defensive ways of coping with anxiety or stress. Speech dis-fluencies, hair pulling, fidgeting, stalling, and evasive abstract responding are indicators of anxiety; verbalized statements are often indicators of a person's underlying attitudes toward significant others. In fact, all the literature concerning nonverbal clues is essentially a lexicon of overt indicators of internal states.

With these perspectives, an approach to goal setting that would appear useful is to state goals with sufficient clarity so that valid observable indicators are available to determine whether those goals have been achieved.

This is precisely the approach Mike's counselor took in helping him set goals. Mike said that his goal was to reduce the confusion he felt about the career choices he was considering—a goal statement that would not have met the behaviorists' standards. What could Mike have said if the counselor had responded by saying, "Can you clarify further what you mean when you say you are confused?" Mike may very well have felt exasperated, unable to answer, and possibly alienated from his counselor. Yet when the counselor asked, "How could we determine when and if we have achieved success?" Mike was able to develop some usable criteria which made sense to the counselor. By asking her question, the counselor was really asking Mike to identify the indicators he would accept of counseling success.

Case study 2:
Janice—studying difficulties

The case of Janice will help to illustrate further these ideas. Janice was a college sophomore encountering serious difficulties in studying. She came to a counselor in the college counseling center and reported that when she tried to study she became very "uptight," and that as a result her ability to study efficiently suffered badly. While she was aware of the vicious cycle (inefficient study patterns → anxiety → greater inefficient study patterns), Janice was not able to control the pattern.

Analysis

What are the helping goals for Janice? To say "improvement of study skills" is in the right direction, but it is too vague. What is meant by improvement? The behavioral approach would suggest a goal statement such as "Counseling will be successful for Janice when she is able to read five consecutive pages of assigned material without removing eye contact and without visually retracing sentences. The time necessary to read any five pages will be reduced from ten to six minutes without loss of comprehension. Janice will take only one break of no more than ten minutes between 7:15 and 9:00 p.m. Goal will be considered achieved when this pattern is maintained for four consecutive days."

While the above is an improved goal statement over the "improvement of study skills" and is impressive by its detail, it misses the heart of the problem—the anxiety involved. The criteria for success are merely the observable indicators that Janice has been helped. We believe it is more advantageous for the practitioner to state goals so that the essential problems to be worked on are included in the goal statement. (Note here that the terms "anxiety" and "anxiety reduction" are not even included in the goal statement.) Therefore, an alternative goal statement for Janice might be as follows:

The essential goal of counseling is to help Janice improve her study patterns. To do this, it would appear necessary to help Janice experience less anxiety while studying. Indicators of success would include: the ability to read five consecutive pages of assigned material without removing eye contact and without visually retracing sentences; the ability to read any five pages in six, rather than the present ten, minutes without loss of comprehension; and being able to study from 7:15 to 9:00 p.m. with at the most one break lasting for no more than ten minutes. An important indicator of success will be when this pattern can be maintained for four consecutive days.

Follow-up

With the help of counseling, Janice was able to improve her study skills, but not to the criterion level specified in the goal statement. As Janice and her counselor continued to explore the problem, it became clear that Janice was feeling intense pressure to excel academically. Her parents frequently criticized her and took the position that since they were putting Janice through college they expected her to do extremely well. At least "dean's list" performance was expected. This, in turn, caused Janice to experience not only high levels of tension but also feelings of guilt. To add to the level of anxiety, Janice's sense of personal adequacy was almost entirely dependent on her academic achievement. What surfaced was that Janice was making this equation: "Good grades = I'm OK. Bad grades = I'm not OK." The counselor hypothesized that these pressures were very much affecting Janice's ability to study, and that Janice would continue to have trouble studying until these pressures were removed. Simply instructing Janice in efficient study techniques would do little to create a lasting change in behavior. Counseling, therefore, focused on two interrelated themes: Janice's relationship with her parents (her feelings toward them and their attitudes toward her), and Janice's sense of personal adequacy. A major breakthrough occurred when the counselor helped Janice find a way to communicate her feelings to her parents. Not only did they reduce the pressure they were imposing on her, but the success of that confrontation helped Janice feel more secure about herself. At this writing, Janice's relationship with her parents is far from ideal, but there has been notable improvement.

Personal learning activity II:
Personal goals

In addition to career goals, each person has goals for self-growth and improvement. Some goals are in the nature of reducing an undesirable behavior pattern or tendency, such as quitting smoking or reducing the tendency to make sarcastic remarks intended to be humorous. Others are in the nature of increasing a desired behavior pattern, such as responding more assertively. The purposes of this three-part personal learning activity are to: help you assess the personal goals you have for yourself, demonstrate the concepts developed in this chapter by helping you apply them to your personal life, and help you apply the concepts in this chapter to your present and future practice as a helping person.

Listed below are thirty-five general personal growth goals people frequently set for themselves. For the first part of this learning activity, scan the list below and identify at least three goals you have either set for yourself at this time, or would like to set for yourself. Write each down at the top of a separate sheet of paper, leaving plenty of room for additional writing on each sheet. You may identify more than three goals, but identify at least three.

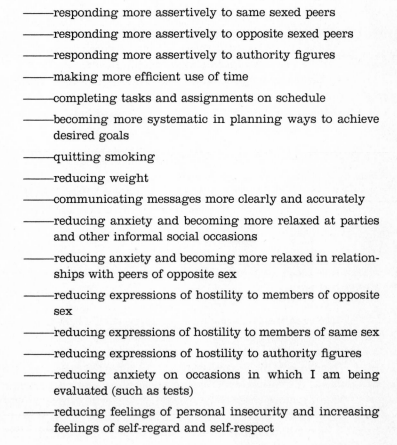

——responding more assertively to same sexed peers

——responding more assertively to opposite sexed peers

——responding more assertively to authority figures

——making more efficient use of time

——completing tasks and assignments on schedule

——becoming more systematic in planning ways to achieve desired goals

——quitting smoking

——reducing weight

——communicating messages more clearly and accurately

——reducing anxiety and becoming more relaxed at parties and other informal social occasions

——reducing anxiety and becoming more relaxed in relationships with peers of opposite sex

——reducing expressions of hostility to members of opposite sex

——reducing expressions of hostility to members of same sex

——reducing expressions of hostility to authority figures

——reducing anxiety on occasions in which I am being evaluated (such as tests)

——reducing feelings of personal insecurity and increasing feelings of self-regard and self-respect

———responding with more patience and less annoyance when others do or say things I don't like or disapprove of

———responding calmly when others communicate criticisms and hostility toward me

———offering more support and encouragement to people I am close to

———responding more effectively so as to maintain and enhance interpersonal relationships

———spending more time with others and less time alone

———responding in ways to prevent fights and arguments

———accepting helpful feedback from others less defensively

———becoming more sensitive to feelings and desires of others

———learning to distinguish more accurately between people I can and cannot trust

———being able to say "no" without feelings of guilt or anxiety

———improving my ability to understand what others are try-ing to communicate to me

———responding more calmly and with less annoyance in frus-trating situations

———reducing the tendency to do things which others find an-noying

———reducing the tendency to dominate and control others

———overcoming the tendency to be controlled by other people's feelings toward me

———making decisions more quickly

———developing more skill in managing and controlling fear when _____

_____

———developing more skill in managing and controlling anger and hostility when _____

———other _____

For the second part of this personal learning activity, imagine that you have actually achieved your desired goal. You have attained the skills you wanted to develop. For each goal, write down three outcomes you would expect to happen now that the personal growth goal has been achieved. For example, if one of your goals was "quitting smoking," you might say,

> *Consequences:*
> ——have more energy and feel less sluggish and lazy
> ——become more active as a participant in sports
> ——become more alert in conversations with others

Write your consequences below the specific goal statement you are analyzing. Please do not proceed to the next part until you have completed this activity.

For the third part of this activity write two observable indicators that you (and perhaps a friend) would use to determine when and if you had achieved your goal. For example, if you wrote down "experiencing less anxiety and more security at parties and other informal social situations," two indicators of successful goal achievement for you might be: (1) "I would initiate conversations with strangers more frequently," and (2) "I would sustain conversations with people for longer periods of time." Write the two indicators of successful goal achievement just underneath the consequences for that goal. (Since indicators are frequently goal consequences, for some goals you may find it difficult to separate consequences and achievements from each other. If so, think of indicators in addition to the consequences you identified in step three of this activity.)

In review, the purposes of this personal learning activity were threefold: (1) to help you assess the personal goals you have for yourself, (2) to demonstrate the concepts developed in this chapter, and (3) to help you apply these concepts to your present and future practice as a helping person.

References

Bergland, B. Career planning: The use of sequential evaluated experience. In E. H. Herr (Ed.), *Vocational guidance and human development.* Boston: Houghton Mifflin, 1974.

Blocher, D. H. *Developmental counseling.* New York: Ronald Press, 1966.

Carkhuff, R. R. *The art of helping.* Amherst, Mass.: Carkhuff Associates, 1972.

Eisenberg, S. Exploring alternative futures: A proactive, developmental curriculum. *Impact,* 1974, *3* (1), 42-47. (a)

Eisenberg, S. Exploring the future: A counseling/curriculum project. *Personnel and Guidance Journal,* 1974, *53,* 527-533. (b)

Ellis, A. Goals of psychotherapy. In A. R. Mahrer (Ed.), *The goals of psychotherapy.* New York: Appleton-Century-Crofts, 1967.

Erikson, E. H. *Identity: Youth and crisis.* New York: W. W. Norton, 1968.

Gelatt, H. B., Varenhorst, B., Carey, R., & Miller, G. P. *Decisions and outcomes: A leader's guide.* New York: College Entrance Examination Board, 1973.

Gordon, T. *Parent effectiveness training.* New York: Wyden Press, 1970.

Hamachek, D. *Encounters with the self.* New York: Holt, Rinehart and Winston, 1971.

Harris, T. *I'm OK. You're OK.* New York: Harper and Row, 1967.

Johnson, D. W. *Reaching out.* Englewood Cliffs, N. J.: Prentice-Hall, 1972.

Jourard, S. *The healthy personality.* New York: Macmillan, 1974.

Krumboltz, J. D. Behavioral goals for counseling. *Journal of Counseling Psychology,* 1966, *3,* 153-159.

Maslow, A. H. *Toward a psychology of being.* (2nd ed.) New York: Van Nostrand, 1968.

Mosher, R., & Sprinthall, N. Psychological education: A means to promote personal development during adolescence. *The Counseling Psychologist,* 1971, *2* (4), 3-81.

Mosher, R., & Sullivan, P. Moral education: A new initiative for guidance. *Focus On Guidance,* 1974, *6* (5), 1-11.

Rogers, C. R. *On becoming a person.* Boston: Houghton Mifflin, 1961.

Toffler, A. *The futurists.* New York: Random House, 1972.

White, R. W. The concept of healthy personality: What do we really mean. *The Counseling Psychologist,* 1973, *4* (2), 3-12.

3. Principles of behavior applied to the counseling process

To be truly effective as a helping person, a counselor must have a firm understanding of human behavior and must be able to apply those understandings in his or her reaching out efforts. The purpose of this chapter is to develop some basic principles of human behavior that counselors can use to understand their own behavior as well as the behavior of the people they help.

The first proposition of the book is that all human behavior, including the behavior of the counselor and the client in the counseling situation, is purposive and goal directed. We consider this statement to be true whether or not there is any awareness as to the purposes and goals of one's behavior. The counselor's primary goal is to achieve the outcome goals of counseling the client, and to behave in such ways as to facilitate progress toward the attainment of those outcome goals.

A second proposition is that in order to attain certain important

32

long-term goals, it may be necessary to first attain certain more im- 2.
mediate goals. As the review of the counseling goals suggested, most
counselors view the establishment of a relationship of mutual trust,
openness, and honesty as one such immediate goal. The counseling
process will proceed only after this relationship has been achieved.
Attainment of this relationship is necessary and instrumental to the
successful attainment of outcome goals. A major task for counselors
is to *anticipate* with each client other process goals for this successful
attainment of outcome goals.

A third proposition is that in any given situation, any given 3.
action in that situation will result in a variety of consequences. Some
will be desirable; others may be undesirable. Some consequences will
be immediate, others delayed. Some will be observable to the actor,
others not observable. Thus, consequences may be analyzed according
to four categories: (1) whether they contribute favorably to, or interfere with, the bringing about of an important goal, (2) whether they
are desirable or undesirable, (3) whether they are immediate or delayed, and (4) whether they are observable or unobservable.

Suppose in the course of counseling, a counselor says to his
client, "Perhaps the reason you turn people off is that you are really
afraid of them." The client thinks for a second and says, "You're right!
I never thought about that before." Insofar as the counselor is concerned, the client's response was an *immediate and observable* consequence of the counselor's response. Suppose the client also thinks to
himself, "Wow, this counselor really understands me well." Since the
counselor could not observe the client thinking that to himself, the
client's thought is an *immediate but unobservable* consequence of his
statement.

Suppose, further, the client goes home and continues to think in
depth about what the counselor had said. As far as the counselor is
concerned, that client's activity is a *delayed and unobservable* consequence of his response. Suppose, even further, the client comes in the
following week and says, "You know, I did a lot of thinking about what
you said to me last week. You really hit the nail on the head. I am afraid
of a lot of people, and I realize that I need to work through my fears
about other people." This last statement is clearly a *delayed and observable* consequence of the counselor's response.

Therefore, counseling effectiveness is related to the counselor's
ability to accurately *anticipate* the consequences of his or her actions
with the client. Since some consequences are delayed and others are
unobservable, accurately anticipating consequences of one's actions
is clearly a difficult task. Nevertheless, the more accurately a coun-

selor can anticipate the impact of his or her behavior with the client, the more effective that counselor is likely to be with the client. Perhaps one way of defining sensitivity is in the ability to accurately anticipate the impact or consequences a person's behavior has on another person's subsequent behavior.

In reviewing the consequences of the client's statement above, most counselors would judge them as favorable. The client has acquired a new and potentially useful awareness; the new discovery stimulated some introspective homework and the client has developed favorable regard for the counselor. When a person behaves in ways that bring about desired goals, or when behavior results in favorable consequences, his or her actions are considered to be effective. However, sometimes an individual's behavior results in consequences that block the achievement of important goals. Ineffective or maladaptive behavior occurs when any of the following conditions result:

——the results of a given action block or interfere with the achievement of a highly valued goal (a counselor statement puts the client on the defensive and the client terminates)

——the results of a given action are the very opposite of an intended outcome (an adolescent who wants another to become his friend insults him; a prospective job seeker annoys the interviewer by his abrasive belligerence)

——the results of a given action are judged by some standard to be undesirable (a parent continuously puts a child into a series of double binds and then wonders why the child shows fear)

A good deal of counseling revolves around the process of helping people change maladaptive or counter-productive behavior to more effective ways of behaving. During the second (or insight) stage of the process, the interaction may well invite the client to focus on issues such as: What is it I really want to bring about for myself? How did I behave? What were the results of my actions? What results do I regard as undesirable? What might I do differently to bring about what I want for me and not what I do not want for me? How can I learn to master these behaviors?

While these questions often form a base for counseling exploration, they also form a base that many counselors use to look at their own counseling behavior. As they listen to the tapes of their counseling sessions, experienced, as well as novice, counselors ask themselves: What did I really want to make happen in this session (or what did I want the client to do)? What makes these results important? What indicators or feedback do I have available to me to determine whether my intended consequences really did happen? What might I have done differently to be more effective in bringing about that which I wanted to bring about?

Often this kind of "efficiency thinking" leads to lasting growth and change. But very often it is also painful. It requires the ability to be open to feedback about one's actions and their consequences and the recognition that one's behavior was not as effective as he or she had hoped. Because it is painful, counselors rarely engage their clients in this kind of exploration early in the counseling process. While this kind of exploration may be important for the client, the client must feel safe enough to do it openly and with minimum defensiveness. The rapport and trust between client and counselor must be strong enough to offer the client support while he or she is going through this process. Exploration around this set of questions often becomes the second stage of the counseling process. The assessment of client readiness to enter into this level of intense focused exploration will be discussed in Chapter 8.

Values and values clarification

Clarification of values about the desirability of given goal events or possible consequences is a critical part of this thinking process. Valuing statements (Raths, Harmin, & Simon, 1966) are essentially statements about the desirability or preferability of the occurrence of an event, an action, or a future consequence of an action. Whenever a person uses words such as "should," "ought," "want," or "hope that," he or she is expressing a valuing statement. Whenever a statement can be changed around without altering its meaning to begin with the stem, "It is good and desirable for me to . . ." a valuing statement has been expressed. Obviously, valuing statements can be expressed in the negative form as, "I don't want," "I ought not," "It is bad and undesirable for me to . . .".

People make valuing statements about their own behavior, the behavior of specific significant others, as well as the behavior of people in specific groups: "My husband *should* help out with household chores more often." "Our son *should* be getting better grades in school." "It is *good and desirable* for high school seniors to think about their post-high school futures." "Taking drugs is *bad* for people." "It is *good and desirable* for people to be aware of the emotions they experience when they experience them."

Often people experience confusion and discrepancy in their valuing statements. Certain of their "should" statements are incompatible with other of their "should" statements. "I *should* be honest with people" and "It's *undesirable* to hurt other people's feelings" is one example that new counselors often experience in their training. Another example: "Clients *should* decide for themselves what is in their own best interest." "Roy is constantly getting into vicious fights. I *should* try to get Roy to stop fighting." In such situations, people are said to be experiencing *valuing conflicts* or *valuing dilemmas*. Counselors experience valuing dilemmas within themselves as they work with people. Also, they often recognize that valuing dilemmas are a part of a client's difficulties. For both, the effort to resolve apparent valuing dilemmas is an important experience in personal growth. Working through apparent valuing dilemmas leads to greater understanding of self, increased ability to take more effective action in the future, and increased ability to take actions that are consistent with personal valuing priorities.

The counselor's value judgments

Here are some examples of valuing conflicts often faced by counselors. Suppose a fourteen-year-old girl seeks counseling because she is "very confused about a lot of things" and generally "uptight." In the course of counseling, feelings of strong anger toward her parents, of which she had not previously been aware, begin to surface. As she begins to recognize these feelings, she also experiences moderately intense levels of guilt about them. How should the counselor value these results of intervention? Should these results be judged as good and desirable for the client? As bad and undesirable? As an inevitable set of events? To answer these questions, the counselor must come to grips with the value judgments he or she is making about the client. He or she must also deal with the personal feelings should such consequences occur. Might some counselors feel guilty about the influence they may have on the client? Might some feel afraid because they are not sure how to help the client work through her feelings of guilt?

Another example: Suppose a seventeen-year-old male high school junior seeks the counselor's help because he is having difficulty getting along at home as well as in school. He has no friends, his grades are poor, and his life is depressing, boring, and lonely. In the course of counseling, the client decides for himself that the best way to cope with these problems is to quit school and join the military. The counselor happens to know that his parents would be very upset with this decision. Again, what counselor value judgments are involved? Does he or she assume the boy capable of making wise decisions for himself and thus accept the decision even if it might incur the wrath of the boy's parents? Does the counselor take the position that finishing high school, no matter how arduous the task, is really in the boy's best interest, and so tries to persuade him to finish? Does the counselor take the value position that people have the right to make their own decisions and that the obligation to themselves is to think through the consequences of their decisions? With this viewpoint, of course, the counselor would want to say to the client, "Well, that is a possible alternative open to you, but before you act on it, I think it might be important to think through the consequences. . . . What are some of the things you think might happen if you choose this course of action?" Once the client has looked at the consequences, the counselor might follow up by saying, "What are some of your feelings about whether those consequences would be good for you or not?" The purpose of this last counselor goal-directed response, of course, would be to help the client clarify for himself some of the value judgments he is making for himself about the consequences of his actions.

There are times when the goals a client wants and desires are goals the counselor values as not in the client's best interest. A good example would be the counselor who values client self-exploration and self-examination while working with a client who does not value these things for self. Counselor and client are in a value conflict situation. They disagree as to what is good and desirable for the client. *Counseling cannot succeed when a value conflict exists between client and counselor as to what is in the client's best interest.* If counseling is to be successful, such value conflicts must be resolved. This means that someone's values must, of necessity, be changed. Thus, the effective counselor must be aware of the value judgments he or she is making as to what is in the client's best interest, aware of the discrepancies that exist between self and client, and must be prepared to resolve such discrepancies.

Earlier literature in counseling held the position that a counselor should not make judgments concerning what was in another person's best interests. That was something the counselor should be trying to help the client work out for him- or herself. While that is still a desirable counselor priority, more recently it has been realized that a counselor cannot avoid making judgments about the client. Whatever a counselor does in the counseling session should be in the best interests of the client. Thus, in order to decide what to do at critical decision points, the counselor must also decide what is in the client's best interests. Since such judgments are inescapable, the counselor must have a set of criteria for deciding. Ultimately, the criteria must be in the counselor's image of the healthy individual, discussed in Chapter 2. What is in the client's best interest is that which will help to resolve the difficulty at hand and at the same time lead to favorable growth in the future. An additional criterion is that the counselor must avoid doing those things that may result in harm or growth-blocking consequences for the client.

In working toward a resolution of the place for the counselor's values in the counseling process, it is also useful to distinguish between the actions of the client during the counseling sessions and the client's actions outside the sessions. As the counselor listens to the client, he or she is also hypothesizing from the data the client offers, assessing the client's behaviors, and making judgments about the significance and meanings of the client's behaviors. It is from these judgments that growth-stimulating confrontations occur. The issue for counselors is not whether such judgments should be made; they are inevitable. As a person with advanced knowledge and understanding of human behavior, it is appropriate for the counselor to make such judgments. To not make such judgments would result in a denial of the very skills the counselor has to offer to the client. The focus of the counselor's attention should not be on whether it is OK to make such judgments, but rather on the specific meanings and significance that are attached to the client's statements, and on what should be done about such judgments once they are made. With mature clients, effective counselors deal with their judgments by using "I messages" and principles of constructive confrontation to present them to their clients (cf. Chapter 6). Their effort is to present their judgments to their clients in such a way that the clients can use the judgments for gainful growth.

Beliefs, values, attitudes, and actions

Any discussion of the counseling process must consider the interrelated notions of values, beliefs, attitudes, and philosophical assumptions. These factors are stressed especially in the client-centered theory of counseling. Within that model are some important concepts related to the role of values in the counseling process. The primary focus of this discussion will be on the relationship between values, beliefs, attitudes, and actions, and what client-centered writers describe as "congruence." When using this concept, the writers seem to be referring to the notion of internal consistency among one's beliefs, attitudes, and values. In the use of this term, it is clearly communicated that they believe it is desirable and good that all elements and components of one's belief system should be internally consistent with all other elements and components of one's belief system. Further, it is desirable that one act in ways that are consistent with one's belief system and avoid acting in ways that are inconsistent with one's belief system. One may really understand the valuing orientation of this position by contrasting it with a position espoused by Ralph Waldo Emerson when he said, ". . . consistency is the hobgoblin of little minds. . . ."

Some important constructs in the counseling literature may be described using this basic model. Enhancing, facilitating, or contributing to a client's growth and development is generally seen as an important counseling goal. Few people, if any, ever achieve complete congruence in the sense described. It may not be possible to achieve a state of complete internal consistency among all the important elements of human functioning. And yet, perhaps, one way to conceptualize growth and development is to see them as a process over time of continually assessing and reappraising one's beliefs, values, attitudes, and actions and continually modifying these components in the direction of greater congruence. Change in the direction of greater congruence or internal consistency may be seen as growth. The process of "self-actualizing" may be seen as the process of coming closer and closer to a state of congruence between self-as-is and self-as-would-like-to-be. If this model is viable, it suggests that service to some clients is to help them become more aware of their values, attitudes, beliefs, and underlying assumptions, aware of the discrepancies among these components, and aware of what changes will result in greater congruity. It must be pointed out that such an approach might be more appropriate for a bright, introspective person interested in greater self-understanding, and less appropriate for a resistant, defensive client. It is also an approach that may be more appropriately implemented at a later, rather than at an earlier, stage of counseling. Premature implementation of this sort of approach may be especially frightening to some people.

Another concept very much related to this basic model is "genuineness." The concept has been used often by a variety of writers with a variety of meanings. Sometimes it seems to mean "honesty," other times, "candid self-disclosure." Perhaps one operational description of genuineness is *being aware of one's values and beliefs, and when one acts, to always act consistently, never inconsistently, with those beliefs, values, and attitudes.*

Using this description of the concept, developing into a genuine person is a process that requires awareness. Clearly, becoming aware of one's beliefs, values, and attitudes is a necessary and instrumental part of the process of becoming a genuine individual. With emotionally stable, introspective, and non-defensive people of adolescent or older age, sensitivity groups are frequently used as an approach to facilitate the growth and awareness process. Counselor education programs frequently require a sensitivity group experience for students precisely on these grounds. Their rationale is that genuineness is an important characteristic of counselors, that becoming aware of one's beliefs, values, attitudes, and underlying assumptions will contribute to the enhancement of this quality, and that a sensitivity group experience is a powerful approach to achieve those self-learning goals. It should be noted that such groups do have a powerful impact on their members, and that with some people, the impact is intense and negative. That is, for some people these groups may be threatening and may interfere severely with their growth and development. For a few, the experience may have a destructive impact.

Awareness

A major strategy of almost all traditional face-to-face counseling intervention systems has been to facilitate some kind of client "awareness." The various systems have differed with regard to what they want their clients to become aware of, but all have agreed that a major way to help clients function more effectively is to help them become "aware of" something. Their underlying operating assumption is that a causal relationship occurs between gaining awareness and improvement of functioning. Thus, client improvement would occur if, and only if, the client were to gain awareness. If clients do not change, it is because they have not gained sufficient awareness. If they do change, it is because they have gained insight.

The assumption of this functional connection between awareness and change has been seriously challenged, especially with the development of the operant conditioning approach, a system that does not assume awareness and defines what is learned as associations between a stimulus and a response.

Part of the challenge has been based on scientific grounds. Many clients considered to have demonstrated awareness did not demonstrate change, and many who demonstrated change did not demonstrate awareness. A second challenge stems from the question, "Awareness of what?" Where each system has differed has been in the kind of things counselors have wanted their clients to become aware of. Thus, psychoanalysts have emphasized awareness of alleged underlying motives the helper assumed to exist; rational-emotive helpers have emphasized awareness of illogical self-feeding statements that disrupt the client's ability to make rational decisions.

Clearly, the kinds of things the counselor hopes to help his client become aware of have a great deal to do with whether or not counseling change can be facilitated. It is one thing to work toward change by trying to facilitate awareness of alleged unconscious processes; it is another thing to try to help a client change undesirable behavior by helping him become aware of the consequences of his undesirable behavior. In each case, the counseling approach of the helper would differ considerably.

Thus, facilitating certain kinds of awareness may be seen as a valuable process goal for certain clients with certain difficulties, whereas, for other clients with other difficulties facilitating awareness is not an instrumental process goal. Facilitating awareness of underlying values is also a desired process goal for some clients, particularly clients who are bright and do not resist the examination of values. As will be developed shortly, awareness of dominant emotions and the situations in which they occur is yet another valuable awareness-based process goal. For clients whose counseling goal is to make important life decisions (career, future education, etc.), becoming aware of the skills that are necessary for effective future performance and of interests that will be necessary for the enjoyment of future positions are essential process goals. It is also essential that clients become aware of their behavioral characteristics that are related to their decision.

Toward an understanding of emotions

Helping clients understand and work through powerful emotional experiences has generally been considered an essential aspect of the counseling process. Empathy may be described as the counselor's ability to understand how the client feels at any given point in the counseling process and how he or she may feel about the situations being described to the counselor. Empathy also refers to the ability of the counselor to respond to the client so as to communicate that the nature and intensity of the emotion experienced is understood by the counselor. Thus, counselors who have some functional understanding of human emotions are likely to be more empathic and impactful than those who do not.

An understanding of emotions begins with the recognition that a distinction must be made between emotions and attitudes or opinions. Emotions are internal experiences such as joy, anger, anxiety, hope, sadness, doubt, confusion, love. Attitudes are beliefs about past, present, and future events. The use of the word "feel" in the following statements will help to clarify this distinction. The word is used incorrectly in the first statement and correctly in the others.

——I feel that counselor education programs should provide intensive training in effective helping

——I feel happy when I know somebody has benefited from a talk with me

——I feel angry when somebody has not lived up to an agreement with me

——I feel anxious when I find out that somebody disapproves of my actions

In the first sentence, the initiator incorrectly labeled his valuing statement as a feeling. In the second, third, and fourth statements, the initiator labeled a feeling he experiences and a class of situations in which he tends to experience those feelings. In this use of the word feeling, empathy refers to the ability to identify and help a person describe feelings he or she is experiencing. Incorrectly labeling attitudes as feelings tends to block the ability to tune in to the emotions being experienced.

Emotions people experience do not simply happen. They are internally experienced responses to situations and are influenced both by the individual's perceptions or beliefs about the situation and by his or her past experiences in situations that are similar. In turn, the emotions a person experiences in a situation have both verbal and nonverbal indicators and influence his or her way of responding to the situation. Thus, emotions function both as responses and stimuli. As responses, they are triggered by definable situations; as stimuli they influence the way a person reacts to a given situation.

The feelings people experience differ in both kind and intensity. Joy is a feeling that differs markedly from anger, and in turn is different in kind from the feeling of anxiety. In contrast, annoyance and rage are both experiences of anger that differ from each other in intensity. A complete understanding of an emotional experience includes being able to describe:

———the emotions that were experienced

———the intensity of the emotions that were experienced

———the situation that triggered the emotions

———the perceptions held about the situation involved

———the behavioral indicators of the emotion experienced (both verbal and nonverbal)

———the feelings that influenced the behavior that occurred in the situation

The emotions of another are not always easily understandable to a second party. To understand the emotions of another, the counselor needs to know the cues to look for and, in turn, what the cues indicate or signify. Four sets of cues are available to the counselor. The most obvious set of cues is the words a client uses to describe his or her feelings. Often clients use jargon to express their emotions: uptight (usually very anxious); my mind was blown (surprised or confused); bugged (annoyed). Experienced counselors learn to become sensitive to these "red flag" words in order to help them more fully understand the emotions experienced by their clients.

A second set of cues is the voice tones of a client. The voice of a person who is angry will often be much louder than normal voice amplitude; the rate of speech may be faster. In contrast, the voice tones of a client feeling depressed will often be much more quiet and subdued; the rate of speech will be slower than normal; words may come out one at a time rather than in sentences. The anxious client will often stutter, stammer, repeat parts of a sentence, and use lots of "you knows."

Facial expressions, focus of the eyes, and motor cues are very good indicators of client emotion. The eyes of a nervous person will have difficulty focusing on any object. There is apt to be an unusually high amount of fidgeting, squirming, and foot wiggling. In contrast, the depressed person is likely to gaze downward and there will be a noticeable absence of body activity. When a person is angry, he or she will show a heightened level of motor activity.

A fourth set of cues is based on inference. Given the circumstances, a client may describe how he or she might feel about a situation. For example, the woman who says she was qualified for a job but that it was awarded to a man instead can be expected to feel both disappointed and angry about this event. The parent who receives a telephone call that her child has been injured on the school playground can be expected to feel very apprehensive.

Table 3.1 will help to relate cues with the emotions that they signify. The left-hand column describes the sources of cues available. The row across the top describes five basic human emotional experiences: joy, anxiety, anger, guilt, and depression. The rectangles inside the matrix refer to the specific cues within the source indicated that signify the particular emotion across the top. The specific cues provide information to the counselor from which to infer the specific emotions experienced by the client as indicated across the top of the table.

Table 3.1   Sources of cues for different emotions

	Emotion				
Source of Cues	Joy	Anxiety	Anger	Guilt	Depression
Verbal					
Voice Tone					
Nonverbal Motor (face, eyes, body movement)					
Inference					

While the words clients use, particularly the red flag words, are the most obvious sources of information, they are not always the most reliable. Defensive clients can most easily cover up and control the sources of cues. The client who was experiencing anger may have learned that anger is not an OK emotion and thus avoid describing this emotion. The most reliable sources of cues are voice tones and nonverbal-motor cues. These are much more difficult to control, especially when emotions are intense, and, therefore, more reliable as emotion indicators. Often when there are discrepancies between cues, counselors will accept the nonverbal cues as the more valid indicators. For example, a client who is shouting loudly about a recent experience of unfair treatment may deny that he or she was experiencing anger about the situation. The stuttering client may not acknowledge experiencing anxiety. In the face of such discrepancies, many counselors will recognize that the emotions are really there, but are difficult for the client to accept as a part of self. Apparently, the experiencing of these emotions is threatening to the client.

The fourth source of cues—inferences from information shared by a client—is the most difficult for counselors to deal with. Inferring a feeling state of another inevitably involves some projection and thus is subject to error. Projection is the process of placing oneself in the situation of another and imagining how it feels to be in that situation. While this can lead to projecting one's own feelings onto a client and thus not perceiving the client accurately, by avoiding this source of cues it is also possible to miss tuning in to some important aspects of the client's emotional experiencing. Experienced counselors try to minimize errors of this kind by basing their inferences not only on how they would feel in the situation, but also on how others they have known have felt in similar situations. Inferences are usually kept tentative, to relate to other sources of cues. Often, too, this source is used as a basis for assessing client openness versus defensiveness to self-examination.

Toward an understanding of anxiety

The experiencing of anxiety may be understood as an extension of the basic principle that human behavior is purposive and goal directed. When people perceive that they are able to achieve important goals, there is a tendency to feel secure and relaxed. However, when people anticipate that they may have difficulty bringing about an important goal or that something harmful may happen in the future, anxiety is experienced. Thus, anxiety is a feeling state experienced in the present that occurs as a result of anticipations of something undesirable or harmful happening in the future. The perceptions behind anxiety are essentially these: "I have a goal that is very important to me. I have doubts as to whether I can bring that goal about for myself. I anticipate either that I do not have the power to bring about that goal, or that my efforts to bring that goal about will not result in success. I anticipate that something harmful will happen to me in the future and I do not feel secure about preventing the occurrence of that harmful event."

In interpersonal situations, for example, a person who wants approval, recognition, affection, or support from another is likely to experience anxiety if he or she anticipates receiving from that other criticism, ridicule, rejection, put down, attack, or any other message which says in effect, "I don't like you" or "I think your performance is less than acceptable." The level of anxiety experienced will be related to how desperately the individual wants approval or recognition, the significance of the other person involved, the likelihood that disapproval or rejection will result, the individual's appraisal of his or her own ability to respond to the situation to obtain approval, and the individual's sensitivity to rejection experiences in past situations.

Anxiety, then, is a reflection of a person's perceived sense of adequacy or inadequacy. In the face of a difficult situation, where one is not sure whether or not a goal event can be brought about, the person feeling a sense of adequacy will say to self in essence: "I am optimistic that I can bring this goal about for myself. I believe that I have the skills to deal with the situation. Even if I do not bring about what I desire, I have the skills to cope with the consequences. Nothing terribly disastrous will happen to me in the future." In contrast, the insecure person's perceptions are: "I am not optimistic that I can bring about this important goal for myself. If I do not bring about this important goal, other consequences will follow, which will be harmful to me. I doubt whether I will be able to deal with these subsequent consequences." The person absolutely convinced of his or her inability will have the following beliefs and perceptions: "I know I cannot bring this goal about for me. It is so impossible that I will not even try. I will simply have to accept whatever consequences come from not bringing about this goal. I am so convinced of this that I will not even worry about the situation."

While every individual experiences difficult, challenging, and risky situations, some seem to experience more pervasive anxiety about those situations than others. The person with basic confidence in self and the ability to bring about important goals has developed a "success identity." The person who focuses on doubts and who in the face of difficult situations experiences high levels of anxiety has developed a "failure identity." The first has lots of "I-can-do-its" that are a part of his or her life-style. The second has many "I-doubt-whether I-can-do-its" and "I cannot-do-its" as a part of his or her life style.

Ways of coping with anxiety

Since anxiety is an indicator to an individual that he or she is anticipating that something bad will happen in the future, the healthiest way to cope with anxiety is to "process it" in awareness. This means developing honest answers to the following questions:

———What situation in the present am I finding threatening?

———What outcomes am I anticipating for the future (failure, put down, rejection, interpersonal friction, loss of something valued)?

———What makes me think these anticipated outcomes are really bad?

———What is the basis for believing these future events really will happen?

———What action alternatives are open to me to act on the present situation so as to either bring about for myself that which I want or to prevent that which I do not want?

———If my anxiety relates to the anticipated behavior of another individual, what is the basis for my thinking that the other individual will really act the way I anticipate? Is it possible he or she might act in ways different from the way I am anticipating?

That is the process for healthy, rational coping with anxiety. No person ever uses this approach to cope with all anxiety-laden experiences and some never use it. There are a variety of defense mechanisms people use to defend self against threatening or anxiety-provoking situations. Note that the metaphor of "defensiveness" implies an attack—defend against attack connotation. Coleman and Hammen (1974) list and describe fifteen anxiety protection defense mechanisms, including: denial of reality, repression, regression, fantasy, rationalization, projection, reaction formation, identification, introjection, emotional insulation, intellectualization, compensation, displacement, undoing, and acting out. Brief definitions of these defenses are provided in Table 3.2. The element that these defensive

Table 3.2 Summary chart of ego-defense mechanisms

Denial of reality	Refusing to perceive or face unpleasant reality
Repression	Preventing painful or dangerous thoughts from entering consciousness
Regression	Retreating to earlier developmental level involving less mature responses and usually a lower level of aspiration
Fantasy	Gratifying frustrated desires by imaginary achievements
Rationalization	Attempting to prove that one's behavior is "rational" and justifiable and thus worthy of the approval of oneself and others
Projection	Placing blame for difficulties upon others or attributing one's own unethical desires to others
Reaction formation	Preventing the expression of dangerous desires by exaggerating the opposite attitudes and types of behavior
Identification	Increasing feelings of worth by identifying oneself with some outstanding person or institution
Introjection	Incorporating into one's own ego structure the values and standards imposed by others
Emotional insulation	Reducing ego involvement and withdrawing into passivity to protect oneself from hurt
Intellectualization	Suppressing the emotional aspect of hurtful situations or separating incompatible attitudes by logic-tight compartments
Compensation	Covering up weakness by emphasizing some desirable trait or making up for frustration in one area by overgratification in another
Displacement	Discharging pent-up feelings, usually of hostility, on objects less dangerous than those which initially aroused the emotions
Undoing	Counteracting "immoral" desires or acts by some form of atonement
Acting out	Reducing the anxiety aroused by forbidden desires by permitting their expression

systems have in common is that they are all attempts to escape (at least psychologically) some anxiety-provoking situation and all involve at least some element of distorting environmental information.

Three other defensive reactions counselors are likely to encounter are discounting, blaming others, and switching the issue. Discounting is the process of minimizing the significance of some person, event, or information. Occasionally, this may sound like a combination of denying and rationalizing: "Jim isn't all that important a person. If I can't get his friendship, it does not really matter that much."

The tendency to blame others is an especially difficult situation to work through. Blaming another when things go wrong takes away responsibility from self and is thus ego-protecting. Switching the issue or topic for discussion is a client's way of telling a counselor that there is something associated with the primary issue of discussion that is threatening to the client. At the same time, this tendency to switch is an indicator both of the client's readiness for deeper level self-examination and level of trust for the counselor.

Toward an understanding of anger

Understanding anger as an emotional response begins with an understanding of the kinds of stimulus conditions that provoke the feeling. Three classes of situations have been consistently identified in the research literature: frustrating situations, situations in which an individual's sense of adequacy and security are being threatened, and situations in which one person's behavior does not meet the expectations or approval or another.

Many people think of frustration as a feeling. However, research on human behavior (Dollard, Miller, Doob et al., 1939) suggests that it is more appropriate to view frustration as a class of stimulus conditions. Thus, a frustrating situation may be described as any situation wherein a person has an important goal and the means to achieving that goal is blocked. Anger is a frequent emotional response to frustrating situations. The intensity of anger experienced (mild annoyance to intense rage) is related to the importance of the goal that is being blocked, the urgency or immediacy of the goal, the person's appraisal as to whether the obstacles involved can be overcome, the level of environmental pressure being experienced by the individual, the person's past experiences in situations similar to the frustrating event, and the individual's sense of basic personal security. Thus, to the driver returning home as usual after work, a red traffic light may evoke only small annoyance. But for the same driver who has received a call from his wife that their child has suddenly become ill, that same red traffic light may evoke a more intense anger. Missing an item on a "pop quiz" may evoke mild self-directed annoyance. For the same student (a senior going to college), missing an item on the ACT exams may evoke intense self-directed annoyance.

It is important to distinguish between two classes of frustrating events: those where the obstacles to goal achievement are perceived as coming from environmental factors and those where a skill deficit is perceived as being involved in the inability to bring about a highly desired goal. When a person perceives that the source of frustration lies external to self (somewhere else in the environment), anger is likely to be directed away from self. When the individual perceives that goal blockage comes from his or her lack of ability, then anger is likely to be directed toward self.

An unusually high level of anger to frustrating situations is often an important sign of an underlying sense of basic personal insecurity. The frustrating event is experienced as a confirmation of the individual's negative attitude toward self—his or her "I am not OK. I can't do it" beliefs. To an outside observer as well as the individual, the observed anger often acts as a cover-up to the underlying insecurity. Behind the surface expression of anger there is often deeper level anxiety. For such individuals gaining control of anger and reducing it requires awareness and control of the deeper level anxiety.

Where the individual assigns responsibility for the frustrating condition is often an important indicator of client defensiveness. As the counselor listens to a client describe his or her anger and its perceived underlying sources, a question that inevitably arises is whether the client is assigning responsibility for the frustrating situation to the appropriate sources. It is not uncommon for teachers and counselors to see students who blame others for their difficulties when the source of difficulty lies within self. For such students, accepting personal responsibility for the frustrating situation is threatening. It is more comfortable to assign responsibility away from self. Clients who respond defensively are generally not aware of the rationalization, denial, repression, and discounting they engage in to avoid personal responsibility. Helping a client work through his or her responsibility-avoidance defenses is often one of the most difficult parts of the counseling process. These principles are demonstrated in the case of Jimmy, at the end of this chapter.

It is a truth in life that people evaluate the quality and acceptability of each other's behavior. Person *A* evaluates person *B* while *B* is also evaluating *A*. An evaluation is a judgmental statement about the acceptability of the quality of another person's actions—whether it has met certain standards or expectations. Behind the expectations are a series of "should" statements: "My husband should get home from work before dinner time." "My wife should understand my moods when I get home." "The children should cooperate with each other." "The teacher should give us clues as to what will be on the exam." "Students should be in the room when class begins." Anger occurs when the imposed "shoulds" are not met. The intensity of anger experienced is related to the closeness of the relationship of the people involved, the importance of the "should" statement to the angry person's belief system, the severity of violation, the persistence of the violation, and the justification for the violation. Thus, in an unusual incident when a well-behaved student inadvertently puts another down, the teacher may experience some annoyance but not nearly as much as would be felt toward another student who does it often and continues to do it after he and the teacher discussed it in private. The teacher would also probably feel more anger toward a student with whom he or she had close rapport than toward a student with whom the relationship was distant.

When anger comes from a perceived violation of expectations and standards, working the anger through usually requires an awareness-based approach. Over time the counselor's role becomes that of helping the individual work non-defensively on issues such as the following:

———If I am angry about the behavior of another, then I am making some "should" statements about that other person's behavior. What are the "should" statements I am making?

———Is it appropriate for me to be making these "should" statements about the behavior of the other individual involved? If yes, then what assumptions and perceptions do I have about this individual? If no, then can I learn to stop applying this "should" statement to this individual and learn to be more accepting and tolerant?

———What *really* is so intolerable to me about this other person's behavior?

———Quite likely my anger is blocking my ability to understand some important aspects of this person's behavior. What might be some explanations for the behavior that I regard as unacceptable?

——Of whom in my past does this person remind me? In what ways are they similar? Different?

Notice that the work of the client is essentially to become aware of the "should" statements behind the anger and the basis for making them. The work of the counselor is to stimulate the work of the client.

This is not to say that anger toward another is always inappropriate. People who believe this often try to deny and repress their anger when they experience it. People do have a right to expect certain things of each other, and when these expectations are not met, a certain amount of anger is not unreasonable. However, we are saying that there are occasions in which the amount of anger experienced is unreasonably high and other occasions in which the anger is inappropriate. The judgment of the appropriateness of the client's anger and anger level need not be made by the counselor alone. Often the appropriateness itself becomes an issue for counseling discussion. More is said about counselor anger in Chapter 6, which is on constructive confrontation.

Toward an understanding of self-concept

"Self-concept" refers to the views a person has about self. At a global level, the term refers to a person's perceived sense of basic adequacy to cope with basic life-space situations and to bring about important life goals. The person with a healthy self-concept takes the following life stance toward self: "I'm OK. I believe I have now, or can acquire, the basic skills to cope with the stresses in life that I can expect to encounter as an alive person. I have important life goals and while I know there will be obstacles along the way, I am optimistic about my ability to achieve them. I experience respect for myself and expect other people will like me and treat me with respect. If and when they do not, their disrespect or dislike for me will not influence me to dislike myself."

These basic views toward self stand in sharp contrast to the person with a low self-concept or low sense of self-worth: "I'm not OK. Often I doubt my own basic abilities to cope with the stressful situations in life I can expect to encounter. Anticipating these stressful situations frightens me and if I confront myself honestly I know I go out of my way to avoid them. The future frightens me because I seriously doubt whether I will be able to bring about for myself that which I really want. As a consequence, whatever thinking I do about my future feels much like fantasy. I do not experience respect for myself. I fear others because I anticipate that they will dislike and reject me, ridicule me, and disapprove of my actions. Criticism adds to my sense of self-dislike. Often I experience myself trying to prove to me and others that I really can do something that secretly I believe I really am not able to do. I find it very difficult to be assertive. On those occasions in which I have tried, my efforts come out as anger and frustration. The dominant emotions in my life experiencing are anxiety, despair, confusion, and anger."

The work of Erikson (1968) suggests that identity formation begins at birth and that basic identity is formulated at a very early age. Once formulated, a person's core identity appears to be remarkably resistant to change in a favorable direction. What seems to occur is that traumatic and stressful events can cause a person with a basically healthy self-image to develop severe doubts about basic adequacy. But even in the face of favorable affirming events, many people experiencing self-doubt and dislike from a very early age do not change their views toward self for the better.

Erikson suggests that the self-image a young person acquires is heavily influenced by the attitudes of his or her parents. By their behavior, parents convey their underlying attitude toward their children. The children pick up the cues and take on those attitudes for themselves. Critical to the identity formation process seems to be the way caring is expressed, the amount and kind of opportunities for curiosity expression and environment exploration made available to a child, and the ways in which correction for misbehaviors is handled. As reviewed in Chapter 4, caring refers to how much one person's present and future well-being matters to another. Caring parents take the attitude, "Your present and future well-being matters enough to me that I am willing to devote time and energy to you and to show an interest in the things in which you show an interest." In contrast, what comes through from the non-caring parent is, "I have many agendas and priorities in my life. You are only one of them. I choose to spend my time on these other agendas, which means your worth and importance to me are relatively low."

Following upon this, caring parents structure the environment of their children so that from the earliest ages there are plenty of opportunities for successful achievement and that achievement is recognized and accepted with happiness and enthusiasm. Curiosity responses to the environment are encouraged and supported rather than blocked and suppressed. Opportunities for taking on responsibilities are also structured into the environment very early, affirming the parent's belief that the child is capable of accepting responsibility and, therefore, is a responsible person. When the responsibilities are taken care of, the child's successful efforts are again recognized and affirmed.

Caring parents also recognize that not all of the child's behavior is acceptable. Some behaviors are quite unacceptable and must be corrected. Rather than using punishment techniques that imply that the child is regarded as stupid and/or evil, caring parents will take the time to explain why a given behavior is unacceptable, what alternatives would be more acceptable, and encourage those new behaviors when they happen. Caring parents will also recognize that misbehaviors are purposive and goal directed for recognition, power, revenge, or display of inadequacy (Dinkmeyer & McKay, 1975) and will take into account the purposes of misbehavior in their correction procedures.

A person's view toward self appears to be a powerful determinant of behavior, personal decision making, and aspirations for the future. In his book *The Productive Personality*, Gilmore (1974) identifies three attributes of exceptionally productive people. They are high achievers, they are unusually creative, and they are leaders. The research he reviews suggests that high performance on all these dimensions seems to be related to a positive self-concept. In short, exceptionally productive people like and respect themselves and are optimistic about their abilities to be successful. They seem to have acquired a success rather than a failure identity. In his review of the relationship between self-concept and academic achievement, Purkey (1970) suggests that self-concept appears to correlate more highly with academic achievement than do scores on tests of "intelligence."

At a more specific level, self-concept refers to what an individual knows and believes about self. A person's specific views about self include a descriptive appraisal of capacities and limitations, interests and disinterests, and dominant behavior patterns. It includes views in the present, and hopes and expectations for the future. Sometimes these self-referent statements are idiographic (me looking at self); at other times they are nomothetic (me compared to others). Here are some examples:

————I am skillful at using my hands for mechanical work

———I do not read as well as others

———I would rather watch a television show that interests me than go to a loud party

———I enjoy playing a guitar, but do not enjoy listening to opera

———I become very angry when I believe I have been unfairly treated, but rarely show my anger

———I wish I could be more assertive

The descriptive statements that people make about themselves usually have evaluative implications. Often people are not aware of the evaluations behind their descriptions.

———I relate very well to peers of the opposite sex (and am proud of that ability).

———I often find myself very concerned about whether other people approve or disapprove of what I do or say (and wish I could overcome this fear).

———I become very nervous when I have to say something in a group. The larger the group, the more nervous I am. (I do not like having this problem and wish I could overcome this fear.)

———People often seem offended by my actions and I do not know why. (This pattern bothers me.)

———I am not very good at playing chess and probably will never be. (This lack of ability does not bother me at all.)

———I find myself worrying a great deal about whether my children really love me. I know they do, but I still worry about it. (I don't like this about me and wish I could overcome my fears.)

———I am well organized and an excellent typist (and feel good about these skills), but I also have a tendency to be crabby with the people I work for. (I do not like being so crabby so often.)

What does "healthy self-concept" mean

Since the term "healthy" is heavily judgmental, the term "healthy self-concept" is heavily value-laden. This leaves the counselor with two options: to suspend the use of the concept, or to use the term with clear awareness of the implied judgments behind its use. The position of the authors is to opt for the latter choice.

Healthy self-concept involves both the global and specific meanings of the term. Respect and liking for self, optimism about one's ability to bring about important future goals, and freedom from unrealistic anxieties about failure are all important characteristics of an emotionally healthy individual. So is the capacity for experiencing confidence in one's ability to make wise, reasoned decisions.

The difficulty in thinking about the meaning of a "healthy self-concept" occurs when one attempts to attach the term "realistic" to self-concept. It is easy to say that having a healthy self-concept includes setting goals that are "realistic" and describing oneself "realistically." Obviously, it is not healthy to set goals that are "unrealistic" (either too high or too low), or to have views about self that are not consistent with reality. But who is a good judge of what is realistic and unrealistic for another individual? For example, it would be easy to say that it is unrealistic for a college freshman with a cumulative college board score of 900 to believe that he or she can actually become a world renowned brain surgeon. The score predicts that admission to medical school is a very unlikely possibility for this individual. Similarly, counselors often believe that the scrawny, uncoordinated kid from the ghetto who aspires to become a star professional football player is engaging in unrealistic fantasy as a way of escaping the unhappiness of his present life space. But an ancient Chinese proverb cautions about such assessments concerning the unrealistic aspirations of another: "It is very difficult to prophesy, especially about the future."

Similarly, counselors often encounter people whose perceptions of their present selves often appear unrealistic. Occasionally, the sociometric neglectee perceives himself to be popular among his peers. A person may perceive himself or herself to be a talented musician when his or her musical efforts are highly displeasing to any and all potential listeners.

Like all discrepancies that are a part of the world of the counselor, the challenge is to ask what the apparent discrepancy means to the individual involved. In this clarification process, the counselor must first investigate his or her own judgments. What is the justification for believing this other person's aspirations are unrealistic? Is the judgment defensible to a critic? What makes it defensible? Is the evidence of reality convincing? There are times when a counselor will be convinced of his or her answer to these questions and other times when he or she will not be sure. Clear and convincing evidence that the client's aspirations or perceptions are not realistic leads to the hypothesis that it is very important for the client to hold on to his or her personal myths. An analysis of what makes the myth important to the client leads the counselor to a greater understanding of the client, and hence the goals and process of counseling for the client. Clarification of the basis for believing that the client's myth is really a myth helps the counselor check out and recognize his or her own judgmental tendencies and how they affect his or her feelings toward and perceptions of the client.

What does improvement of self-concept mean?

Counselors often say that the primary goal of counseling for a given individual is to increase his or her self-concept. Since self-concept has both global and specific dimensions it is clear that this goal is very ambiguous. Sometimes it seems to mean helping a person move from a general "I'm not OK" to an "I am OK" life stance. At other times, it seems to mean developing a more optimistic outlook on one's ability to achieve important future goals. With other clients, when the goal "self-concept improvement" is analyzed, it turns out to mean setting goals that are more realistic or more acceptable to someone else in the client's environment.

When the goal of counseling is left this ambiguous, counselor and client alike have no way of assessing whether progress is being made or when the goals of counseling have been achieved. As a result, the counseling process often becomes aimless and without focus. Frequently, both client and counselor leave the session experiencing a sense of futility. Nothing useful has happened and something should have.

The problem is not difficult to overcome, but it does require some cognitive restructuring for counselors who fall into this trap. The solution is for the counselor to specify more clearly what is meant by self-concept improvement for the specific client being helped. This can be done in a variety of ways. One is to focus on the question, "If this client's self-concept were to improve, what concomitant changes in his or her behavior would I be able to observe?" Frequently, the concomitant changes that are specified become goals in and of themselves. Often working on the more specific changes first can bring about a more global change in beliefs about self.

Another solution to this problem is for the counselor to intentionally leave out the term "self-concept" in his or her thinking about the client. Purposefully leaving out an ambiguous term forces clarification, specificity, and greater elaboration. This thinking strategy also helps to surface some implied "if-then" statements.

For example, the counselor may go through a thinking process as follows: "Here is a client who has a low self-concept, and for whom self-concept improvement is an important goal. . . . Let me see if I can be more clear and specific. Here is a client who does not like self and who believes others do not like him either. If I can show the client that others really do like him, then perhaps that will lead him to liking himself more. . . . No, Mark is a client who discounts any favorable data he receives. He would discount the idea that others like him. Perhaps we ought to explore in more depth how he learned to think the way he has about himself. Perhaps his views are coming from some painful experiences in his past. We both need to understand more fully the nature of his relationships with his parents and how they might be affecting his present views about himself."

In sum, self-concept is an important concept involved in understanding human behavior. Used carefully and tentatively, the concept can help to understand and account for the behavior patterns of another, and to generate ideas for approaches to helping. Indiscriminate use of the term without recognition of its vagueness can lead to superficial thinking about the client and the goals for helping. Clarification of the specific meaning of the term for the individual client involved can lead to specificity of goals and possible helping approaches.

Case study 3:
Jimmy—an angry young man

The case of Jimmy will help to illustrate these principles. Jimmy was a twelve-year-old student in the sixth grade. He had always been smaller than the other boy students of his age. He was the fourth of five children in a family characterized by continuing turmoil and instability. Often the father would leave the home situation for extended periods and when he reappeared he was often drunk and broke. Mother received unemployment compensation in addition to Aid to Dependent Children. The apartment in which they lived was in very poor repair and seriously overcrowded. The older children (two boys and one girl) frequently squabbled with each other. Somehow in the family constellation Jimmy emerged as the scapegoat. Many of the communications to him from his older siblings were in the form of ridicule and put downs. Jimmy's response to these criticisms would be to try to hit the other person involved.

In his school performance, Jimmy's work was "marginal passing." His grade equivalent for measures of reading and verbal skill were generally about two grade levels below his actual grade level. Yet, many of his teachers reported that in some ways Jimmy showed important signs of being "street smart." He often showed clever ways of manipulating a situation to his own advantage.

Jimmy had a long history of fighting in the school. Often incidents that the teachers regarded as "insignificant, even by the norms of Jimmy's peer group" would trigger Jimmy to instigate a fight. When queried about it afterward, Jimmy would always indicate that the fight was the fault of the other students involved; the responsibility for starting the fight lay with them, not him. Earlier in his school career, teachers observed that this was rarely the case. However, in the last year or so teachers observed that on a few of the fighting occasions groups of students would "bait" Jimmy into a fight. Jimmy never avoided the bait even though he generally came out the loser.

Partly as a matter of self-preservation, partly because it was a project for a counseling course, and partly because he cared, Mr. Washington, Jimmy's teacher, decided to try to do something about Jimmy's behavior. Mr. Washington had somehow managed to develop a better rapport with Jimmy than his previous teachers. Using this relationship, Mr. Washington was able to establish a contract with Jimmy that included both contingency and parallel elements to it. If Jimmy agreed to go an hour without a fight, then he could do any classroom activity of his choosing. Mr. Washington also agreed to spend fifteen minutes a day "rapping" with Jimmy on an individual basis about any issue Jimmy chose. There would be no criticisms or hassles of Jimmy's behavior in these rap sessions. The original contract was fulfilled and several new contracts were subsequently established, fulfilled, and reevaluated. In each contract, Jimmy's agreement was to go for a progressively longer period without fighting. In this way, Mr. Washington had helped Jimmy gain control over his own fighting in the classroom when his teacher was present. However, Mr. Washington could not get the change in behavior to generalize to settings outside the classroom.

In supervision, the nature of Mr. Washington's interactions

with Jimmy during the rap sessions was analyzed. It was clear that Mr. Washington really cared for Jimmy and very much wanted Jimmy to control his anger because the fighting would result in some very bad long-range consequences in Jimmy's future: eventually he would probably be expelled from school and subsequently would enter a life of crime. However, Mr. Washington rarely used "I messages" in his interactions with Jimmy. Nor did he respond to the feeling dimensions of what Jimmy said. As a result of the supervision discussion, Mr. Washington agreed to respond in a reflective way to a feeling Jimmy expressed and would respond with an "I message" at some point in their next interaction.

The results were dramatic. Once during their interaction, Mr. Washington said to Jimmy, "I sense you felt very hurt and angry when your brother criticized you and wished he would have been more understanding of your feelings instead." This led to a much deeper level of discussion about how Jimmy feels inside when he is criticized and some of Jimmy's feelings about his older siblings. Mr. Washington did not try to talk Jimmy out of his feelings, but limited his responses to "Tell me more about . . ." and "Help me understand more fully." Although there were still strong elements of denial in Jimmy's statements, there was also a shift toward greater ownership of feelings.

It also surfaced that Jimmy really did not like getting into fights. Sometimes it felt to him as though he just could not control himself. At other times, he would say no other solutions made any sense. Toward the end of their conversation, Mr. Washington used an "I message" to offer what he regarded as an important self-disclosure, "I want you to know, Jimmy, that I really care about what happens to you now and in your future. As I see it, you recognize that fighting does not always solve your real problems and frequently adds to them. I am wondering if we could work together to help you get control over your fighting." This led to an intensive discussion about whether Jimmy believed it was possible and desirable for him not to fight.

This interaction seemed to be a major turning point. Several days later Jimmy said he was not sure whether he could stop but that he would try if Mr. Washington could help. Mr. Washington used role play and encouragement to help Jimmy find other ways to handle the situations in which he was being baited. Over time, fights in the classroom stopped and fights on the playground were reduced. Jimmy still had not established any close friendships, but there was some tendency for the students to be less resistant to including Jimmy in group activities.

Analysis

Understanding Jimmy's fighting and underlying anger begins with the recognition that Jimmy did not like himself and was largely unaware of his own self-dislike. He almost never received messages from significant others to the effect "We think you are OK and likeable." To the contrary, the messages he received were "We think you are not OK and that you are unlikeable." Like all people, Jimmy wanted very much to belong, to be liked, and to receive recognition. Being put down and excluded, the life stance he was taking was "I am not OK and am disliked by others. I do not belong. The only way I can get recognition is by fighting." At a deeper, probably subconscious level, Jimmy was also dealing with "I don't belong, but want to. Not belonging when I want to is frustrating and it hurts. I am angry about being excluded, rejected, and put down."

Jimmy also showed the typical defensive pattern of assigning responsibility for his difficulties to others. No matter what happened, it was not his fault. While some might construe this as lying, it is quite possible Jimmy genuinely believed this. To admit he was responsible and even to explore alternatives to fighting would be a threat to what little sense of self-regard he experienced. When the motivation for anger lies at this level, counseling exhortations to think rationally about the long- and short-range consequences will have little impact. In fact, Jimmy resisted these earlier efforts by saying, "Fighting is the only way that works for me. The others in my class know they can't push me around or make fun of me."

If the experiencing of anger came from a threat to Jimmy's basic security and long-term frustration over not being able to achieve the goals of belonging and acceptance, then fighting as a way to cope with the frustrating situations came from exposure to significant role models who consistently demonstrated to Jimmy that fighting was *the* solution to this problem. Further, Jimmy's fighting was supported on a partial reinforcement schedule—the most difficult to break. Two reinforcers seemed to operate. Sometimes Jimmy would win the fights. If he lost, it meant he just had to fight harder and better. Second, the fighting would temporarily stop the put downs and ridicules.

Jimmy's belief system also supported the fighting. The conclusion he had come to was "Fighting is the only way for me to get what I want." It was a well-defended belief system. Jimmy could cite examples to support his beliefs. Indeed, Mr. Washington frequently wondered if Jimmy's beliefs were not accurate. So long as Jimmy held on and defended his beliefs no lasting change would occur. Yet, the harder people tried to change his beliefs the more resistant Jimmy became to changing those beliefs. If Jimmy were to be reached at all it had to be at a different level. The level of contact that stimulated work was communication at a feeling level.

What really made the difference in Mr. Washington's efforts? Perhaps more than anything else was Mr. Washington's expressions of caring. By paying attention, actively listening, and risking some honest self-disclosure, Mr. Washington was communicating in essence, "Underneath the fighting behavior there is a person who is OK and likeable. If I did not like and care I would not bother to invest the time and energy or take the risks that I have." To a young person hungry for recognition such expression of caring must have meaning.

Mr. Washington learned he could not talk Jimmy out of his beliefs, so he did not try. Further, his position was that there may be times when Jimmy may need to fight. So one of the things he tried to do after making in-depth contact was to help Jimmy learn to discriminate when fighting was OK and when it was not. This helped reduce the generalization. Once Jimmy was willing to try to control his fighting, the discrimination activity plus role playing helped Jimmy learn that in certain situations there were alternatives which he was capable of implementing. Mr. Washington hoped that this new recognition would generalize. While there was some generalization, Jimmy did not apply this new discovery as far as Mr. Washington would have liked.

References

Coleman, J. S., & Hammen, C. L. *Contemporary psychology and effective behavior.* Glenview, Ill.: Scott, Foresman, 1974.

Dinkmeyer, D., & McKay, G. *Systematic training for effective parenting: Instructor's Manual.* Circle Pines, Minn.: American Guidance Service, 1975.

Dollard, J., Miller, N. E., Doob, L. E., Mowrer, O. H., & Sears, R. R. *Frustration and aggression.* New Haven: Yale University Press, 1939.

Erikson, E. H. *Identity: Youth and crisis.* New York: W. W. Norton, 1968.

Gilmore, J. V. *The productive personality.* San Francisco: Albion, 1974.

Purkey, W. W. *Self-concept and school achievement.* Englewood Cliffs, N. J.: Prentice-Hall, 1970.

Raths, L., Harmin, M. M., & Simon, S. *Values and teaching.* Columbus, Ohio: Merrill, 1966.

4. The process of counseling

Effective counseling can take fifteen minutes; it can take a couple of sessions (as with Mike); or it can take months (as with Janice). In earlier chapters, counseling has been described as a *process*. The purpose of this chapter is to describe and analyze some of the components of the process that are the core ingredients of all counseling efforts.

The term "process" helps to communicate much about the essence of counseling. "Process" means an identifiable sequence of events taking place over time. Usually there is the implication of progressive stages to the process. For example, there are identifiable stages in the healing process of a serious physical wound such as a broken leg. Similarly, there are describable stages in the process of human development from birth to death. Although the stages in this process are common to all human beings, what happens within each of these stages is uniquely different for each individual.

63

The parallel applies to counseling. Although the specific events, dynamics, and content of exploration differ with each person to whom the counselor reaches out, the stages of the process are similar for most clients. Generally, the stages include: (1) the initial meeting; (2) exploration of client's concern and facilitative relationship development; (3) goal specification, identification, and assessment of factors related to goal achievement; (4) development and implementation of an approach to goal achievement; (5) evaluation of results; and (6) termination and follow-up. Chapter 5 will focus on the first two stages; later chapters will focus on subsequent stages.

To understand counseling as a process, it is also important to distinguish between outcome goals and process goals. As described in Chapter 2, outcome goals are the intended results of counseling. Generally, they are described in terms of what the client desires to achieve as a result of his or her talks with the counselor. In contrast, process goals are those future events the counselor considers helpful or instrumental in bringing about outcome goals. Outcome goals are described generally in terms of new client actions that will occur after the counseling sessions and outside the counselor's office; process goals are primarily events that take place during the counseling session and in the counselor's office. They are events that the counselor considers helpful and instrumental to outcome goal achievement.

Sometimes process goals are described in terms of counselor actions; at other times process goals are described in terms of effects to be experienced by the client. For example, a counselor may say, "If I am to help this client, I must actively listen to what he is saying and understand the significance of his concerns for his present and future well-being. I must understand how the attitudes he is describing influence the way he behaves toward significant others. I must understand the surrounding circumstances that relate to his concerns and I must understand the reinforcing events that support his present behavior." All these are process goals that relate to the counselor's behavior.

As he listens to an audio recording of his first session, a counselor may also think, "If I am to help this client he must feel a greater trust for me than he now appears to be experiencing. The client seems to be talking a good deal about issues and events that do not relate to his primary concern. If our sessions are to be worthwhile, he must focus more intently on his primary concerns. Perhaps the client is afraid to look at, and talk about, his primary concerns. If so, it will be important to help him gain control over these anxieties. How can I help the client feel more trust and less anxiety?" Experiencing trust, focusing more fully on primary concerns, and controlling fear are all process goals described in terms of effects the client should experience. The last sentence in the counselor's thinking raises the crucial question: "What can I do; how can I behave so as to facilitate these important process goals?"

Some process goals appear essential for all counseling relationships; others appear to be specific to clients, goals, and type of intervention. Some of the process goals common to almost all counseling relationships include establishing a relationship of trust, safety, and open communication; setting specific outcome goals; exploring underlying feelings, beliefs, and values; and developing useful awarenesses and insights. Some of the process goals especially appropriate for career choice counseling include identifying careers, seeking out information about the different identified careers, assessing personal talents, interests and preferences, and acquiring firsthand experience about the work involved in different career fields through real or simulated experiences. Using our first two case studies as examples, the counselors for both Mike and Janice considered it important to develop trusting relationships and to set clear goals. However, a process goal that was an essential part of counseling for Janice, but not Mike, was the working through of feelings of hostility and insecurity that related to having been conditionally acceptable to parents.

Three kinds of process goals that seem to cut across most counseling approaches and which seem to be appropriate for most clients are *relationship establishment, self-examination,* and *awareness facilitation.* As Truax and Carkhuff (1967) point out, almost all approaches to interpersonal helping work on the assumption that if counseling is to be effective, then the client must experience a sense of trust toward the counselor. He or she must have the belief that it is "OK" to talk about self, personal concerns, doubts, confusions, and innermost feelings to this other person. While it may sometimes be painful to have to look at and get in touch with those feelings, still, nothing disastrous will happen as a consequence. The counselor will neither betray nor use the information shared, to hurt or harm. It is worth the risk, because sharing thoughts and feelings will lead to helping achieve the goals established for this counseling experience. People who emphasize the relationship aspects of counseling, such as Rogers (1961) and Truax and Carkhuff (1967) say that the offering of empathy, genuineness, and positive regard helps to facilitate this sense of trust and full communication. More will be said about this in later chapters.

Self-exploration

The word "explore" is a verb that means "to transverse or range over, for the purpose of discovery." It also means "to look into closely, to examine, to scrutinize." *Self-exploration* then is the action process of learning and discovering new things about self. Most theories of counseling agree that self-exploration and examination is a critical part of the helping-growth process for most clients. The theorists may disagree as to what parts of self are important to discover. For example, while Ellis (1974) believes that the focus of self-exploration should be around dimensions of rationality, Perls (1969) and Rogers (1961) believe that the here and now affective dimensions of the client's experiencing should be the primary focus for exploration. They may also disagree on approaches and techniques the counselor should use to stimulate such exploration. For example, while Rogers reflects, Perls very actively and almost immediately confronts his clients. The critical point, however, is that all these helpers want to bring about the same process goal—intensive client self-exploration, which in turn they all believe will lead to growth, emotional control, greater self-respect, clearer decision making, and more effective behavior.

As notions about effective helping emerge and evolve, self-examination and exploration continues to remain a critical part of the process of intensive counseling. Behaviorism (Bandura, 1969; Ullmann & Krasner, 1965) has been the only major system for which self-examination has not been a central process goal. However, recent literature from this orientation (Mahoney, 1974) suggests that self-examination is becoming increasingly important in this system as well.

To help make clearer the meaning and significance of the process of self-examination, a few of the questions around which counselors often stimulate self-examination are:

——How do I describe myself?

——How do I describe my interpersonal behaviors?

——What situations and experiences would cause me to experience joy? Nervousness? Intense anxiety? Anger?

————What are my visions and expectations for the next five years of my life? What information forms the basis for those visions?

————Regarding my personal future, what are my fondest hopes? My greatest fears? About what area of my future do I feel most insecure?

————As I look at my dominant behavior patterns, which ones am I happy about? Which patterns do I most want to change?

————What feelings do I experience in the presence of authority figures? If they are negative feelings, what experiences in my past have contributed to my development?

————Under what conditions am I a high risk taker? A low risk taker? What does this information mean about me?

————Under what conditions am I most apt to have difficulty controlling my emotions? What emotions am I most apt to have difficulty controlling?

————What "ought" or "should" statements am I most apt to make about other people's behavior? What do I experience when my "should" statements are not met?

————What "should" statements about my own behavior give me the most difficulty?

Carkhuff (1969) points out that self-exploration is not an all-or-nothing experience, but rather that there are levels of depth associated with the process. The level of depth experienced by the client involves two dimensions: the kind of information shared and the work or encountering the client does with the information. At *Level 1*, the client simply does not share any significant information about self and demonstrates no evidence of engaging in the process of looking at his or her behavior. At *Level 2*, the client shares some information of a personal nature in response to counselor queries, but also guards other more important information. At this stage, the client is reporting the information to the counselor, but not working with it or trying to understand its significance. There is a great deal of guardedness and defensiveness involved in the client's engagement. Little is offered in a spontaneous or initiated manner.

At *Level 3*, the client shows a tendency to initiate information in a voluntary manner, but again seems to be reporting it in a mechanical manner rather than working it through. The significance of the information seems to be dissociated from self. If the concern is of an interpersonal nature there is not a full ownership of the responsibility for one's own behavior in the situation. There may well be a tendency to place responsibility for the difficulties on the others involved in the situation rather than to look at one's own behavior.

At *Level 4*, information is initiated with much more spontaneity. Much less information is guarded or monitored. Deeper, more significant information that may be painful in nature is shared. There is a clear tendency for the client to "work" with the information that surfaces: to understand it, to relate it to self, to explore its meaning and significance. The client is listening and "tuning in" to self. The counselor will notice "introspective avoidance" at certain critical points where the information becomes unpleasant or painful. The client will move away from the issue being discussed or move to a less intense encountering of the material that has surfaced.

At *Level 5*, the defensive patterns characteristic of the previous levels are gone. Information that emerges is dealt with without avoidance. The client is actively engaged in "reaching in" to understand what is there and the significance and meaning it has. The client regards self-exploration as an exciting venture that has painful experiences associated with it but that are endurable. A large proportion of attention is focused on self and is likely to be focused on present-versus-past experiencing. Few clients and few counseling sessions achieve this level of intimate intensity. When it is achieved, all participants in the process feel drained afterward.

A frequently raised question about this model is whether the counseling process must reach *Level 5* for counseling to be successful. Just as there are levels of self-exploration, so are there levels of counseling impact. The general principle is that the greater the level of self-exploration the more powerful will be the counseling experience for the client. The deepest levels of self-exploration will result in the deepest levels of growth and change.

Conversely, the further away from *Level 5* the client remains the less powerful will be the counseling experience. Below *Level 3* counseling will be of very little impact or significance to the client. If the interaction process reaches and is maintained at *Level 3*, counseling is likely to be of benefit to the client if the concerns are of a vocational choice and decision-making nature. Most of the counseling experience for Mike was at *Level 3*. For clients whose goal involves emotional control (such as Janice) it appears that communication at *Level 3* can be of some help, but that it will be necessary to achieve *Level 4* for the gains to be powerful and lasting. This statement is offered as a tentative hypothesis—to be supported or modified by the evidence of further research. Chapter 5 will discuss what counselors may do to achieve the more intense stages with their clients.

Awareness facilitation

The key to the process of self-exploration is that it leads to new discoveries and awarenesses. For most counseling systems, awareness stimulation is another critical process goal of counseling. A common assumption behind this set of approaches is that counseling is more likely to be successful and beneficial if the client can acquire new awarenesses and insights, especially new insights about self. The deeper and more profound are these self-based insights, the more impactful and powerful will be the counseling experience.

While awareness facilitation may be an important process goal, the various theories would seem to differ considerably on what specific kinds of awarenesses are worth helping a client acquire. In part, the awarenesses considered important reflect the assumptions and principles about human behavior acquisition and change that lie behind the theory. The awarenesses emphasized by the client-centered approach and the rational-emotive approach describe some of the different kinds of awarenesses that are considered important. These are not necessarily incompatible. Thus, it is not desirable for the reader to classify self in terms of which awarenesses he or she prefers. Rather, the intent should be to expand one's awareness about the range of possibilities.

Carkhuff (1969) believes that counseling is effective when the client is experiencing a developmental process of exploration → awareness → new action. The effective counselor is a person who has developed the mastery level understanding of this process, who has experienced it for self, and who can help others go through it. As the client shares thoughts and concerns, he or she begins to explore or examine feelings, beliefs, underlying motives, values, and underlying assumptions. If there is openness in the relationship as the client explores, he or she is also working to *clarify* for both self and counselor what is vague and confusing, to relate different ideas and information to each other, to resolve conflicting and discrepant ideas, and to understand the source of feelings and underlying motivations for behavior. With continuous examination and exploration, the client develops new insights or awarenesses and then begins to work on how the new insights can apply to making personal life decisions and to behaving in new ways.

Sometimes the new insights emerge gradually; at other times they surface like a sudden discovery experience. The overall process is much like the discovery learning model described by Bruner (1960). In this model, the counselor's task is not to teach new insights, but rather to help the client discover new awarenesses and insights that will help to make important decisions, gain control of undesirable feelings, and change undesirable behavior. While the specific insights to be gained depend on the client, the goals of counseling, the client's life history, and present circumstances, in general, the kinds of insights that are considered most important are awareness of how one views self; how one is viewed and perceived by significant others; dominant feelings one experiences and occasions on which those feelings are experienced; how one's dominant interpersonal behavior patterns affect significant others; the relationship between stated values and actual behavior; the underlying motives for one's behavior (in Maslow's terms, "the personal needs one is attempting to satisfy"); and the assumptions about self, significant others, and life space that lie behind the client's behavior.

The assumptions behind this approach are that unhappy feelings and beliefs are often suppressed; that even though they are suppressed they powerfully affect an individual's actions in sometimes negative ways; that becoming aware of such unhappy feelings and perspectives helps to gain control over them; that such control will enable a person to change behavior for the better.

These were precisely the assumptions made by Janice's counselor. He believed that in order to study more efficiently, it was important for Janice to become aware of underlying feelings of fear that related to the possibility of failure and poor performance. Awareness of these repressed feelings would enable Janice to control them, and such awareness was thus considered a very important process goal.

As will be developed in Chapter 5, the counselor attempts to help the client achieve these insights by active listening, by summarizing, by reflecting important feelings that emerge, by offering "I messages," and occasionally by confronting. In this context, high level empathy responses are those that accurately identify feelings, beliefs, and assumptions and their significance to the client. Low level empathy responses are those that fail to identify accurately feelings, beliefs, and values that are expressed and fail to recognize the underlying significance of what the client is sharing. High level empathy responses facilitate in-depth exploration and new insights; low level empathy responses block the process of awareness development. It is important to stress and affirm that self-awareness and discovery is the essence of this process; reflection responses are just one verbal tool that can make the process happen. There are other verbal tools that can also powerfully facilitate this process.

While awareness and insight are also considered important process goals in the Rational-Emotive approach, the specific awarenesses to be learned are different in the framework of this system. A primary assumption of this approach is that people will tend to act in self-defeating and counter-productive ways in the presence of certain activating events (A). However, it is not the events themselves that cause the self-defeating behaviors, but, rather, the things that people say to themselves and generally about themselves in the presence of that event. The assumption made by this approach is that in the presence of certain activating events people will say certain things to themselves—beliefs (B) that are irrational and self-defeating. The essential process goals in this system's approach are to help the client gain insights and awarenesses about these internal (B) events and their behavioral consequences (C). More specifically, the process goals of Rational-Emotive counseling are for the client:

> ———to identify behaviors that are self-defeating and the activating events where they are most likely to occur or to occur most strongly

> ———to become aware of the internal statements and assumptions and beliefs (B events) one is making to self in the presence of these identified activating events

> ———to become aware of the irrational aspects of one's assumptions and beliefs

> ———to become aware of how the irrational beliefs are leading to counter-productive behaviors

> ———to become aware of new assumptions and beliefs that would be more rational and sensible

> ———to change the assumptions one makes from irrational to rational

> ———to work and practice, through homework and trial and error, on behaving in ways that are consistent with the newly acquired beliefs and assumptions

As in the client-centered approach, the important process goals are awareness and insight based. However, the specific awarenesses and the reasons they are considered important differ markedly. Some of the irrational assumptions to which people adhere and which contribute to their unhappiness are:

1. *It is essential that one be loved or approved by virtually everyone in his or her community.* (This is irrational because it is unattainable, and leaves one taking a servant stance in his or her interpersonal relationships.)

2. *To consider oneself worthwhile one must be perfect. If one does not behave to perfection then he or she is unacceptable, inferior, and inadequate.* (Again, irrational because it is impossible. No one can be perfect in all of his or her endeavors. Trying to justify oneself on the basis of the quality of his or her achievements can only lead to galloping anxiety and insecurity. "I'm not OK until I prove to myself and others that I am OK" is an extremely self-defeating life stance.)

3. *It is a terrible catastrophe when things are not as one wants them to be.* (Sometimes events and circumstances are bad and cannot be changed. But many people "over-catastrophize" the degree of badness involved. Ellis and his followers work hard to help their clients control the tendency to do this.)

4. *There is always a right or perfect solution to every problem, and it must be found or the results will be catastrophic.* (It is irrational to believe that there is a perfect solution to every problem or that one can predict what will happen with certainty.)

In this approach to counseling, the counselor takes the position that he or she knows what is rational and sensible, and, thus, that two major process goals in counseling are to uncover what is irrational and to convince the client as to what is rational. Counselors taking this orientation thus exercise very strong controls over what happens during the counseling process.

Summary

Counseling may be seen as a process having a series of stages which include the initial meeting, exploration of client concern and relationship development, goal achievement, development and implementation of an approach to goal achievement, evaluation of results, and termination and follow-up. Each of these stages will be analyzed further in subsequent chapters.

Process goals are those which a counselor considers helpful and instrumental to the attainment of outcome goals. Three process goals considered important by most counselors are relationship development, client self-examination, and insight facilitation. Some essential aspects of relationship development have been explored in this chapter and will be developed more fully in Chapter 5. The insights emphasized in the Client-Centered and Rational-Emotive approaches were analyzed in this chapter to illustrate what is meant by insight facilitation. Additional insights will be developed in subsequent chapters.

References

Bandura, A. *Principles of behavior modification.* New York: Holt, Rinehart and Winston, 1969.

Bruner, J. S. *The process of education.* Cambridge, Mass.: Harvard University Press, 1960.

Carkhuff, R. R. *Helping and human relations, Vol. II.* New York: Holt, Rinehart and Winston, 1969.

Ellis, A. *Humanistic psychotherapy: The rational-emotive approach.* New York: McGraw-Hill, 1974.

Mahoney, M. J. *Cognition and behavior modification.* Cambridge, Mass.: Ballinger, 1974.

Perls, F. C. *Gestalt therapy verbatim.* Lafayette, Calif.: Real People Press, 1969.

Rogers, C. R. *On becoming a person.* Boston: Houghton Mifflin, 1961.

Truax, C. B., & Carkhuff, R. R. *Toward effective counseling and psychotherapy.* Chicago: Aldine, 1967.

Ullmann, L. P., & Krasner, L. *Case studies in behavior modification.* New York: Holt, Rinehart and Winston, 1965.

5. Dynamics of the first counseling session

Prior to the first counseling session, client and counselor are relative strangers to each other. In school settings, a student may have learned something from other students about the counselor's reputation. He or she may have been in a class visited by the counselor or may have been introduced during a new-student-day orientation program. The counselor may have heard of the student from teachers, may know something about the student from the cumulative record, or may know of a student's reputation by his or her school activities. But the two parties are likely to know very little about each other. If counseling is to be a helpful and worthwhile experience, both parties must come to know each other at a level much deeper than a casual acquaintanceship, must learn to respect and accept each other, must trust each other and feel safe about communicating openly and providing information to each other, must identify and agree upon a problem or concern on which to work, and must begin to develop a

74

sense of mission as to the outcome goals of their interactive efforts.

For the counselor, the essential process goals of the first session are to:

——stimulate open, honest, and full communication about the concerns needing to be discussed and the factors and background related to those concerns

——work toward progressively deeper levels of understanding, respect, and trust between self and client

——provide the client with the view that something useful can be gained from the counseling sessions

——identify a problem or concern for subsequent attention and work

——establish the "gestalt" that counseling is a process in which both parties must work hard at exploring and understanding the client and his or her concerns

——acquire information about the client that relates to his or her concerns and effective problem resolution

For most clients additional process goals also include:

——stimulating self-examination

——generating some specific task for the client to do, or some specific issue to think about before the next counseling session

The purposes of this chapter are to analyze factors, conditions, and circumstances related to the attainment of these goals and to describe ways that counselors can achieve these goals. It is important to recognize that these are continuing rather than terminal goals. In a sense, these goals are never fully attained; rather, counseling is a process of working toward continuously deeper levels of these goals. The analysis begins with a discussion of the different entering perspectives and orientations that clients bring to the counseling setting.

In previous chapters, it has been stressed that people generally come to counselors because they have a problem. They need help in dealing with their problem and view the counselor as a possible source of help. The problem may concern a decision that needs to be made about some future course of action and that the client is experiencing some conflict and confusion about which course of action to take. Sometimes clients seek a counselor's help to acquire information about self and environment that will lead to making an important decision. Other clients seek a counselor's help because they encounter difficulties in their environment and need help coping with these difficulties. At other times, clients recognize that their own behavior in given situations is dysfunctional and wish help in acquiring more effective ways of behaving. Not infrequently, clients recognize that something unhealthy is going on within themselves and they need help in changing these disturbing patterns. A few examples include: experiencing high levels of anxiety or anger which are difficult to control, experiencing a negative view toward self and one's potential for achievement of important goals, experiencing a fear of failure, experiencing a fear of success, experiencing a loss of hope, and not having a sense of mission about a desirable personal future.

Not only do clients come for help with a range of problems and concerns, they also come to a counselor with different levels of readiness and commitment to working on their difficulties. Sometimes clients seek out counselors on their own volition, but frequently people are pressured by significant others in their lives to seek a counselor's help. Obviously, the first is more committed to working than the second. The focus of this chapter will be on reaching out to the voluntary client. In Chapter 7, the dynamics of working with the nonvoluntary and reluctant client will be discussed.

The important point is that clients enter a counseling relationship at different levels of readiness for counseling. Under the most favorable conditions a counselor would hope that a client would enter the relationship fully and unconditionally trusting the counselor, with complete understanding of the problems to be worked on, ready to talk fully and openly about self and factors that relate to the problems, ready to *work* toward a greater understanding of self and to use those understandings as the basis for making decisions, coping effectively, and changing.

Such clients are rare. Even with voluntary clients, it is more likely that the client is not sure whether the counselor can be trusted and wonders whether the counselor will have the ability to understand and help. Not being sure, many clients test their counselors. If the counselors pass the test, counseling proceeds. If not, disengagement and termination are the result. One of the most frequent tests is to present a problem that is not the essential one for consideration. If the counselor appears to understand, seems trustworthy and safe to talk with, and offers helpful contributions, the counselor has passed the test and a deeper and more significant problem emerges.

Often clients enter counseling with a dependency orientation. They present their problem and then leave it to the counselor to do the work necessary to solve the problem. The client becomes the passive recipient of the counselor's helping efforts. In this orientation, the client places the responsibility for doing the work on the counselor and away from self. This entering perception is an inaccurate view of the counseling process and one that seriously interferes with the chances for counseling to be worthwhile. Counseling must be seen by both partners as a process where both must work hard at sharing, understanding, exploring, becoming aware, and clarifying.

Rather than being open, many clients enter counseling from a defensive posture. To be defensive means to avoid thinking and talking about things that are painful and uncomfortable or to avoid sharing information that could make one look less adequate to others. Many clients resist sharing important information and thoughts that are threatening. Indeed, one of the paradoxes of counseling is that clients are most resistant to sharing the material that is most important. One of the challenges of the first session is to help clients talk without fear and defensiveness about the things that are really bothering them.

Another entering perspective held by some clients is that to seek out the help of a counselor means that a person is disturbed, in trouble, or somehow unable to handle his or her own difficulties. Some clients enter counseling, therefore, with a sense of embarrassment about the idea that they need to turn to someone else for help.

The nonvoluntary client who has been pressured into counseling by someone else, is likely to be hostile, belligerent, and defiant. Some such clients express their hostility openly. They tell the counselor they were forced into counseling and that they are unhappy about it. Others express their hostility in more subtle and passive ways: by not communicating, by leading the discussion away from self, or by bringing up a safe issue that does not relate to the problem to be discussed.

Dealing effectively with the first session includes being able to deal with these less than optimal orientations.

Stimulating open communication

Stimulating open communication means that the counselor must help the client share fully all the information that is relevant to the concern and problem. This includes not only the easily observable, factual information, but information about what the client is experiencing in his or her affective world: inner feelings, beliefs, values, assumptions, and opinions about self and significant others; hopes, expectations, and fears about one's personal future; understandings about factors and conditions in one's present, personal life space; events in the past that may have led to present difficulties; feelings of fear, conflict, confusion, doubt, and anger; and a vision in a values clarification sense as to what the client wishes to bring about for self in the future as a result of the counselor's assistance.

The Johari Window, originally developed by Joe Luft and Harry Ingham (Luft, 1963) helps to visualize further what is meant by open communication and some of the difficulties involved in making communication happen.

Figure 5.1 shows that in any relationship between two people there are four types of information. The first cell refers to information

Figure 5.1   The Johari Window[*]

	KNOWN TO OTHER	UNKNOWN TO OTHER
KNOWN TO SELF	(Public) 1	(Private) 2
UNKNOWN TO SELF	("Bad Breath") 3	(Unknown) 4

Source: Basic design from *Group Processes: An Introduction to Group Dynamics* by Joseph Luft, by permission of Mayfield Publishing Company (formerly National Press Books). Copyright © 1963, 1970 by Joseph Luft.

[*]For the most comprehensive explication of the Johari Model, see *Of Human Interaction*, by J. Luft, Mayfield Publishing, Palo Alto, Calif., 1969.

an individual knows about self, which the other member also knows about that individual. In casual acquaintances, this is generally public or easily observable factual information or information an individual is not reluctant to disclose to most others. In more intimate relationships, this may be information known by the parties in the relationship, but not known to members outside the relationship.

The second cell refers to information a person generally chooses not to disclose: fears, anxieties, doubts, sex life, quarrels with significant others, feelings of conflict, and confusion. The third cell refers to information others have about an individual that he or she may not have about self. This type of information, sometimes humorously referred to as the "bad breath" area, generally refers to the impressions one individual has about the other and explanations for the other's behavior. The fourth cell usually refers to curious aspects about self to which neither party has good answers or information: Why do I lose control over my anger? Why is it I cannot stop smoking?

It may be seen, from Figure 5.1, that stimulating open communication is a matter of helping the client feel secure and unthreatened about moving material from Cell 2 (information known to self but unknown to the other) into Cell 1 (information known to both self and a significant other, in this case the counselor). For most clients this is not easy; the material to be shared may never have been shared with anyone. Often the feelings of fear and anger and certain "unacceptable" beliefs that are part of this window have never been shared because they are difficult for the client to face. It is not infrequent for effective counselors to hear clients report that they have never before shared that information with anyone else. When this happens, the feeling is often one of relief more than of anxiety.

Use of the Johari Window also helps to understand levels of depth in interpersonal relationships as well as the meaning of trust. Any information an individual knows about self can be located in either Cell 1 or Cell 2. Any information an individual knows about another can be located in either Cell 1 or Cell 3. People actively choose to disclose or keep private information about themselves (material in Cell 2). People also actively choose whether to share or hold back information and impressions they have about another (Cell 3). The strength of a relationship between any two people can be assessed on the basis of how much and what kind of information each would actively choose to share with the other (move from Cell 2 to Cell 1). The more information and the more significant the information a person actively chooses to share, the more intense is the relationship and the deeper is the level of trust. Conversely, distrust may be seen as directly related to the amount and kind of material a person actively chooses not to share with another. The difference between close and deep relationships and superficial relationships is the amount of personal information each is willing to share with the other. Clearly, it is important for the counselor to be a person with whom it is possible for many people to develop deep interpersonal relationships.

Trust is a matter of actively choosing to share personal material. The more material a person is willing to share with another, the deeper is the level of trust. Whether a person chooses to trust or not depends on his or her anticipation of what the other will do with the information once it is shared. If the anticipation is that harmful consequences will occur, the information will be inhibited. In contrast, if the anticipation is that no harmful consequences will occur, and, additionally, that some beneficial ones might occur, the information is more likely to be shared.

Trust and deep human relationships do not simply occur. Effective counselors make these events happen, primarily by showing the client by their own actions that nothing disastrous will occur by taking the risk to share. The evolution of relationships and of trust can easily be understood from a behavioral approach. Once the risk to trust is taken and the results of taking the risk are both beneficial and not harmful, inhibitions about trusting with deeper, more significant information are extinguished. Taking the risk is reinforced and generalizes to the sharing of other information. This information is shared and the extinction-reinforcement process continues.

This model suggests that trust is an experience between people that evolves and emerges gradually. Once developed, open communication and trust, whether maintained or destroyed, depends on what the counselor does with the information that is shared.

Information clients are reluctant to share

As stated earlier, most people enter counseling with only a vague idea of what to expect. The counselor is a relative stranger and they are unsure as to what level and how deeply this unknown person can be trusted. Additionally, some clients have learned from past experiences to take an optimistic view of people's credibility. People should be assumed worthy of trust until they are proved otherwise. Others have learned that people should not be trusted until they can prove that they are worthy of trust. Given two clients with the same information about self, one client may be willing to share that information and the other may be unwilling.

For every individual, sharing or keeping information private about self is an important right of choice. Effective relationships with people include the ability to discriminate between those who can be trusted and those for whom trust would be dangerous. In the relationship between client and counselor, because the counselor is a relative stranger, from the client's perspective trust may be a risk.

At the same time, there is generally information about self that most clients are reluctant to share. Any information that could result in the client being punished, criticized, or made to feel stupid is generally inhibited. Examples include use of drugs, acts of violence or vandalism, violation of laws and rules, and making a decision or taking a course of action that on hindsight was regrettable or highly inappropriate.

The sharing of painful feelings and events related to those feelings is also difficult for most people. Most people would prefer to repress or suppress feelings of guilt, embarrassment, humiliation, rage, or intense anxiety rather than to allow them into awareness. To share them means to allow them into awareness, and that is painful. Examples might include incidences of ridicule or humiliation by peers, failure to perform adequately as a sex partner, and actions which are perceived as cowardly. Adolescent males are especially reluctant to share any information concerning events in which they or others perceive their actions to be unmanly. Especially in the early stages of the counseling process, most clients are reluctant to share inner fears about a basic sense of adequacy or about the adequacy of their performance in situations where competent performance is especially important.

In the process of growth most people develop a moral code—a set of moral standards about proper moral conduct. These standards emerge from a combination of values transmitted by the family and culture, and personal values clarification experiences stimulated by conflict situations. Many people are reluctant to talk with others about occasions in which they perceived themselves as having violated their standards. Perceived violation of personal standards triggers feelings of guilt, and guilt is a very painful feeling to allow into awareness. Furthermore, the more central the valuing code, the stronger the reluctance will be to discuss the events related to the perceived violation of the code.

There is a strong cultural norm in our society that says that what goes on within a family unit should be kept private and within the family unit. Whatever "dirty linen" occurs should not be aired in public. Thus, clients are often reluctant to share information within the family unit that may affect their personal lives. For example, it has been estimated that each year in the greater Cleveland area alone about 120,000 students experience the separation of their parents. For most, this is a very traumatic experience that can trigger feelings of anxiety about having to choose between the parents, anger about abandonment, possible guilt for having contributed to the situation, and fear about loss of stability in one's home environment. Yet, very few of these students consider approaching their counselors for help in working through these difficult feelings and in learning to cope effectively with the situation. Attitudes about the ability of their counselor to be of help is, of course, one factor; but another important factor is that this is viewed as a family matter and, therefore, should be kept private.

Generally, what inhibits people from sharing such information is the anticipatory anxiety that if such information were disclosed, "very bad" consequences would occur. The anticipated consequences are generally: possible punishment, possible embarrassment or humiliation, possible anguish at having to face painful situations, or violation of an important personal standard. Essentially, the most facilitative way to develop trust is to show the client that these anticipated results of sharing will simply not happen in the counseling situation; since the bad consequences of sharing will not happen, there is no reason to be afraid. Quite to the contrary, it is possible that if the risk is taken positive consequences might occur.

How good counselors inspire trust

While there are some behavioral "dos" and "don'ts" involved in facilitating the development of trust, inspiring trust is more a matter of implementing a set of assumptions about self and one's professional role. The counselor who wishes to be trusted must ask himself or herself a series of very searching questions:

———Why should a person, especially a person who may know very little about me, trust me?

——What makes me believe I am worthy of another person's trust?

——If bonds of trust begin to emerge between this other person and me, and this other person entrusts me with important information, what might I do that could betray this trust?

——If I am pressured, under what conditions would I consider sharing with another person information a client has shared with me?

The most obvious way a counselor could betray trust is to reveal information shared by the client to someone else. It would be easy to say that a counselor should never share with anyone else that which is shared with him or her in the privacy of the counseling situation. However, that standard is not feasible and, in a number of instances, may not even be wise. Paradoxically, the counselor who values being trusted will ask self: "Under what specific instances will I disclose information shared with me?" He or she will then establish a set of clear criteria to decide between appropriate and inappropriate circumstances. In Section B of the Ethical Standards of the American Personnel and Guidance Association, the following guidelines are offered:

——The counseling relationship and information resulting therefrom must be kept confidential, consistent with the obligations of the member as a professional person. (paragraph 2)

——When the member learns from counseling relationships of conditions which are likely to harm others over whom his institution or agency has responsibility, he is expected to report the *condition* to the appropriate responsible authority, but in such a manner as not to reveal the identity of his counselee or client. (paragraph 7)

——. . . when there is clear and imminent danger to the counselee or client, or to others, the member is expected to report this fact to an appropriate responsible authority, and/or take such other emergency measures as the situation demands. (paragraph 8)

Thus, it can be considered appropriate to disclose information shared in counseling, if the circumstances meet any of these criteria:

——if there is a strong possibility that the future physical well-being of either the client or another person would be seriously threatened by holding back the information shared

———if there is a strong possibility that the future commission of a serious crime could be prevented

———if the information shared indicates that a serious crime has been committed

But there are other critical situations not well covered by these professional guidelines. For instance, in school settings, teachers frequently refer to the counselor students who are underachieving, who demonstrate feelings of intense hostility, who are identified through sociometric procedures as social isolates, who are having family difficulties, or who are troubled and distressed. Referring teachers often want to know if action has been taken and whether change can be anticipated. They believe that as the referral source they have a right to some information and not infrequently feel professionally insulted when the counselor demurs. Sometimes teachers feel concerned about what may have been said by the student about them. Also, parents often believe they have a right to know why their child is seeing a counselor, especially if the student has been in trouble. School principals often justify their right to know on the grounds that it is their responsibility to maintain the safety of the people in their building.

Clearly, the counselor walks a tightrope on the issue of keeping information private. On the one hand, it appears necessary if the counselor is to have any chance for being effective in his or her professional efforts. Once it is known that the counselor does not keep information private, people will be unwilling to trust the counselor. On the other hand, the counselor's effectiveness depends on the good-will and respect established between self and fellow professionals. If alienation occurs, the counselor's effectiveness is also severely strained.

There are some things counselors can do about these apparent dilemmas. The first thing is to develop a clear set of criteria for deciding under what specific conditions, and to whom, information will be disclosed. It is generally wise to follow up on this with a policy statement, made available to prospective clients as well as to colleagues. It is even more helpful if such a policy statement can be developed by a guidance committee having representation from all the people to whom the counselor is accountable. (In a school setting this includes students, teachers, administrators, and parents.) Then, in difficult situations, when it appears that the client may be at a point where he or she may wish to share information, the counselor can inform the client of the conditions under which he or she would be in a position where sharing would be necessary. In so doing, the counselor is protecting the client's right to choose to share information or to keep it private, with full understanding of the possible consequences. Rather than feeling alienated, many clients appreciate the candor the counselor has offered, and recognize and appreciate that the counselor has done some serious thinking about this important matter.

If the client subsequently chooses to share such information, a major part of subsequent counseling *must* be an exploration and agreement (preferably with a contract) about what will be disclosed and to whom, and how it will be done so as to protect the client's best interest under the circumstances. This part of counseling may well take the form of negotiating so that an approach can be developed wherein the needs of all parties are met. (See *Teacher Effectiveness Training*, 1970, for some helpful ideas on how to facilitate this process.) If the client chooses not to share, the counselor may wish to arrange for a referral to another setting in which the communication obligations are not the same.

A second step counselors can take concerning this dilemma is to develop understanding between self and colleagues concerning conditions of disclosure. The policy statement described previously can be of significant help in such discussions. Once developed and agreed upon, the counselor can refer to it, indicating that he or she feels ethically obligated to respect the guidelines developed. While a few colleagues may feel some resentment, many will respect the counselor for maintaining professional standards. Additionally, when a referral is made, before the client is seen, it is helpful to clarify with the referring person what kind of feedback, if any, the counselor is willing to offer. This may not be as difficult as it sounds. In school settings, some teachers may desire details and specifics, but many will simply want some recognition that they have tried to be helpful along with some assurance that efforts have been taken to deal with the concerns they have identified. This can be done without discussing specific information. When the referred client is seen subsequently, the issue of who should tell what to whom must be discussed and negotiated as described previously. More will be said about this in Chapter 7 on nonvoluntary clients.

Being clear about one's own valuing position in the use of information is an important factor in the development of trust, but not the only factor. Often counselors have the feeling that they can be trusted, but the client shows an unwillingness to trust. The indicators of low levels of trust are the same as the indicators of client defensiveness: evading important issues for discussion, sharing peripheral facts but not internal feelings, assigning responsibility for difficult situations outside of self, presenting a peripheral rather than a central problem, and a direct expression to the effect "I would rather not discuss that matter." Clearly, if the counseling process is to be of value for the client, these defensive barriers must be overcome.

There are two basic approaches available to the counselor to deal with these barriers: to do nothing, and to "process the problem" with the client. Some counselors prefer to do nothing. Their view is that if they continue to experience caring and regard for their client and show it, the client will eventually see the caring, and, over time, deeper levels of trust will naturally develop. They also believe that if a client is not ready to trust, pressing too hard for a deeper level of trust may be threatening to the client and will thus be counter-productive. The client may become intimidated and "close out" counseling.

Counselors using a direct approach believe that if trust and open communication have not developed over a reasonable period of time, it is important to "process the problem." In essence, to "process the problem" means to present it as an issue for discussion in as non-threatening a manner as possible. Leaving the development of trust to chance may or may not bring about its occurrence. Often when a client does not trust a counselor, it is because he or she has learned not to trust people or is generalizing (or transferring) learned distrust to the counselor. The learned distrust may be toward people in general or it may be localized to adults or authority figures. Or it may be based on secondhand information the client has heard about from others.

Whatever the reason, counselors taking this orientation believe that examining the level of trust in the counseling relationship leads to helping the client examine his or her sense of trust toward people in general. Thinking through who should and should not be trusted is an important developmental issue for all people that, in turn, can lead to intensive examination of one's interpersonal relationships. Thus, processing the level of trust is important for the specific counseling relationship and is an important growth issue for the client. While the risk of intimidating the client is a possibility, the risk can be minimized if supportive approaches are employed. These counselors reason that the risk is worth the gain that may result.

Counselors taking this orientation stimulate the processing in a variety of ways. Sometimes observation-supportive statements are used:

Clare, I can see that it's hard for you to share these feelings. I want you to know that it's OK to share them. I won't think less of you, I won't report what you share with me to anyone else, and I won't use the information in any way that will be harmful to you.

Another example:

Sometimes people who talk with me about personal matters aren't sure whether it's OK to be fully open with me. Sometimes this occurs because they are not sure what I will do with the information once I receive it. Sometimes people are concerned that I might think less of them once they tell me certain things about themselves. That is not how I react. If I am to be of help, I must try to understand rather than to judge.

Another approach that is based on a combination of "I messages" and principles of constructive confrontation (to be discussed in Chapter 6) is illustrated by the following example:

Bill, I have noticed that since we have started our discussion, I have been doing almost all of the talking. You have said "yes" or "no" occasionally, but have shared very little with me. I would like very much to be able to help you with your concerns. But for me to do so, it is important that I understand you and the issues you are concerned about. I know it might be difficult, but I think it would help a great deal if you could tell me about yourself and help me understand.

In each case, the counselor responded in a sensitive way to the client's observed or inferred feelings. Each counselor did not accuse nor punish the client for unacceptable behavior. Each counselor demonstrated the importance of counselor self-disclosure to the counseling process. In the first two examples, the counselors shared some personal and important viewpoints about counseling. In the third example, the counselor shared important feelings being experienced. In all examples, these were shared through the honest use of "I messages."

To summarize this section: the developments of progressively deeper levels of open communication and trust are essential parts of the counseling process and vital process goals of the first counseling session. Level of trust is indicated by the amount and kind of information one person is willing to share with another. The level of trust that develops depends in large part on the sharing person's anticipations concerning what the receiver will do with the information once it is obtained. Open communication is likely not to occur if the sharer anticipates that sharing the information will result in hurtful consequences. Thus, inspiring trust really becomes a matter of developing clear guidelines for deciding what will be disclosed to whom and under what conditions. Once these conditions have been developed, it becomes the counselor's responsibility to communicate and to act congruently with these even under pressure. Suggestions were offered as to approaches to help clients develop trust for the counselor.

Caring and acceptance

Another core condition necessary if counseling is to have a favorable impact is that the counselor must experience an honest sense of caring for the client. The caring must be demonstrated to the client and the client must perceive it. Honestly felt caring is likely to be communicated naturally. Effective counselors do not try too hard to demonstrate caring; if it is felt it will be demonstrated as a natural part of their interaction.

Essentially, caring is the honestly experienced belief toward another that "your present and future well-being matter to me. It is important that whatever concerns and difficulties you are experiencing are worked through and resolved so that you can experience a more enjoyable present and look forward to a more optimistic future. Your well-being is important enough that I am willing to commit time and energy, and even take some reasonable risks, if necessary, to be of help to you."

To counselors with this view, the most obvious indicator of caring is how intently they are able to engage in active listening to their client. Staying in touch with the client's message and working to understand the underlying meanings a client's communications have for his or her life space is very hard work. All counselors find their attention straying at points in the process. They find themselves tuning into things and events outside the counseling process and outside the client's life space. Caring means being able to monitor oneself to know when attention is drifting away from the client and making an internal commitment to get back.

Another personal assessment indicator is to think about the risks one would be willing to take to help the client. One kind of risk relates to the question of counselor self-disclosure to the client. The question here is "If it will help my client, am I willing to take the risk to share something personal about myself with the client?" Another risk is in the area of constructive confrontation. Providing unhappy or uncomfortable feedback to another is often an important part of the counseling experience that is as painful for the counselor as the client.

Another indicator of caring is whether the counselor is willing to participate in that painful experience if it will help the client. Most effective counselors will honestly say that they recognize that a confrontation with a client is important, but choose not to do so because they do not experience enough caring for the client to go through the pain of the experience.

A third indicator experienced counselors use to assess caring is to ask themselves, "What kinds of follow-up or follow-through am I willing to take on my client's behalf"—that is, a commitment to another person's well-being often involves follow-through action.

Indicators of lack of caring include a lack of concern about the client's present or future well-being, an inability to engage in intense active listening, a lack of interest, a choice to not expend any time or energy beyond the minimum of one's job, a reluctance to take follow-through action, and an unwillingness to take reasonable risks that could result in the client's benefit. Just as there are levels of trust, so are there levels of caring. All counselors have limits as to how far they will go to implement their sense of caring. Very few are willing to sacrifice their jobs or risk their lives at critical points. Few are willing to make themselves available at all hours of the night for extended periods. There is nothing to feel guilty about on this matter. These observations only confirm an important truth that all counselors must acknowledge: while caring is important, there are limits to the level of caring and to the implementation of caring.

Another truth about caring is that every counselor encounters clients about whom he or she must honestly say, "I must simply admit that I do not experience feelings of caring for this person. This person's present and future well-being simply make little difference to me." To a person who perceives self to be a "caring individual" those are hard feelings to face; but to pretend caring when it is not present is dishonest and defensive. Introspective counselors try to cope with these feelings by allowing them into awareness. Recognizing these feelings, they must ask themselves what is involved that is causing them to feel this sense of dislike and lack of concern. Most recognize when they experience these feelings it is because they have observed qualities and characteristics in their client that they find unlikeable. For example, some counselors recognize that caring is not experienced toward manipulative people, people who communicate attitudes of bigotry, people who express consistent hostility, or people who are unconcerned about how their actions influence others. An important part of a counselor's personal growth involves being continuously aware of feelings of non-caring, recognizing the interpersonal qualities related to those feelings, becoming aware of what is behind those feelings, and making a commitment to gaining personal control over them. When counselors process their feelings this way, they often find that their feelings toward the client are generalized from unhappy past experiences with someone whose behavior patterns were similar to those of the client. Thus, when feelings of non-caring are experienced, it is the counselor's responsibility to own these feelings and not to make the client responsible for them.

Many counselors wonder what to do when they find themselves experiencing only minimal levels of caring. The first approach to coping is to try to work these feelings through as suggested above. Some experienced counselors use their feelings to process the counseling experience. They present their feelings openly to the client and attempt to use their feelings as feedback for the client. Sometimes the results are gratifying; sometimes such approaches do not work. Minimal levels of caring stay minimal. Under these circumstances, the counselor must simply accept the feelings and acknowledge their presence without feeling ashamed or guilty. He or she must make a choice among three options: (1) to try to refer the client to another counselor, (2) to disengage, or (3) to provide levels of help consistent with the felt level of caring. The options are presented in the order of their desirability.

It is worth reemphasizing that if such feelings are experienced with an occasional client there is no reason to be ashamed of them. Such feelings are part of life, and understanding them is part of growth. On the other hand, the counselor who finds self experiencing feelings of non-caring and nonacceptance on a regular basis should engage in some intensive self-examination as to what makes the acceptance of others so difficult.

Facilitative and blocking responses

Research on human interaction (Truax & Carkhuff, 1967; Raths, Harmin, & Simon, 1966) suggest that some helper responses seem to facilitate in-depth interaction, self-examination, and beliefs and values clarification, while other responses seem to block that process. Early in the stages of a helping relationship, counselor responses that will block open communication include:

———put downs and personal criticisms (You have got to be kidding when you say that! Come now! Get serious!)

————criticisms of viewpoints and beliefs (Your reasoning makes no sense at all here)

————rejection of feelings (Come on now. There is no reason to feel nervous about tomorrow's exam. You really should not feel anger toward your mother)

————advice giving or pressing for a given course of action, especially before relevant facts are known (I think you should assert yourself on this matter and tell your boss you do not like the way you are being treated)

————opinion giving, especially if offered so that there is no room for another to present an alternative point of view (Learning a skilled trade is the only plan that makes sense in today's economy)

————asking a series of data gathering questions or interrogating (What are your interests? Do you prefer outdoor or indoor activities? Do you prefer being with people or being alone when you are nervous?)

————asking "why" questions that require justifications (Why did you tell your wife at the party that you did not like her smoking when you knew it would embarrass her?)

————taking sides with people in conflict (Mary, I think Bill is right about this matter. You do show a lot of scorn for his ideas)

————support giving in a patronizing way (Lots of people close out others when they have important things on their minds. It's normal; don't worry about it)

————lecturing, moralizing, sermonizing (When I was a child . . .)

Other responses seem to facilitate communication and stimulate a more in-depth intense level of thinking. Communication channels are opened and broadened when helpers make responses such as these:

————summarizing (I want to be sure I understand what you have told me . . .)

————interchangeable responses, especially those which are worded so as to reflect feelings and beliefs (I hear you saying that you are angry that your wife does not respect your privacy)

——clarification-requesting responses (Could you tell me more about these feelings of confusion you get when you are alone? Could you give me another example of a time when you got so angry you wanted to hit the other person involved?)

——responses whose intent is to clarify feelings, beliefs, values, and assumptions (Is that something you are proud of? How might you express your commitment to that point of view? Let's see if we can figure out the assumptions behind that point of view. Were you upset enough that you really wanted to disengage from the discussion?)

——"I messages" (I am curious as to how you dealt with that difficult situation. I am eager to know more about your thinking on this issue. I am wondering about how your parents reacted to this news. I am pleased to know that things worked out so well for you. I am disappointed that things did not work out as you had hoped. I am concerned about the fact that you are engaging in unprotected sexual activity. I am confused about what you are saying to me. Could you clarify what you are saying so that I can understand more fully)

——low-level inferences (I am sensing that you were really disappointed that your boyfriend did not call you. I have a hunch that it was very difficult for you to be assertive in this situation)

——combinations (I hear the anger you are feeling. I am sensing you were especially disappointed that your parents did not tell you sooner about their decision. I am wondering if you took their actions to mean they thought you weren't mature enough to understand the problem)

Ways to communicate empathy

Ever since Rogers (1942) talked about the counselor's ability to walk in the moccasins of the client, the communication of empathy has been considered an important part of offering effective help. Empathy means the ability to understand not only the surface aspects of a client's message, but also the related feelings and perceptions that are an underlying part of that message. Empathy also includes the ability to understand the special personalized meanings and significance a client attaches to what he or she is saying.

Communicating empathy requires the ability to engage in intense active listening; that is, the ability to absorb and retain information the client is communicating and to relate information to other information shared earlier. It requires the ability to receive the information the client is communicating without distorting it. It requires the ability to "tune in" or pay special attention to the feelings, beliefs, values, underlying assumptions, and phenomenological perspectives of what the client is saying.

Effectively communicated empathic responses help to achieve a number of interrelated process goals of counseling. An effective empathic response affirms to the client "I have understood not only the overt part of your message but also the underlying significance that it has for you." The affirmation of being deeply understood supports further and more in-depth exploration. It takes caring to do the work of active listening; therefore, accurate empathy responses indicate caring. Finally, an effective empathy response focuses the client's attention on the feeling and affective dimensions of what is being communicated, and thus stimulates in-depth self-examination and more intensive exploration. Accurate empathy acts as a gentle, supportive confrontation that moves counseling from surface discussion to in-depth encounter. Thus, people who are afraid of intense encountering relationships with others also find it difficult to offer high levels of empathy.

Typically, clients report events and circumstances that are part of their lives, but attach feelings to those events as a secondary matter. (My roommate borrowed my textbook yesterday without asking me and it kind of annoyed me.) Effective empathy responses are stated so as to highlight the *feeling* aspects of the client's message. Their purpose is to help the client become more fully aware of underlying feelings, to clarify confusing feelings, and to explore what is behind those feelings. They help the client to label accurately both the kind and intensity of the feeling experienced.

An empathy response should not only focus on, and highlight, feelings, but should also describe the circumstances that led to those feelings. The key is to make the *feelings* the highlighted part of the message. Carkhuff (1969) suggests the following paradigm (model for responding) as a way to get started: "Sarah, I hear you saying you are feeling _____ about _____." Using the example above, one can say, "Sarah, I hear you saying you are feeling annoyed about your roommate taking your book without asking you first." This can be expected to help Sarah express some underlying feelings as, "Yeah. She has done this several times. She is getting to me and I don't know what to do about it or how to handle the situation."

Carkhuff (1969) distinguishes between *interchangeable* empathy responses and *additive* empathy responses. Interchangeable responses are those which accurately capture and reflect back to a client the essential part of his or her message. While they do not add meaning to the client's stated message, neither do they subtract any significant data from the message. Thus, they are considered interchangeable. In contrast, "additive responses add significantly to the feeling and meaning of the expressions of the client in such a way as to accurately express feeling levels below what the helpee was able to express. . . . The counselor responds with accuracy to all of the client's deeper as well as surface feelings" (Carkhuff, 1969, p. 175). Since the additive levels go beyond the client's stated message, the components which are added are inferred or hypothesized from what the client has said. This being true, the additive parts must be stated tentatively rather than with certainty. Using an extension of Carkhuff's model, the following paradigm is suggested: "Sarah, I hear you saying you are feeling _____ about _____. I am also sensing _____." The third blank contains the inference. Using the above example, several inferences are possible:

———Sarah, I hear you saying you are annoyed about your roommate taking your book without asking you first. I am sensing that you wanted to say something to her, but did not know how to go about doing it.

———Sarah, I hear you saying that you were kind of annoyed about your roommate taking your book without asking you first. I am sensing that to you her act was one of disrespect and disregard for your rights.

———Sarah, I hear you saying that you were annoyed about your roommate taking your book without asking you first. I am sensing, too, that while you very much wanted to express those feelings to your roommate you held back.

In each type of response, the counselor highlights or emphasizes the feeling aspect of the client's message. In the interchangeable example this helped Sarah "tune into" a deeper aspect of her feelings—a sense of frustration and annoyance toward self about not being able to do anything about the event. In each of the additive empathy examples the counselor was careful to distinguish between what he or she *heard* (actually received in transmission) from what was *inferred* (hypothesized based on the information offered). Presenting inferences tentatively allows the client more room to react and makes it much easier for the client to use that which the counselor has offered. Using the second additive example, Sarah may have said, "Well, I really did have many of the same feelings. But with my boyfriend I was feeling a great deal of fear about losing his friendship. With my roommate, it's more that I am afraid that if I say something she will do something vindictive." If the counselor had made the inference part of the response more dogmatically, Sarah may well have been blocked from expressing her follow-up thoughts.

Another paradigm that Carkhuff suggests is "feeling _____ about *(description of situation)* and would like *(description of desired future event)*." As suggested in Chapter 1, counseling is a process of exploration in the present to help the client bring about something desirable in the future. The above model is especially useful in helping the client clarify personal desires for the future. Since feelings of anger, anxiety, and disappointment in the present come from anticipations about the future, a helper response, such as the one above, helps to clarify the sources of those feelings.

Using the case of Sarah, "Sarah, I hear you saying that you are feeling annoyed because your roommate took your book without asking you first and that you would like for her to stop abusing your rights when she does things like this," this response can be especially facilitative in moving from feeling exploration to future action exploration. It also helps acknowledge that something deeper than the event itself is involved in the situation.

Carkhuff (1969) and Means (1973) both emphasize that additive responses offered too early in the process can have a disruptive influence on the counseling relationship. Such responses may go beyond where the client is at the present time and thus threaten or intimidate the client. At least the client will become very self-conscious and monitor what he or she says. At worst, the client might become so threatened as to terminate. Both suggest that the counselor must gauge his or her empathic responses to the client's level of readiness for self-disclosure and self-examination. Additive responses tend to focus on aspects somewhat more anxiety provoking.

Use of reflective and interchangeable responses must be put into its proper perspective. Many times trainees say, "I hate it when all people do is sit there and reflect life like parrots." At other times, trainees develop the idea that making interchangeable responses is the way one is supposed to respond as a counselor. In both cases the essential process goals of interchangeable responses are missed. The purposes for offering such responses are to help the client focus on feelings, to clarify them, to explore what is behind them, to use this new information to understand self more fully, and to use these new understandings of self to gain greater control over feelings and to cope more effectively with difficult situations. Persistent use of such interchangeable responses will lose their intended impact. Counselors should limit the use of such responses to occasions when they want their clients to focus on a specific set of feelings that seem to have special significance. Used in a discriminating manner this way, an occasional interchangeable response can have a very powerful impact.

The critical point to keep in mind is that exploration of feelings is the important process goal to be achieved. Interchangeable responses are just one verbal tool for achieving this impact. There are other such verbal tools. For example, if the exchange with Sarah occurred during the second session and a base of trust and open communication had been established during the first session, the counselor might simply have offered responses such as the following:

———Sarah, let's work on understanding your annoyance

———Sarah, can you get in touch with what it was about the situation that most annoyed you

———Sarah, you say you were feeling annoyed. But as I listen to your voice it sounds to me as though you were very angry about what happened. Is it possible you were also afraid in that situation?

All this could be followed up with an exploration of Sarah's passiveness and, subsequently, some assertion training.

In the earlier moments of counseling, interchangeable responses used at carefully chosen choice points can facilitate in-depth exploration and movement toward greater openness. However, before trust and open communication have been fully developed, it is well to use additive empathy responses with caution. The inferential-interpretive aspects of these responses can be intimidating, pushing the client farther than he or she is ready to go.

Changes in the Johari Window

The Johari Window, referred to earlier in the chapter, may help to describe the self-awareness dimension of the counseling process. As the client begins to talk about self to the counselor, the amount of information known by both the client and the counselor expands and the amount known to the client, but not to the counselor, contracts. This process can be diagrammed as in Figure 5.2, where the size of Cell 1 increases and the size of Cell 2 decreases.

Figure 5.2   The process of sharing, as illustrated by the Johari Window

	KNOWN TO COUNSELOR	UNKNOWN TO COUNSELOR
KNOWN TO SELF	1	2
UNKNOWN TO SELF	3	4

Source: Basic design from *Group Processes: An Introduction to Group Dynamics*, by Joseph Luft, by permission of Mayfield Publishing Company (formerly National Press Books). Copyright © 1963, 1970 by Joseph Luft.

As the interaction continues, the counselor begins to formulate impressions and hypotheses about the client: motivations for the client's actions, hypotheses as to how the client's behavior affects significant others in his or her life spaces, assumptions behind the client's ideas, and explanations for the emergence of strong feelings such as anxiety, anger, doubt, and confusion. Many of these hypotheses generated by the counselor are not part of the client's awareness. They may be viewed as in Cell 3. In later stages, an important part of the counseling process may be that of sharing these hypotheses and observations with the client. Here, too, the use of "I messages" and principles of constructive confrontation are the bases for the counselor's approach to sharing. As the counselor makes these observations and hypotheses available to the client for thought and exploration, the movement is from Cell 3 to Cell 1. As the client begins to receive and consider the feedback data, he or she learns progressively more about self. Some of the unknowns begin to become more understandable. Over time what has happened through this process can be diagrammed as in Figure 5.3. Client and counselor have both come to understand the client more fully, and much of the unknown about the client and his or her behavior has been reduced. The process is one of guided self-discovery. It is sometimes painful, but often exciting.

Figure 5.3   **Change in information about self as a result of receiving feedback from the counselor, as illustrated by the Johari Window**

	KNOWN TO COUNSELOR	UNKNOWN TO COUNSELOR
KNOWN TO SELF	1	2
UNKNOWN TO SELF	3	4

Source: Basic design from *Group Processes: An Introduction to Group Dynamics* by Joseph Luft, by permission of Mayfield Publishing Company (formerly National Press Books). Copyright © 1963, 1970 by Joseph Luft.

Summary

Counseling begins when one person asks another for help in dealing with a problem or making an important decision. The purpose of this chapter has been to explore some of the conditions necessary during the first session to make subsequent helping efforts effective. The essential process goals of the first counseling session were described. They include stimulating open, honest, and full communication about the concerns needing to be discussed and the factors and background related to those concerns; working toward progressively deeper levels of understanding, respect, and trust between helpee and helper; providing the helpee with the view that something useful can be gained from the helping sessions; identifying a problem or concern for subsequent attention and work; and establishing the "gestalt" that counseling is a process where both parties must work hard to understand the client and his or her concerns. For the counselor, an additional process goal is that of acquiring information about the client that relates to his or her concerns and for effective problem resolution.

These represented the organizing framework for the chapter where issues and concerns related to the achievement of these goals were discussed. The Johari Window was used as a model to describe the meaning and dynamics of open communication and the role of open communication in stimulating client self-awareness. Issues and concerns related to establishing trust were examined; the role of caring, acceptance, and active listening was considered; and helping responses that block and facilitate were identified. Finally, empathy as a helper quality that stimulates open communication and in-depth exploration was discussed.

References

Carkhuff, R. R. *Helping and human relations, Vol. I.* New York: Holt, Rinehart and Winston, 1969.

Gordon, T. *Parent effectiveness training.* New York: Wyden Press, 1970.

Luft, J. *Group processes: An introduction to group dynamics.* Palo Alto, Calif.: National Press, 1963.

Means, B. L. Levels of empathic response. *Personnel and Guidance Journal,* 1973, 52, 23–28.

Raths, L., Harmin, M. M., & Simon, S. *Values and teaching.* Columbus, Ohio: Merrill, 1966.

Rogers, C. R. *Counseling and psychotherapy.* Boston: Houghton Mifflin, 1942.

Truax, C. B., & Carkhuff, R. R. *Toward effective counseling and psychotherapy.* Chicago: Aldine, 1967.

6. Principles of constructive confrontation

There are times during the counseling process when the counselor recognizes that the client must become aware of, and deal with, information that has uncomfortable or painful implications. Sometimes the unpleasant information may be factual in nature: expectancy tables that predict very low probabilities of success for a desired future course of action, low performance on an important national test, or rules and regulations that act as constraints for a given course of action.

At other times, the counselor may have feelings, inferences, or impressions about the client's behavior and may believe that client growth and change can be stimulated by offering the inferences acquired. For example, a counselor may observe that a male client has frequent difficulties with female authority figures, but fewer difficulties with male authority figures. The counselor may also hypothesize that this difficulty relates to the client's relationship with his mother (a classic case of client transference or generalization of feelings from their original source to new targets). The counselor may also observe that the client is not aware of this connection and that an awareness may help the client reduce his hostility. The counselor may decide that offering the observation and related inference may be an effective way to stimulate this awareness.

On still other occasions, some things may be happening in the counseling process that block counseling movement. For example, the client may be evading an important area of discussion, may be talking excessively about safe topics to avoid moving into difficult areas, or may be reporting feelings and experiences rather than working to try to understand them (all examples of client defenses). The counselor recognizes that little movement can occur until these obstacles are overcome and that to overcome these obstacles the problem must be "processed" or discussed openly.

All of these are examples in which the counselor must ask the client to face and deal with uncomfortable material. The process of presenting the material to the client is called "confrontation." Johnson (1972) describes constructive confrontation as:

. . . a deliberate attempt to help another person examine the consequences of some aspect of his behavior. It is an invitation to self-examination. A confrontation originates from a desire on the part of the confronter to involve himself more deeply with the person he is confronting. Confrontation is a way of expressing concern for another person and a wish to increase the mutual involvement in the relationship. . . . The purpose of a confrontation is to free the person being confronted to engage in more fruitful or less destructive behavior. (p. 160)

True confrontations are painful for both parties involved. The offering of a confrontation is a conscious decision of the counselor and, thus, a true act of caring. By confronting, the counselor is saying that he or she cares enough for the client to go through the stress and pain in order to bring about a change of behavior and growth. Johnson illustrates this point by asking who "is the true friend: the person who ignores the destructive behavior of another . . . or one who risks rejection by confronting the other . . . with the consequences of his behavior in order to help him not make the same mistake over and over again? If you are a person's friend, do you ignore his interpersonal mistakes or do you confront him with his mistakes in a way which facilitates his learning not to make the same mistake in the future?" (Johnson, 1972, p. 159).

Confrontations are a risk; a confrontation experience inevitably changes the nature of a relationship. If the caring involved in a confrontation is not perceived or accepted, or if confrontation is done to ventilate anger rather than to provide useful feedback, alienation is the likely result. If the counselor genuinely cares, and if his or her motives are based on caring, and the concern and the caring behind the act is understood, then the relationship is likely to move to a deeper, more open, and more intensive level.

Guidelines for appropriate confrontation

The act of confronting is a choice, not an impulse. Like all critical choices, the counselor must develop a set of criteria for deciding. The following are guidelines for deciding about the appropriateness and efficacy of a confrontation:

1.   *The first rule of confrontation is: do not confront another person if you do not intend to increase your involvement with him or her.* (Johnson, 1972, p. 160)

Confrontations are intense experiences that demand honest and examined communication from the helper. Intense introspective work must precede a confrontation. What to say, why it is important to say it, what the real motives for saying it are, how the client will react and work through his anger and fear are all part of the initial introspective work. Once offered, it is the responsibility of the counselor to help the client deal non-defensively with the data: to understand it, to internalize it, to become aware of the implications, and to consider what it means for future choices and behavior. To do less is not an act of helping; it is probably an act of hostility. If more intensive involvement is not desired or if honest and intensive caring is not experienced, do not confront. This is then an act of hostility or vengeance.

2.   *Confront only if you experience feelings of caring. Do not confront if you do not experience feelings of caring.*

To reaffirm earlier observations, caring is a concern and a commitment to the present and future well-being of another. The only honest reason for offering a confrontation is the belief that awareness of the information in the confrontation will enhance the present and future well-being of the helpee. If the caring is not present, the purpose for confronting is not to help, but to express or ventilate hostility. In that case, the helper is using the client to satisfy his or her own needs and not those of the client. The writers can think of a number of occasions where the possibility of confronting was considered and rejected because not enough caring was experienced toward the helpee. In short, the honest feeling was "I honestly don't care enough for this individual to invest time and energy to make the confrontation a beneficial experience for the other involved. Also, I do not care to extend my involvement or deepen or intensify my relationship with this person at this time."

3.   *Confront only if the relationship has gone beyond the initial stages of development or if basic trust has been clearly established.*

Confrontations can be effective only if the client experiences a sense of regard, caring, and respect from the counselor, and if those feelings are experienced toward the counselor. It takes time for such feelings to develop between people. If those feelings are not present, the information offered in the confrontation will be discounted by the client, and alienation between the parts is a likely outcome.

4.   *If the conditions above are present and the client is not ready to deal with the information non-defensively, then the counselor has two basic options: to avoid confronting or to help the client become ready to use the information once it is offered.*

Defensive clients do not accept confrontations very well. They discount the information given by the counselor, by rationalizing, justifying, leading away, verbally attacking the counselor, or by minimizing the importance of the consequences involved in the situation. A person who discounts such information is unlikely to use it for growth, change, and decision making. Getting a client ready means making sure his defensiveness, which could result in discounting the information, is under control. Johnson points out that if at the moment of confrontation "a person's anxiety level is high or his motivation or ability to change is low, the confrontation will not be utilized as an invitation for self-examination, and, therefore, it should not take place" (Johnson, 1972, p. 160).

How to confront constructively

Confrontations are a risk at any time. The less optimal the previous conditions the more risky and less beneficial the confrontation is likely to be. So one of the preparation acts is that before confronting the counselor must assess the strength of the relationship supports for the confrontation. The following questions will help toward this processing:

————What is the extent of my caring for this individual?

————Do I wish to extend my involvement with this person and develop a more intense relationship than what is being experienced now?

————What is the level of openness between us? Shallow, moderate, or deep?

————What is my estimation as to what the client will do with the information once it is presented? Will he or she receive it openly or defensively?

————How important is it that the client receive this information? What bad consequences might occur if the client did not receive the information? Just how bad are these consequences? Is the prevention of these consequences very important?

Having made the decision to confront, the approach will then be based on the nature of information to be offered. If the information relates to facts, then the information must be described in a straightforward, non-guarded fashion. Usually, counselors present the information and let the client react to it. As the client reacts, the counselor listens carefully for indicators of openness or defensiveness. If the defensiveness is high, the counselor may simply repeat the information to be sure it was received accurately, or may draw out implications that the client fails to see in self. Sometimes a response, such as the following, can help support a client during a confrontation experience: "I understand this information is not particularly pleasant; nonetheless it is important that we work it through together." If the facts are in printed form, then it is always well to have the printed material available for observation.

Confrontations based on counselor hypotheses, inferences, or feelings are more difficult because they are more subjective and, therefore, prone to defensive reactions from the client. There are three essential guidelines for offering such confrontations:

1.   *Present the data on which the inferences are based before stating the inference.*

Frequently, the data will be in the form of observed client behavior. This means that the client's behavior that forms the bases for the counselor inferences must be described in clear, specific, and unambiguous terms, that is, concretely rather than diffusely. Counselors sometimes wish to take the emotional "sting" out of their observations and try to do this by couching their statements in guarded messages. While perhaps well-meaning, this is an ineffective procedure because the information is not presented in a way so as to help the client really work with it.

2.   *Distinguish between observations and inferences and make that distinction verbally clear in the message to the client. State inferences tentatively.*

Inferences are abstractions or tentative conclusions from data being presented and, thus, may or may not be accurate. Presenting an inference to the client as though it were fact assumes that there is no doubt as to the accuracy of the inference. A counselor who does this is giving him- or herself too much credit. Additionally, it crowds the client and makes it difficult for the client to accept. Some counselors do this simply by distinguishing between "hearing" (the observation) and "sensing" (the inference). For example, "Bob, I hear you saying that you can accept the idea of your son becoming a policeman rather than a lawyer. But I am also sensing that his decision is very disappointing to you."

3.   *Use "I messages" throughout the confrontation statement.*

"I messages" own inferences and feelings; "you messages" attribute them to the client. "I messages" make it much easier for the client to accept the information presented and invite work around that information. "You messages" frequently sound accusatory and, hence, evoke defensiveness.

In the previous example, the counselor used the word "I" twice in the statement to the client. The counselor might well have also said (with an underlying accusatory tone), "Bob, you say you can accept your son's decision. But that decision is clearly very disappointing to you." In this counselor response, the word "I" was not used. Additionally, the inferred feeling of disappointment was presented to Bob as though it were a fact and as though Bob should feel guilty for having such feelings. The expected client response from this counselor statement would probably be, "No, not really. Why, what makes you think so?" Not only has feeling exploration not occurred, but Bob has shifted the focus of attention to the counselor and away from self. It is much easier for Bob to defend and attack whatever the counselor subsequently says.

The following are some examples of counselor confrontation responses. In each case, a potentially effective counselor response is followed by an ineffective counselor response, which violates one or more of the guidelines above. In each case, the basic client concern may easily be inferred from the counselor statements.

Effective:	Sharon, I can see that you are angry about your husband's treatment of you. I am sensing that it is very difficult for you to let him know you are angry.
Ineffective:	If you are so angry toward your husband, why don't you tell him (stupid)?
Effective:	Rich, this is our fourth session. During our meetings you have shared with me some things about yourself. But I have also noticed that whenever we talk about how it feels inside when your wife becomes angry you move away from sharing those feelings. Frequently, you change the subject. The feelings you experience may very well be painful, but it is important that you share them with me.
Ineffective:	Rich, come on. We have gone over this ground several times and each time we go in circles and never get anywhere. The reason that is happening is that you just simply are not leveling with me.
Effective:	Margaret, during our last two sessions we have agreed that you would do some homework. Each time you have come to

the next session you indicate you have not done the homework. I find myself wondering why you are not doing the homework when we both recognize it is a very important part of the counseling experience for you.

Ineffective: Margaret, this is the second time you have come to counseling without doing your homework. What is really happening here?

Effective: Joe, from what we have discussed so far, it seems that when you clown around with your classmates it is your way of trying to get them to pay attention to you. In turn, I think you hope this will lead to making friends. Yet, I have the impression that things rarely work out that way for you. For example, when you tried to clown around with me, I was feeling uncomfortable and was wishing you would stop.

Ineffective: Joe, your clowning around is really getting you into a lot of trouble. Rather than admiring you, everybody is getting tired of it and really annoyed with you.

There may be a number of occasions in which the counselor can express feelings in the form of an "I message" as a way to stimulate gainful movement.

———Tom, I have noticed during our talks that you never mention your father. I am curious as to what kind of relationship you and your father have with each other.

———Marsha, I am sensing a very uncomfortable barrier between us. Whenever we get close to important material you seem to dodge or run away from it. I have the sense you are not sure whether it is all right to trust me.

———Floyd, right now I am experiencing feelings of exasperation and I would like for you to know where they are coming from. I am trying hard to help you understand what it is you do that turns people off. It seems that whenever I try to help you examine what went on with another person, you switch topics. I would like very much to help you understand your relationships with others, but I find it very difficult to do so when you move away from the focus of discussion. Perhaps other people experience feelings similar to those I am experiencing.

———Eloise, I want you to know I appreciate the openness with which you have shared this painful material.

———Shirley, I am sensing your decision to send your young child to live with your mother while you teach and finish graduate school is a very painful area for you. I am not sure whether you would like to share it or not and I am finding myself unsure as to whether to follow up on it or not. If you prefer to keep that area private, I can understand and accept your decision. If you feel OK about sharing it, I would like to understand.

Figure 6.1   Johari Window before confrontation

	KNOWN TO COUNSELOR	UNKNOWN TO COUNSELOR
KNOWN TO CLIENT	1	2
UNKNOWN TO CLIENT	3	4

The arrow indicates the flow of communication during a confrontation experience.

Source: Basic design from *Group Processes: An Introduction to Group Dynamics* by Joseph Luft, by permission of Mayfield Publishing Company (formerly National Press Books). Copyright © 1963, 1970 by Joseph Luft.

Confrontation and the Johari Window

Use of the Johari Window (Figures 6.1 and 6.2) helps to understand the process of constructive confrontation. As the counselor listens to the client, inferences and hypotheses about the client and his or her concerns arise. These hypotheses are known to the counselor, but not to the client, and, thus, may be considered as part of Cell 3 in the Johari Window. The counselor may decide that sharing these hypotheses may help the client engage in self-examination and lead to useful insights about self. Making such information available to the client for consideration and work is the act of moving the information from Cell 3 to Cell 1 where it is available to both client and counselor.

Diagrammatically, the process may be viewed as shown in Figure 6.1 on page 108.

Figure 6.2   Change in the Johari Window after confrontation

	KNOWN TO COUNSELOR	UNKNOWN TO COUNSELOR
KNOWN TO CLIENT	1	2
UNKNOWN TO CLIENT	3	4

Source: Basic design from *Group Processes: An Introduction to Group Dynamics* by Joseph Luft, by permission of Mayfield Publishing Company (formerly National Press Books). Copyright © 1963, 1970 by Joseph Luft.

Providing feedback in this fashion offers the client new information with which to work. Notice that moving information from Cell 3 to Cell 1 is an act of the counselor. Moving information from Cell 2 to Cell 1 is an act of the client. The first is confrontation; the second is self-disclosure. Confrontation in this manner is an inherent part of the insight stimulating part of the counseling process.

Dealing with counselor anger toward client

A part of the counseling process that is especially difficult and that represents a time for processing and, possibly, confrontation occurs when the counselor experiences negative feelings such as annoyance, disappointment, anger, or rejection toward the client. A first principle relating to the experiencing of such feelings is that *such feelings are the responsibility of the counselor, not of the client.* Dealing effectively with anger begins when the counselor allows the feelings into awareness. Since the experience of anger toward a client is assumed to be bad and undesirable, counselors often try to cope with their anger by suppressing it (pretending it is not there and blocking it out of awareness). Repression and suppression are generally ineffective ways to control uncomfortable emotions.

Anger and disappointment generally occur when one person's behavior does not meet the expectations of another, or when one person lets another down. The person whose expectations were not met in the situation is likely to feel anger toward the person whose behavior did not meet those expectations. Anger also occurs when one person's behavior is unacceptable, hurtful, or intolerable to another. Anger is frequently a mask for underlying feelings of fear, apprehension, and anxiety. With these principles in mind, once a counselor is aware of feelings of anger, he or she must "process" it, or try to become aware of its underlying sources. The counselor can do this by raising some important questions to self:

1. Precisely what client behaviors do I find disappointing or unacceptable? What alternate behaviors would be more acceptable?

2. If I am experiencing anger toward the client, then I am making judgments about the acceptability of the client's behavior. The client is not living up to my standards or expectations. What are the standards or "should" statements I am imposing on my client? Is it reasonable for me to impose those standards?

3.   Am I experiencing fear behind my anger or disappointment? If so, what is it that I am really afraid of?

4.   Do I want to express my anger either as an emotional
whip or as a way to protect myself?

5.   How do I understand and account for the client's behavior that is related to my anger? What meaning does the
client's behavior have for him or her?

The purpose for raising these questions is to check out the basis
for the anger. Counselors going through this process often discover
that their anger is a matter for them to work through on their own
rather than to attribute it to the client. Often counselors discover that
they are transferring or generalizing anger feelings from some other
sources in their lives. The client reminds them of someone else in their
lives toward whom they feel anger. On still other occasions, counselors discover that their surface anger is really a mask for covering
up fear underneath the anger, and that the expression of this anger is
a form of defense. They may also discover that they would like to use
their anger as an emotional whip—as a means for controlling the
behavior of the other person involved.

However, there may be occasions in which the counselor has
checked out his or her anger and still finds that the experience of
anger is not unfair or unreasonable, and that it would be unfair to self
to believe that such feelings should not exist. Under such conditions,
the counselor has three basic options: not to disclose such feelings, to
present the feelings in whatever way they seem to surface, or to
present them as information to the client according to the guidelines
for constructive confrontation.

To new counselors, this often appears to be a difficult problem.
They believe "I should be honest with the client and if I am feeling
angry then I should honestly express my feelings. But if I express my
feelings the client may well feel hurt and rejected and whatever rapport has been built up will be destroyed."

Once the principles of constructive confrontation are understood, the answer to this question is not difficult. Feelings of anger,
disappointment, discomfort, or distrust must either be presented according to the principles of constructive confrontation or not at all. If
they are to be presented, they must be offered as therapeutic or gainful
material to help the client. It is not appropriate to express these
feelings for ventilation or catharsis, for revenge or emotional whip-
ping. Whether or not the counselor presents his or her feelings de-

pends on the same factors for deciding to confront or not—whether the client is ready to use the information presented and whether the information will help the client grow, learn, or develop more rewarding behavior. An example follows:

Ed, I understand that you told your teacher you were with me yesterday instead of being in class. I think you were using me and our relationship. I very much resent being used that way and am especially disappointed because I thought there was trust between us.

Summary

Confrontation may be seen as a counselor's act of presenting important information to the client. The information may be about important environmental facts or counselor impressions concerning some aspects of the client's behavior. What makes a confrontation experience uncomfortable is that the information to be presented usually has negative connotations for the client. Especially in insight forms of counseling, confrontation is an important part of the helping process.

Since confrontations can be for better or for worse, it is important for the counselor to have guidelines for offering confrontations effectively. The guidelines developed in the chapter include: (1) confront only if you intend to increase your involvement with the individual, (2) confront only if you experience feelings of caring, (3) confront only if the relationship is not in an early stage of development or if the development of basic trust has been established, and (4) if the client is not ready to receive confronting information openly, then the counselor must prepare the client before the confrontation is offered.

Additional guidelines about offering counselor impressions about the client's behavior include: (5) present the data first on which the inferences are based, (6) distinguish between observations and inferences and make that distinction clear in the verbal message to the client, and (7) use "I messages" throughout the confrontation statement. The Johari Window was used to understand confrontation as a part of the counseling process, and counselor anger was considered a special aspect of the confrontation experience.

References

Johnson, D. W. *Reaching out.* Englewood Cliffs, N. J.: Prentice-Hall, 1972.

7. Working with reluctant clients

Much of what has been said in the previous chapter has been built around the assumption of voluntary or self-referral clients who are willing to initiate their own talk on an issue of concern. Getting the counseling process going with such clients is easy: the counselor simply begins with a statement that provides the client with an opportunity to share. "How can I help?" is one such example. Responses such as summaries and reflections of feelings and beliefs, leads such as "Tell me more about . . ." and "I messages" help to facilitate further exploration.

Who is the reluctant client?

Not all clients are self-referred. Many times counselors must work with clients who would prefer not to be with the counselor. The reluctant client is any person who, if given the choice, would choose not to be in the presence of a counselor and who would prefer not to talk about self. In school settings, this may include students whom the counselor has identified as being in academic difficulty or students referred by other members of the professional staff. In family counseling situations, it is often the case that one member comes reluctantly because he or she is pressured. Similarly, parents not infrequently insist that their unwilling children talk with a counselor and wish for the counselor to "straighten out the child's silly thinking and show him the right and proper course of action."

Since they enter the experience under pressure from someone else, the perspectives of entering reluctant clients are likely to interfere with the chances for effective counseling movement. Some may not be sure why they are being asked to see the counselor. Since the counselor is often identified with the authority structure of an institution, many may hypothesize that they are in trouble and will be punished. They will enter with an orientation toward self-protection, ready to assign blame somewhere outside of self. Many may enter with a sense of resentment toward the person who pressured them into seeing the counselor in the first place and will transfer that resentment to the counselor. Often such clients will not perceive a need for help and, thus, will not come prepared to engage in introspective work. Not experiencing an awareness of the need for help, they will not view the counselor as a helping person and, thus, will be unwilling to engage in self-disclosure and open communication. For most, behind the belligerent, defiant façade are intense feelings of anxiety.

Reluctance from such clients is expressed in a variety of ways. Some show open defiance: "I don't want to be here and you can't make me do anything I don't want to do." Others express their defiance in more passive ways: by showing an unwillingness to communicate anything beyond terse answers to direct questions, or by leading the discussion away from self and into innocuous topics. Still others try to manipulate the counselor into talking about self so they will not have to take any responsibility. Clearly, all these reactions interfere with open, honest communication and subsequently with the chances that counseling can be an experience of much benefit.

Counselor emotions toward the reluctant client

As Dyer and Vriend (1975) describe, in the presence of reluctant clients counselors often experience non-facilitative emotions. Many will feel high levels of anxiety. For some, the anxiety will occur because they want very much to be successful and anticipate failure. Other counselors who have high needs for acceptance may perceive the actions of the reluctant client as personal rejection. Anxiety for other counselors may come about because they feel insecure about their ability to deal with the client's defenses. Still other counselors feel anxious because they experience ambivalence about whether it is proper for them to offer counseling to a client who does not desire it.

Many counselors experience high levels of anger toward reluctant clients. As developed in Chapter 3, anger occurs when one person does not live up to the "should" statements that another is imposing on him or her. The counselor experiencing anger toward the reluctant client is quite probably imposing some expectations that the client is not meeting. In turn, the anger toward the client is an important indicator to the counselor that he or she is imposing expectations on the client, possibly without awareness of doing so. Here are some typical examples:

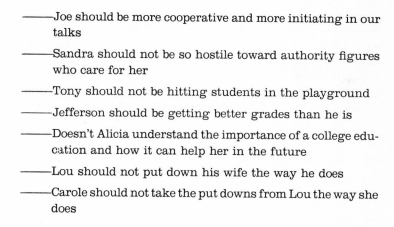

———Joe should be more cooperative and more initiating in our talks

———Sandra should not be so hostile toward authority figures who care for her

———Tony should not be hitting students in the playground

———Jefferson should be getting better grades than he is

———Doesn't Alicia understand the importance of a college education and how it can help her in the future

———Lou should not put down his wife the way he does

———Carole should not take the put downs from Lou the way she does

The frustration → anger hypothesis in Chapter 3 also helps to understand counselor anger. The counselor may have several important goals in mind for the client: opening communication, stimulating insights, helping the client work through resentments, clarifying the client's illogical reasoning, preventing some dangerous future event from happening to the client. The client's unwillingness to communicate openly blocks the achievement of any of these goals and becomes a source of frustration for the counselor.

Some counselors will experience anger because of a perceived loss of status and control. Their attitude is that they should have control over the situation. By his or her acts of reluctance, the client is demonstrating power and control over the counselor. Not only are the client's actions a challenge to the counselor's adequacy, but, for those counselors who need to be in control, the roles are reversed. The surface anger may be covering up underlying anxiety.

Most beginning counselors and many experienced counselors find either or both feelings described. The feelings often block the counselor's ability to reach out effectively. Thus, to deal with the reluctant client, the counselor must first deal with self. He or she must non-defensively allow feelings into awareness and search to become aware of the perceptions about self and client that are behind these feelings.

Working with reluctant clients: A valuing issue

Whether counselors should be expected to work with nonvoluntary clients is an important issue. Some say counselors should work only with those who want the counselor's help. Particularly in school settings, others argue that, as a professional in the setting, the counselor should be expected to work with students encountering academic difficulties or who have been observed by other professionals to have behavior problems. In some settings, this means that the counselor becomes responsible for enforcing school rules and for administering punishment for inappropriate or unacceptable behavior.

There is a real difference between working with students whose behavior patterns suggest some difficulties and administering punishment. Obviously, it is unreasonable to expect that the person who administers punishment will also be perceived as a person to whom one can turn for help and trust. It is the view of these authors that it is appropriate for school counselors to work with students whose academic performance is well below that which can be expected, based on their scores on nationally standardized tests. It is also appropriate for counselors to work with students whom teachers observe to be social isolates, who are not relating well to their peers, who are demonstrating high levels of generalized hostility to authority figures, who often come to school heavily influenced by drugs, or who show by their behavior that they have no sense of personal direction or commitment to a personal future.

Behavior patterns such as these are generally symptoms of underlying problems. Often adolescents engaging in such behavior do not feel accepted by their peers or significant adults in their life spaces. Their behavior is an ineffective effort to get recognition and attention. For other adolescents, behavior patterns such as these reflect underlying feelings of resentment and hostility for perceived unfair treatment. For still others, the behavior reflects a loss of identity, a sense of basic personal insecurity, and a dislike for self. The person who cares for self will do those things that are necessary and instrumental to taking care of self. The person who does not care for self may choose not to do those things that will best take care of self. Counter-productive and self-defeating behavior patterns are often important indicators and reflections of loss of self-regard and respect.

Thus, the long-range process goals of counseling should not be to punish or hassle unacceptable behavior, but rather to help participants develop an understanding of the underlying reasons and motivations for the behavior. When this is accomplished, the counseling process can subsequently be devoted to helping the client find more effective ways to cope with the problems and satisfy the underlying needs. As with all counseling situations, open communication and sharing in the initial stages of counseling is a key to effective long-range intervention. Punishing undesirable behavior may temporarily suppress it, but will have little effect in creating a lasting change for the better.

There are some important observations and assumptions behind the counselor's decision to work with a reluctant client and these need to be examined. One observation is that either the counselor, a third party, or both are judging the acceptability and appropriateness of the client's behavior. As developed in Chapter 3, to make such judgments implies that the judging person has sound criteria for imposing them. The basis for all such judgments ultimately rests in the counselor's views about the characteristics of the healthy individual. The counselor's model of the healthy individual then forms a standard not only to evaluate the behavior patterns of the client, but also to understand the factors supporting what on the surface appear to be unhealthy or undesirable patterns. What may appear as unhealthy on the surface may turn out to be reasonable coping upon further understanding of the client and his or her situation. Nonetheless, counselors do make such judgments and it is not inappropriate for them to do so. Heavy drug use, extreme discrepancy between potential and performance, and continuous episodes of fighting and loneliness are patterns to be concerned about by any reasonable standards of emotional healthiness.

This position is not easy to implement. Many clients are angry and defiant precisely because they find significant others making such judgments. At issue to them is the question, "Who is in control of my life: me or someone else?" Often the reluctance seen in counseling is a resistance to being controlled. Making judgments about the appropriateness of the client's behavior may put the counselor in the same position as other authority figures in the client's life—a person to be feared and distrusted. What can make a counselor different from others who judge is what is done with the judgments once they are made. Often others attempt to coerce and pressure. A counselor's effectiveness lies in his or her ability to communicate caring and trust, to not indicate a moralizing posture, and to avoid using coercive tactics to get the client to conform to someone else's norms.

Another observation is that intervention into the life of a reluctant client is based on a preventive approach to counseling. Seeing undesirable patterns, the counselor, in essence, is saying that if continued, these disturbing patterns will lead to a very bad, perhaps serious, set of outcomes in the client's future. The purpose for intervening in the present is to change behavior so that these potentially bad outcomes will be prevented. It is indeed presumptuous for one person to believe that he or she knows the future outcomes of another's behavior and is willing to make an outsider's evaluation of those outcomes. Nonetheless, there are some client behavior patterns, such as those described earlier, for which such presumptions may be appropriate.

Structuring: The key to working with reluctant clients

Clearly, the conditions necessary for counseling to be of benefit are missing with the reluctant client. If counseling is to be of any value at all the counselor must increase the client's readiness for the counseling experience. Another way of saying this is that the counselor must teach the client how to be a good client. The most reasonable way to bring this about is through structuring. Structuring is a matter of providing the client with information as to why he or she was asked to come to the counselor's office. In general, the guidelines for structuring are the same as those that apply to the process of constructive confrontation. This means that the counselor must clearly inform the client as to the reasons and goals for the session, must present the data related to the problem situation in descriptive rather than inferential or abstract terms, must be willing to use "I messages" to share personal feeling level reactions to the situation, must present the problem from a constructive rather than a punitive orientation, and must allow the client an opportunity to react to the problem being presented. All this information must be presented in an honest, straightforward fashion without the use of guarded messages.

Many counselors find it difficult to structure. Often such sessions have the atmosphere of calling a person "on the carpet" for something he or she did that was judged as unacceptable. The data to be presented sound accusatory and counselors fear that any presentation will put the client on the defensive. The result is that often the client attempts to justify or explain away the problem or to assign responsibility for the problem to someone else ("Johnny was the one who started the fight, not me").

Since a defensive reaction from the client is quite likely, a part of the "working-through-readiness development" process will normally include dealing with client defenses and resistances. Counseling techniques for working through defenses follow the same classification levels of constructive confrontation: mild, moderate, or intense. Mild techniques are those which help a client talk more openly with the counselor about some issue of significance that is "comfortable air space" for the client: "Joe, share with me some of your thoughts about your personal future." The counselor's hope here is that talk around a non-threatening topic will lead to the development of greater trust and openness and subsequently make it easier to discuss more threatening issues. The danger with this approach is that clients may suspect that the counselor has a "hidden agenda" and subsequently they will become more suspicious and reluctant.

Moderate techniques tend to confront the resistance directly, but will address that part which is least difficult for the client to accept: "Maryanne, take the risk to share with me what is *really* irritating you in this situation. Let's see if we can work on understanding it together." In the case study at the end of this chapter, Mr. Wilson's approach with Dana exemplifies a moderate technique.

Intense techniques for dealing with client resistances are identical to direct confrontations and follow all the guidelines of constructive confrontations. Some intense approaches directly describe and label the client's reluctance; other approaches add an interpretation, and attempt to confront the client with the underlying significance and meaning of his or her behavior. An example of the first approach would be: "Jack, right now I am experiencing a great deal of discomfort. I would like very much to help you, but it is also clear that you are reluctant to discuss the problem. The matter really is a serious one, and it is important that we talk openly with each other. So let's simply agree to level with each other." The following are some examples of interpretational approaches: "Sarah, perhaps the real meaning of your silence is that you are afraid to take the risk to change." "Phil, I sense your unwillingness to communicate with me is your way of telling me how much you despise and distrust adults."

Examples of each level have been offered to illustrate some of the different ways counselors attempt to work through client resistance. Clearly, the mild approaches appear the least risky, and the intense approaches appear the most intimidating. No single approach will work best for all clients. Part of a counselor's sensitivity lies in the ability to make diagnostic guesses as to which approach is likely to be most effective for the particular client involved. Another dimension of a counselor's effectiveness lies in the capacity to implement each of the approaches. Many counselors resist the more intense approaches because they are afraid of the perceived consequences—possibly threatening the client, causing a total alienation in the relationship, and prematurely terminating the counseling experience. While these consequences are possible, the intense approaches can also have a powerful impact for the client. The direct confrontation can lead to a more intense and deeper level of self-examination. In a way much more powerful than the other approaches, intense confrontations establish that: counseling is a process of hard work for all participants, a major share of the responsibility for work lies with the client, the counselor is a person who cares enough to take "helping risks" and who expects honest communication from the client, and that open communication and honest looking at self are OK and need not be feared. All of this is predicated on the idea that the counselor's motive for using an intense approach is to stimulate favorable counseling movement and not to ventilate personal anger.

Working with referral sources

To analyze the process of structuring, it is important to distinguish between clients who are identified for counseling by the counselor and those who are referred to a counselor by a third party. In both cases, the counselor must be clear about the reasons for the requested visit and must be clear and specific about the facts related to the request. However, when accepting a referral from a third party, a good deal of prior preparation must be done with the referral source. Often referral sources are vague about the reason they wish a counselor to work with an individual. Just as it is important for counselors to help clients clarify their problems, it is also important to help referral sources state their observations in clear and specific terms. It is also important to help referral sources distinguish between their observation and their inferences. It is not sufficient for a teacher to say, "Katherine has changed a lot during the last marking period. Where she used to be carefree, she now seems to be very worried about something. I think you should see her." The counselor must help the teacher describe the behaviors and circumstances that led to the inference that Katherine seems to be worried. "Can you tell me about some of your observations of Katherine's behavior that have given you the impression she is worried?" is an example of a counselor response that can facilitate such clarification.

Often the counselor has options in referral situations. Sometimes he or she may decide not to accept a referral. In other cases, such as students misbehaving in classrooms, the counselor may try to help the referral source in a consulting capacity. If after hearing the description of a concern, the counselor decides to accept a referral, several issues need to be worked through with the referral source. Sometimes the working-through process takes on a process similar to that of bargaining and negotiating. In almost all cases when the counselor structures, he or she will need to identify the referral source. The referral source must be told this during the referral discussion. Some referral sources may be very uncomfortable about this possibility, and it may be necessary for the counselor to explain carefully why identifying the referring person is important. During the referral discussion, the counselor and referring person must also agree on what information in the referral discussion the counselor is to share with the client. The counselor may wish to try role playing: possible initial structuring statements to help the referring person clarify what information is acceptable to share with the client. Often, as an additional benefit to the role playing, the referring person can provide useful feedback on effective ways to structure, traps to avoid, etc.

The two parties must also agree in advance about what kind of feedback the counselor will offer after the counseling session. As discussed in Chapter 5, this is a difficult dilemma for the counselor. Referring persons generally want some feedback, yet the counselor wants to offer the client an opportunity for private communication. Some counselors handle this dilemma by simply expressing their problem to the referring person: "I can well understand your desire for feedback. You care for Katherine and want to know that something is being done to help her. But it is also important for me to help Katherine develop a sense of trust. This means I must let her know that I will keep private whatever she shares with me. I hope you will understand the importance of not betraying Katherine's trust. This will mean that I may not be able to offer much feedback." Often referring persons are especially concerned about what the prospective client will say about them (Does the student think I am unfair? A poor teacher?). It is well for the counselor to anticipate with the referring person that he or she may be the focus of discussion in the counseling session, again to help clarify feelings about that possibility.

Case study 4: Dana—low grades

Dana was a sixteen-year-old student in the tenth grade. From her standardized achievement tests it was expected that her academic achievement would generally be in the B to $C+$ range. Indeed, up until her sophomore year her performance had been in that range, with one A in Social Studies and another in Family Living. During the first marking period of her sophomore year, she received three C's and two D's. Entries in her anecdotal records from two teachers indicated that Dana had frequently not turned in her homework and that the homework she had turned in was poorly done. The same pattern appeared during the second marking period. In contrast, during the previous year several teachers had commented that Dana came to class well prepared, that her class assignments were well done, and that her homework was always in on time.

In a routine check of student records, Mr. Wilson, the tenth-grade counselor, noticed this sudden change in Dana's performance pattern, and decided it was important to discuss his observations with her. She came to his office as requested, appearing quite nervous and apprehensive. After greeting her, his initial statement to her was as follows:

Mr. Wilson: Dana, I am sure you are wondering why I have asked you to come to my office, and I can see that you are nervous about what to expect. I am not going to punish you for anything, so please try to relax. [*pause*] Routinely, I check the records of the tenth-grade students to see how well they are doing in their schoolwork. I check to see which students are doing well and which are having difficulties. In checking your records, I noticed that whereas last year your grades were in the B to $C+$ range, this year your grades are in the C to D range. Last year you received two A's; this year, none. Also, last year several teachers observed that you were prepared for class and got your homework assignments in promptly. In contrast, this year several of your teachers have observed that you have frequently not been prepared and your homework assignments have frequently not been in on time. Now I don't think it makes much sense to lecture you on the importance of good grades for your future. At the same time, the changes I just described do concern me. I thought it might be useful to discuss this problem and to see what can be done about the situation.

Dana: Well, I know my grades are not as good as they were last year, but I think I can do better next marking period.

Mr. Wilson: Can you help me understand that more fully?

Dana: Well, things haven't been going well at home lately. My parents both work. More often it seems that when they are home together they are always fighting. I think they are probably going to separate pretty soon. At first it bothered me a lot, but lately I have been trying not to think about it. But it's really hard to do that. Anyway, I guess the situation has been affecting my schoolwork.

Mr. Wilson: I'm sorry to hear about what's happening between your parents, Dana. Seeing parents going at each other really can be difficult to accept. Share with me some of the

thoughts and feelings you have had about
their quarreling.

From here, Dana shared a variety of concerns, including the
wish that her parents could put things back together, the feeling of
caring for both of them, and the fear that she might have to choose
between them someday soon. At one point, Mr. Wilson asked Dana if
she thought she were the subject of some of the quarrels. This brought
a flood of tears and an affirmative answer. What eventually surfaced
was a feeling of responsibility for contributing to the parents' difficulties and a concomitant sense of guilt. Dana and Mr. Wilson explored
this together. Eventually, Mr. Wilson helped Dana recognize that the
behavior she thought was contributing to the family difficulties in
reality had little to do with the parents' problem. Dana had been
attributing her behavior to the cause of her parents' problem, but it
was not so. In turn, this helped Dana overcome her sense of guilt.

This session ended with Dana agreeing to do more thinking
about the thoughts and feelings she was having about her parents'
fighting and an agreement to meet the next week. At the next meeting,
Dana shared more thoughts and also the observation that she had not
been able to do much schoolwork. Mr. Wilson acknowledged this
problem and indicated that after she got her feelings into the open she
would be able to control them better and thus be able to devote more
energy and attention to learning.

At the beginning of the fourth session, Dana told Mr. Wilson that
her parents told her they were separating and that she would have to
choose with whom to live. They discussed this for a long time. Mr.
Wilson helped Dana clarify her thoughts and also helped her communicate her decision to her parents. Dana's marks did not improve
during the next marking period. But a month after the actual separation, Dana came to Mr. Wilson and indicated that she was now living
with her mother, that her father seemed to understand and accepted
her reasons, and that she is now able to concentrate more fully on her
schoolwork.

Analysis

Dana's case is an example in which taking a risk to reach
out to a reluctant client was rewarded. Many factors motivated Dana's
reluctance. She did not know Mr. Wilson very well. She knew of him
by his professional title, but knew almost nothing about his individual

qualities. The problem that was disturbing her was one she regarded as a private family matter—certainly not one to be shared with a stranger. Yet, the pressure of her worry, concern, and guilt were enough to motivate Dana to respond to an invitation to talk with Mr. Wilson.

Mr. Wilson's initial response to Dana was the key to the entire counseling process. He reviewed the data that came to his attention and how he obtained it in the first place. He verbally observed the sudden shift in Dana's academic performance. Instead of giving her a sales pitch on the importance of good grades, he took the interpretation that the sudden shift might be a sign of some underlying problem. His assumption was that to really help Dana the important thing was to explore whatever underlying problems might exist.

Dana's response to Mr. Wilson's initial statement was defensive; she did not share her real concerns. But subsequently she did share in response to his desire to understand more fully. Dana's response here was a critical decision for her. She might well have said, "I would rather not talk about it" or "I just had trouble getting started this year." Dana's choice to disclose her anxiety suggests two hypotheses: First, somewhere inside she must have been experiencing a desire to talk with someone; and second, even though Mr. Wilson was a relative stranger, she must have perceived him as trustworthy enough to take the risk to share. Several factors may have influenced her decision: First, Mr. Wilson shared a good deal with her in his initial response to her. In being open, he was acting as a role model and also saying in essence, "It's OK to be open." Second, his request to understand more fully came across as an invitation, not an inquisition. Quite possibly, Dana accepted this as an expression of caring. Third, his interpretation of Dana's change in schoolwork as an indicator of a possible problem, rather than the lazy behavior of an immature child, may have said to Dana that he was an individual who understood people and who related to students as adults. The fact that he took the time at all to notice and to do something about what he noticed in themselves were expressions of caring.

His response, "Share with me some of the thoughts and feelings you have had about their quarreling," was also very sensitive. It provided Dana with an opportunity to bring out some painful feelings she had been harboring. His assumption here was that awareness of feelings and their sources can lead to control of the feelings and their effects on daily life behavior.

Was counseling successful for Dana? If the standard for success is immediate improvement in grades, then the answer is no. Grades did not improve immediately. But immediate improvement in grades would hardly seem a valid standard for evaluation in Dana's case. She needed to sort out a variety of feelings and perspectives before she could fully devote her attention to her studies. We have no evidence that any of her outward behavior changed either. Dana did thank Mr. Wilson for his help. She said she was glad they had talked over her concerns and that he had been helpful to her. The research literature in counseling effectiveness points out a variety of reasons to be suspicious of client self-report as a sole measure of effectiveness. But, in this case, it would seem the best indicator available.

If valid indicators of success are difficult to come by, it is also clear that counseling was not a failure. Too many powerful processes of self-examination were put into motion to come to that conclusion. Mr. Wilson's approach helped Dana clarify, and more clearly understand, thoughts and feelings that were confusing and frightening to her. The problem for the researcher is that it is difficult to measure processes such as "self-examination," and "clarification of feelings and beliefs." Yet, it would be difficult to deny the importance of these counseling experiences for Dana.

Some will question whether it was wise for Mr. Wilson to have accepted Dana's explanation that her sudden change was due to parent quarreling. In the face of pressure, many students use this as a defensive excuse for their performance—a justification lacking in validity. If Dana had been making up this story, Mr. Wilson may have been deceived and conned. The client would have entered frightened and left laughing.

Indeed, this is a difficult problem for counselors. To accept a story is to reinforce a client's efforts to use deception. To confront a possible deception when it is not risks alienation. The client correctly concludes that the counselor does not trust him or her. In this case, Mr. Wilson took the risk to accept and was rewarded. The same judgment the next day with a different client may have turned out differently.

There is no real answer to this dilemma. The best guideline is that, if a client is intentionally deceiving, this fact will eventually surface in the form of factual discrepancies. When and if clear discrepancies emerge, a confrontation will be necessary.

References

Dyer, W. V., & Vriend, J. *Counseling techniques that work.* Washington, D.C.: APGA Press, 1975, Chap. 5: Counseling the reluctant client.

8. Goal identification and assessment of client characteristics

Counseling has been defined as a human transaction process to help individuals achieve goals—future events that a person wants to make happen. Some goals that are appropriate for counseling have been identified in Chapter 2, along with a basis for helping the counselor distinguish between goal-directed activities that are healthy, and activities that are not. This basis for helping offers the counselor criteria upon which to decide whether or not more specific goals will be helpful for an individual client. The standard is how the specific goal, once achieved, will contribute to the client's future growth.

In order to attain certain outcome goals, certain process goals must first be attained. The effectiveness of counseling is directly related to the counselor's ability to describe both outcome and process goals and to develop counseling strategies to attain those goals. These concepts become especially important in the third stage of counseling—goal identification. It is during this stage when client and counselor systematically identify and evaluate the outcome goals of counseling and where the counselor begins to formulate process goals for counseling and strategies to achieve those goals.

This stage begins only after the development of deep levels of open communication, trust, caring, and acceptance has been established. Thus, it is appropriate to identify the establishment of an effective facilitative relationship as an important process goal, which must occur early in the relationship, if later counseling goals are to be attained.

This third stage—the goal and strategy identification stage—may be seen as having four important and interrelated components.

1.   The establishment of target or outcome goals of counseling

2.   The determination and consideration of client characteristics that might influence the counselor's strategy

3.   The thinking through of those process goals that must be attained if later outcome goals are to be reached, and the sequence in which those process goals might occur

4.   The development of a strategy (or plan of action) to be implemented to help the client achieve the identified goal

Goal identification

Describing the goals of the counseling process is frequently a difficult task. Outcome goals are often described in such terms as self-exploration, self-understanding, greater self-awareness, and self-actualization. These terms are too vague, unclear, and unspecific to be satisfactory. *The indicators of counseling success must be identified in terms that describe new client behaviors that are observable.* Examples include: reacting with less anxiety or anger in situations that previously triggered these emotions; responding to interpersonal situations in ways that bring about greater interpersonal respect and caring rather than alienation; using assertive response skills in situations where one's rights have been jeopardized; expressing one's point of view on controversial issues with fluency and clarity, or taking new actions that are consistent with a newly arrived at decision.

A client may report that as a result of counseling he feels better, has more confidence, and more fully understands himself and his world. While these changes may in fact have occurred, they are not descriptions of behavior change and, hence, not adequate indicators of counseling success. On the other hand, if a client were to say, "I feel a greater sense of confidence as a result of counseling. This has had a real influence in the way I function with people. In contrast to the way I functioned before, I now find myself engaging in a sustained conversation with people; my speaking is more fluent; I can more strongly assert my positions on issues even where I am aware others will disagree; I look straight at people when I am talking to them instead of at the floor; I smile more frequently; and I have stopped that continual pattern of saying negative things about myself," then the client has described changes in his overt behavior that were what he and the counselor were trying to attain. While it cannot be certain that such changes were the result of counseling, at least there is an indication that favorable changes did occur and it is quite possible that it was, in fact, a result of the counseling intervention. The important point to realize is that counseling success must be described in terms of behavioral change.

While that principle holds in general for all counseling intervention, the specific behavior changes and the counseling strategies implemented to achieve those changes are specific to each client. This statement is also consistent with the counselor's involvement in the decision-making process. A major service many counselors provide is in helping clients make decisions about future plans and actions. In schools, many counselors try to help students decide which career field to enter after graduation. For other students, it is what institution of higher education to attend and in which potential discipline to major. Other students are seriously trying to decide whether they should stay in school or drop out. For students who come to a counselor for help in making such types of decisions, the counseling goal is to help students decide on the course of action that they believe will be in their best future interest. The indicators of counseling success are still described in terms of some kind of behavior change. It may be a statement to the effect, "As a result of our discussions, I am quite clear about what course of action will be in my future best interest." The ultimate criterion in decision-making cases, however, occurs when the client states the decision at which he or she has arrived, then actually takes action to implement the choice made, and, upon follow-up, communicates to the counselor that the decision made turned out to be the wisest that could have been made. In the next chapter, a more complete analysis of the decision-making process will be presented.

Counselor responses
that facilitate goal setting

An essential task for the third stage of counseling is that of clarifying and agreeing upon the outcome goals of counseling. As developed in Chapter 2, the general proposition is that if counseling is to be successful both client and counselor must have a clear idea as to what it is they are trying to accomplish and must agree as to the desirability of the clarified goals. Two counselor responses that can be especially helpful in stimulating the goal-setting clarification process are a future-focused counselor reflection and Counselor Tacting Response Leads (CTRLs).

Clients frequently state their concerns from a present orientation, but often are not clear as to what they would like for the future. A future-focused counselor reflection can help to bring about clarification as to what is desired for the future. Generally, such a response has two components: a summary of present concerns and an extrapolation of what would appear to constitute future improvement. For example, with a couple encountering marital difficulties during the goal clarification stage, the counselor might say, "We have discussed some of the difficulties that each of you sees as being a part of your present relationship. From what each of you is saying I sense both believe that learning to communicate more openly would be an important improvement." Such a counselor response is mildly confronting and helps both clients clarify whether that is what they really do believe and whether "learning to communicate more openly" is a goal to which they are willing to commit time and hard work.

Counselor Tacting Response Leads contribute to the goal-setting process in three ways: (1) by inviting clients to describe abstractions in more specific terms, (2) by helping clients to associate behavioral events with specific environmental circumstances, and (3) by helping clients put limits and boundaries on over-generalizations. Using the example of the couple above, it is important for each partner to clarify what he or she means by "improved communication." An example of a Counselor Tacting Response Lead to bring about this clarification is: "Bob, I would like to understand more fully what open communication means to you." Also, it is important to identify the situations where each has the least and the greatest difficulty communicating openly. For this clarification, a counselor tacting response lead such as the following would be helpful: "Susan, tell me about a recent time when you found it especially difficult to communicate openly." Later, the following counselor tacting response lead can be helpful: "Tell me about a recent time when you had no difficulty communicating openly." Since counseling for this couple will involve helping each to communicate more effectively with the other on occasions where it is especially difficult (and, therefore, most important), it is important that both clarify what they mean by more open communication and to identify the circumstances where it seems most difficult.

Not infrequently clients use over-generalizations to describe their concerns: "I'm always getting into fights." "I can never do anything right." "I'm always being criticized." "Men can't be trusted." During the early part of counseling, it is important to help clients express their feelings in a cathartic fashion. But to move counseling from catharsis to work that will have long-range benefits for the client, it is necessary to help the client put limits to such over-generalizations. Here, too, a CTRL can be very helpful: "Tell me about a recent time when you felt unfairly criticized." This counselor response can lead to helping the client recognize times when his efforts were not criticized. In turn, this can help the client change his view toward self as a person who is sometimes, but not always, criticized. The examples below offer further clarification of the effects of this kind of response:

Client:	I just can't seem to concentrate. It's really affecting my schoolwork. My grades are slipping and I know I'm not doing well, but no matter how hard I try, I can't concentrate.
Counselor:	Tell me what you mean when you say you are unable to concentrate.
Client:	Well . . . I daydream . . . about things I would rather not think about.
Client:	I just don't seem able to do anything right. No matter how hard I try, it's never good enough. Somebody is always criticizing the way I've done it. Nobody ever tells me I've done anything right, and now I feel like I can't do anything right at all.
Counselor:	Tell me about a recent time when someone criticized you.
Client:	Last evening when my father came home from work. I had to cut the grass in the

	afternoon and he found fault with that. He always finds fault with whatever I do.
Client:	Elevators! I never go on them. Like I've said, I haven't ridden on one in months. I always walk while everyone else rides. We went to Chicago since the last time I saw you. Everybody went to the restaurant on the top floor of this huge building but me. I didn't go; my stomach would have been in knots.
Counselor:	Yeah. As we have talked now, would these feelings about elevators apply to anything else.
Client:	Yeah . . . to airplanes, and sometimes to trains and buses. . . . I would say, to an extent, almost anything I can't get out of when I want to that is moving.

Determination of client input

Following the identification and establishment of counseling goals, the counselor must make some assessment of the physical and psychological input which the client brings to the counseling process. There are some tools and techniques to be used in this assessment. The necessity and extent of the assessment, however, is directly dependent upon the established goal. For example, vocational planning and decision making would require considerably more client input assessment than a study habit problem, but less than a problem in the area of personality disorder. The use of various tools is dependent upon the counselor's level of training, educational background, and experience.

Physical/psychiatric assessment

If, for any reason, the counselor suspects some *physical* incapacity or disability that might hinder the client's development toward his or her desired goal, then a referral to a psychiatrist or physician is essential.

Basically, a referral for a medical or psychiatric diagnosis is appropriate for any of the following reasons: (1) the counselor suspects that the goal or target behavior is beyond the client's potential, due to some physical cause; (2) the counselor suspects that the problem identified has as its cause something physical; (3) the counselor suspects that the problem can be treated best through medical intervention; and (4) the counselor believes that a medical report is necessary for continuing the counseling process.

Psychological assessment and diagnosis

Assessment refers to the process of describing the attributes and characteristics of the client. Assessment is always based on what the counselor observes of the client's behavior. Sometimes his observation occurs informally in the course of the counseling sessions. As the counselor listens to the client, he makes *inferences* about the client based on what the client has said. For example, if the client were to say, "I just never seem to be able to do anything right; I can't seem to make friends; I'm doing poorly in school; I'm overweight; my parents are always criticizing me; even worse, my younger sister is more popular and does better in school; my parents really favor her," the counselor, then, might infer that the client sees himself as inferior and worthless and having a low sense of self-worth. At other times, this observation is done more formally through the use of various structured testing procedures.

Sometimes assessment is based on whether certain characteristics are present or absent. At other times, dimensions or continua are used to characterize the client. When these are used, assessment is generally based on how this client compares to other people; for example, people of his own age, his own sex, and people in the same situation as the client. Some of the more important dimensions on which counselors base their assessments will be described.

Level of intellectual functioning or intellectual development

The concept "intelligence" is deceptively simple, for it has many meanings and connotations: a numerical score on a test purported to measure "intelligence," the ability to think abstractly, the ability to survive in a hostile environment, the ability to solve difficult problems. A variety of tests, group and individual, are available, which purport to assess intellectual development. In counseling situations, counselors frequently base their inferences about their client's level of intellectual development on such factors as the vocabulary the client uses, the correctness of his grammar, his demonstrated ability to think in abstract terms, etc. Some counselors believe that assessment of a client's level of intellectual development is essential, for their counseling strategy will be based on this assessment. Thus, their strategy with children would be different from their strategy with adults, because the two differ with respect to their level of intellectual development. Other counselors believe that level of intellectual development is not related to their counseling strategy and, hence, such an assessment is unimportant.

Emotional states

Human emotions are vital factors of human behavior and, as such, are considered to be important components in the counseling process. Helping clients to more fully understand their feelings about important experiences and situations is frequently considered an essential process goal for many clients. Since this is so, most people who write about counseling believe it is important to understand, and be sensitive to, the dominant feelings the client expresses, and to particular situations that will influence the client to experience certain of these strong feelings. Particularly important emotions that counselors are sensitive to include: anxiety or some sort of fear, anger, hostility, hate, some form of aggression, depression, sadness, or some form of misery, guilt, and happiness and joy.

The counselor may ask himself many questions concerning the emotional behavior of his client:

1.   Are there particular feelings that are more predominant than others in this client's functioning? Does he have an unusually strong tendency to "blow his stack" or to be depressed?

2.   Are there particularly "critical situations" that will influence the client to have particularly intense emotional reactions?

3.   Life space is full of potentially emotion-eliciting situations. Compared to other persons, how does this client respond to these key "emotion-eliciting" situations? For example, when a peer expresses strong verbal hostility, how does the client re-

spond emotionally? How does he respond to criticism from a person in an authoritarian position?

4.   Emotions can be described along an "intensity" dimension, from low to strong intensity. Given the same frustrating situation, for example, some clients will express mild annoyance, others will express strong, violent rage. When a particular client feels something or expresses an emotion, the counselor may well ask, "How intense was that emotional reaction?" Being sensitive to client feelings means responding not only to a particular kind of emotion, but the intensity of the emotion as well.

Since a client's emotions are not always clearly observable, counselors must infer about a client's emotions by what is observable: the verbal and nonverbal behavior in the presence of the counselor and the description of important situations. Recalling the concepts developed in Chapter 3 will help counselors assess the kind of quality of emotion experienced by clients. Thus, when a client discusses a situation and it is appropriate to describe that situation as "frustrating," the counselor can hypothesize that the client probably responded with anger, anxiety, or depression in that situation. Some form of anger is an especially frequent response to frustrating situations. When a client describes situations in which his safety, security, or well-being are jeopardized, fear is a likely concomitant emotional response. Should a counselor hear a client describing a situation where he broke or is considering breaking an especially significant moral or ethical code, the counselor might hypothesize that the client is experiencing feelings of guilt about that situation. Since a counselor's ability to respond to a client's emotions depends upon how accurately he infers the emotions, the assessment of a client's feelings is an important counselor activity.

Self-concept

Another significant component of human functioning about which counselors frequently make assessments is the client's set of beliefs or attitudes toward self—his or her self-concept or self-theory. Several important dimensions may be involved in discussing a client's beliefs about self. Are these beliefs favorable or unfavorable? Are they realistic or out of proportion to what might be realistically expected? To what degree are a person's ideals about self discrepant or inconsistent with his or her actual beliefs about self?

What implications might this discrepancy have for the client's ability to function effectively? The basic model here is that a favorable change in a client's belief about self may result in a favorable change in his or her ability to engage in a more rewarding behavior. For such a client, an appropriate counseling strategy might be to work toward a change in self-image. This would influence other favorable changes to occur.

Interpersonal relationship characteristics

A considerable proportion of human behavior is interpersonal in nature. Speech, for example, is behavior whose purpose is to communicate with others. One might reasonably expect that interpersonal relationships are frequently the root of the presenting problem for many clients. A variety of dimensions has been developed to describe interpersonal behaviors. One is related to trust versus mistrust. Does the client demonstrate trust or does he arbitrarily distrust everyone (including the counselor)? Can he or she accurately discriminate between those for whom trust is appropriate and those for whom trust would result in undesirable consequences? Honesty versus façade is another interpersonal dimension. Does he or she present self honestly in interpersonal relationships, or present a façade for the purpose of making a certain kind of impression? Whether the client is outgoing or withdrawn is another interpersonal dimension. Of major importance is the relationship between certain emotions and interpersonal situations. Is the client tense in interpersonal situations or generally relaxed? What kinds of interpersonal situations are especially stressful for him or her?

Client expectations

A significant factor concerning client functioning is the set of expectations held, that is, predictions concerning what will happen in certain situations. With some clients, certain predictions are inappropriate and unrealistic. A client's entering expectations concerning the counselor and the counseling process may be the difference between the success or failure of the counseling intervention. If so, an essential part of the counselor's strategy may be to deal with these entering expectations. Later, the counseling process and appropriate counseling strategy may be to help a client modify his expectations about certain important life situations. For example, a client who expects punishment from adults in general and who manifests strong fear in the presence of adults may be helped considerably by looking at those expectations and modifying them so that he learns that he may expect encouragement and support from some adults.

Personality construct dimensions

A wide variety of personality construct dimensions may be invoked in the assessment of clients. One important construct is the dimension of "openness versus closedness." Is the client guarded, defensive, resistant, or is he or she open, honest, and candid? How willing is he or she to be completely honest with self as well as with the counselor?

A related dimension is that of repressor-sensitizer. Repressors are people who block from awareness potentially stressful or threatening ideas. At the other extreme, sensitizers are people who are extremely concerned about their perceived inadequacies, inabilities, etc. The rigid-versus-flexible dimension refers to the degree to which a client is willing to look at alternatives. Clients whose behaviors are described as rigid are those who have fixed and unalterable beliefs. Clients who are described as flexible are those who seriously examine alternative positions with which they are confronted. For some clients with some kinds of counseling goals, assessment along these dimensions will influence the counselor's strategy. For other clients, the counselor's intervention strategy will be independent of such assessment.

For clients whose presenting problem has to do with making decisions about careers and education, an essential part of the counselor's role is to help them assess their skills, talents, abilities, and interests. This means helping clients describe themselves with respect to their comparative strengths and weaknesses. With respect to intellective functioning abilities, many tests, both group and individually administered, are available. Other tests, such as the *Differential Aptitude Test* (1966) and the *General Aptitude Test Battery* (1947), are available to assess more specific kinds of skills. (The latter is administered by the United States Employment Service.) Other tests are available to help client and counselor assess very specific skills, such as reading rate, reading comprehension, musical talent, etc. For a complete compendium of such tests, the reader is referred to *The Seventh Mental Measurements Yearbook* (1972). For readings on the use, application, and interpretation of tests, the reader should refer to works dealing with psychological testing, tests in counseling, personality measurement and assessment, and psychological measurement in general.

Client "interests" constitute another set of variables that are very much related to career and educational choices. Interest usually refers to the degree of preference a person demonstrates for certain kinds of activities. Some people prefer hiking through the woods to reading a book; for others, the preference is vice versa. Still others prefer building and constructing things with their hands, to either of the other two activities. Clearly, a person's preference for or interest in certain kinds of activities would appear to be related to the kinds of careers where a person would find enjoyment (assuming he has the talent to perform well in various job roles). The *Kuder Preference Record* (1954) and *Strong-Campbell Interest Inventory* (1974) are available instruments designed to help client and counselor consider the client's comparative interests.

Level of aspiration is yet another dimension many counselors believe is important in helping clients consider decisions. Making reliable and valid assessments concerning this dimension can be difficult. Many high school seniors verbalize high levels of aspiration to significant adults in their lives, but once in college and away from home, they fail to act consistently with those stated levels of aspiration. Clients whose levels of aspirations are out of proportion to their talents represent challenging cases to counselors. Both types of discrepancies are challenging. For the client who has much talent but little ambition, the counselor may feel a strong push to try to raise the client's level of aspiration. At times, this may represent a serious discrepancy in value judgments concerning what is in the client's best interest. At other times, this "inappropriately" low level of aspiration may reflect some serious client inhibitions. On the other hand, the counselor may see some clients with limited talent but with very high levels of aspiration, as people who will eventually encounter a series of devastating failure experiences.

Several essential points must be made about evaluation, assessment, and testing. The act of assessing is a behavior of the counselor, and, like all other counselor behaviors, "assessing activities" is purposive and goal directed. With respect to involvement with the client, counselor assessment and diagnostic activity can be justified only if the counselor's in-counseling activities will in some way be influenced by the assessments and diagnoses he or she makes. In the past, many counselors and psychotherapists engaged in the practice of "psychological voyeurism"—tests were administered, and diagnoses, evaluations, and assessments made. Assessment became a goal in and of itself. Insofar as the client is concerned, assessment is only a process goal to help facilitate the achievement of outcome goals. If the counselor's in-counseling activities will not be influenced by the assessments he or she makes, he or she has no business making such assessments. The only exception to this rule is the use of tests and other assessment procedures to gather data for carefully designed research projects.

Many counselors believe that tests have more undesirable than desirable consequences in the long run. They believe that taking information from a test influences the counselor in that he treats the client as a member of a category rather than as an individual. This "stereotypes" the client. For example, suppose a counselor was counseling with an adolescent boy and learned that his score on a highly respected test of intelligence was in the "well-below-average range." How would the counselor react to him? Would the counselor's differential reaction be on the basis of categorizing the client? Would that be in the client's best interests? Would such categorizing enhance or interfere with the counselor's effectiveness? The point these critics make is that it is extremely difficult to avoid categorizing an individual and making inferences and predictions about him once test data have been obtained. Such a tendency violates the assumption of individuality and uniqueness, which counselors believe is the essential and vital factor of their effectiveness.

Following the determination of client psycho-physical input, the counselor has the responsibility to develop a strategy, which would facilitate client growth toward the identified goal. Initially, this requires the counselor's consent and confidence that the identified goal is worthwhile for the client and that the goal is realistic and can be achieved. Three conditions must hold for this consent to occur:

First, the stated outcome goals must be consistent with the counselor's professional ethics. A serious dilemma here might be exemplified by the client who comes to the counselor for help in finding ways to avoid a responsibility. Clearly, in order to make any decision, the counselor must have a clear understanding of the ethics, values, and operating principles that guide his or her behavior and influence decisions.

Second, the counselor must be competent to help the client attain his or her goal. The dilemma for counselor trainees is clear. To help the client, the counselor must believe he or she is competent. Yet trainees, having had little counseling experience, have no basis on which to judge their competence.

Third, the strategy used to help clients must be consistent with the counselor's code of ethics. One can easily modify a client's compulsive hair-pulling behavior by shaving his head, but generally this would not be considered an ethical form of intervention.

If the help sought by the client is in the counselor's realm of competence and if there is no question of the counselor's professional, ethical, or personal position, then the counselor proceeds to develop a strategy for counseling intervention. If the help asked for by the client is beyond the counselor's competence, the client must be told and referred to another helping practitioner. If no referral sources are available, or are not available at the time, it is the responsibility of the counselor to continue to work with the client, staying within the framework of those things that he or she can perform competently. If for some ethical or personal deliberations the counselor is not willing to give the client the assistance he or she seeks, the referral source is an alternative open to the counselor. Three other alternatives are possible:

1.   The counselor may openly and candidly explain to the client why she or he is not willing to help, and allow the client to decide whether he wants to continue the process, knowing how the counselor feels about the goal

2.   A secondary goal may be established that can become the focus of the counseling process

3.   The counselor may attempt to persuade the client to consider another outcome goal, which would be consistent with the counselor's sense of ethics

As conditions currently stand, referral may be more easily accomplished in some areas of the country than others. One factor is the unavailability of referral sources; that is, there may be no one available at the time to whom the counselor can send the client. Second, though there may be a referral source, the counselor may feel there is no one more competent than he or she, regardless of the referral source's job title or function. In any case, it is the responsibility of the counselor to see the client, if that is the desire of the client. Under these circumstances, the best alternative may be for the counselor to continue to maintain the relationship that has been established, and, by this relationship, provide the client with an opportunity for self-exploration and support.

In suggesting a referral, the counselor may leave it up to the client to make his or her own contact with the referral source, or may make the initial contact for the client, with the client's permission and understanding. Some follow-up is necessary, either with the referral source or the client, in order to determine if the counselor's further assistance is necessary in any capacity.

Counseling strategies

Once the outcome goals have been clarified and agreed upon, the counselor's major task becomes that of developing an intervention strategy or specific plan for helping the individual client involved. The planning process includes taking into account characteristics of the client to decide: what issues are important for further exploration, what new insights are important for the client to acquire, what new perceptions and cognitive restructurings might be facilitative, and what specific approach or combination of approaches would appear to have the greatest chances for success.

Thus, there are several *action-related* questions which counselors must ask themselves: "How am I to proceed so as to have the greatest chance in achieving the outcome goals we have mutually agreed upon?" "What strategies or courses of action are most likely to result in the attainment of these outcome goals?" "What actions on my part might interfere in attaining these goals?" "Is there a sequence of things that must first occur (process goals) if counseling is to be successful?" "If so, can I clearly describe these process goals that are necessary and instrumental in attaining outcome goals?"

Since the attainment of counseling goals is directly related to the way the counselor behaves in the presence of the client, these questions clearly demand that the counselor focus on his or her own in-counseling behavior. The key question is, "What sort of counselor behaviors will have what kind of impact, on which kind of clients, at what stage in the counseling process?" A counselor's skill is directly related to:

1.   The ability to accurately anticipate the kind of impact he wants to have on his client

2.   The ability to behave in such ways as to have the intended impact

The state of professional knowledge in the behavior intervention disciplines is a very long way from specifying the answers to questions a client may have about specific concerns. However, the mandates and responsibilities of counselors still remain. Further, there are some general process goals which may be considered relevant and appropriate for many clients with certain varieties of concerns. There are also certain kinds of strategies that appear potentially more effective for certain client concerns. In the next chapter, a variety of counseling strategies and the model of human behavior upon which these are based will be examined.

Client education
to counseling procedures

There are times in the counseling process when it is desirable and/or necessary to educate the client to the counseling procedures that will be used to facilitate client growth toward the desired objective. It may be necessary that the client be aware of the procedure, the reasons why the counselor has decided to select such a procedure, how the client will feel during the procedural process, what it means for the client to reach his desired objective, and whether it will facilitate growth. Explanations, demonstrations, and reading materials are all appropriate forms of client education. At specific times, however, it is not desirable to educate the client to the procedures to be used. An example of this is the counselor who has decided to verbally reinforce the client's expressions of more positive self-report. The procedures and treatments will be discussed later.

Client commitment to strategy

At this point, with the understanding the counselor has of the client, client input, and client-desired objective for counseling, along with counselor agreement and assessment of these factors, it is necessary for the counselor to help the client commit himself to the assistance offered in facilitating growth toward the desired goal. Most clients have several areas or matters in which they seek assistance. Out of the process stage of goal identification, the counselor helps the client to isolate, or at least identify, the one area in which he or she desires to be helped. The client must commit self, verbally, to working in this area.

The focus is in one area, in which some specific help can be given, rather than on a broad approach. This client commitment may be termed a verbal "contract."

The criteria for assessing a successful third stage

In order for the counselor to assess success in helping the client to identify a goal of counseling and to establish effective counseling strategies, the following criteria are offered, in question form:

1.   Did I help the client to speak in a specific manner by:
    a. defining the terms he used
    b. relating to specific historical events
    c. taking a look at any physiological reaction he or she may have experienced at the time of the specific event
    d. helping him or her to compare and contrast behavior in various settings and under different circumstances

2.   Did I help the client to state a goal for his counseling experience?

3.   Was this goal stated in behavioral terms?

4.   Am I sure the client has no physical incapacity or disability which might hinder his development toward the goal? If there were some questions, did I proceed in an appropriate manner as described?

5.   Do I have data that are gathered through psychological assessment and that are necessary and dependent upon the client's stated goal?

6.   Do I believe the client's goal is realistic and achievable? If not, did I follow an appropriate course of action?

7.   Limited by my competencies, can I help the client toward his goal or must I take another course of action, such as referral, or must I simply maintain the facilitative relationship? If not, did I follow an appropriate course of action?

8.   Do I feel ethically and personally that I can and want to help the client reach his or her goal? If not, did I follow an appropriate course of action?

9.   Is the strategy I have chosen proper and within my realm of competencies?

10.   Does the client understand (if appropriate) what I am going to do to help him?

11.   Is the client committed to accepting my stated assistance in facilitating growth toward his desired goal?

Summary

The primary goal of this stage in the counseling process is the preparation of the counselor and client for the strategy implementation stage of the counseling process. The client, with the counselor's aid, has determined the goal for counseling. The counselor has assessed the physical and psychological characteristics the client brings to the counseling process, which are related to attaining the goals of counseling. The counselor has consented to help the client and has developed a strategy for such help. The client has been prepared for the procedures to be used and has made a verbal contract in this regard. This stage having been satisfactorily completed, and, while maintaining the facilitative relationship, the counselor and client are ready to move into the next stage of the counseling process.

References

Bennett, G. K., Seashore, H. G., & Wesman, A. G. *A manual for the differential aptitude test's fourth edition.* New York: The Psychological Corporation, 1966.

Buros, O. K., Ed. *The seventh mental measurements yearbook.* Highland Park, N.J.: Gryphon, 1972.

Kuder, G. F. *Kuder Preference Record—Personal.* Chicago: Science Research Associates, 1954.

Strong, E. K., & Campbell, D. P. *Strong-Campbell Interest Inventory.* Stanford, Calif.: Stanford University Press, 1974.

U. S. Department of Labor. *The general aptitude test battery.* Washington, D. C.: U. S. Department of Labor, Employment Service, Occupational Analysis, and Industrial Services Division, 1947.

9. Counseling strategies and methods

This chapter will consider the various strategies available to the counselor to help achieve the kind of change he or she and the client have agreed upon as desirable. Since strategies for change are based upon principles of human behavior acquisition, the approach will be to articulate some of these basic principles and then to describe the kinds of strategies based upon these principles. The format for this chapter, then, is to describe those principles of behavior development that apply to the counseling process.

Before developing these principles, it is crucial to emphasize that the *timing* and sequence of application are factors that are vital to the successful application of these principles. Premature application may result in disastrous impact. These principles can be applied productively only after an effective relationship has been attained and the goals of counseling have been clearly described.

Principles and strategies not based on awareness as a process goal

Principle 1: People learn new behaviors by receiving verbal instructions from significant others

Some obvious examples of this principle would include parents teaching their children which behaviors are appropriate at home and a sports professional teaching a novice to execute the skills of a sport. This is also the model upon which most classroom activities are based. Students allegedly learn by being verbally instructed by the significant other labeled, "teacher," through simple instructions, information, directions, and commands that are given clearly and intelligently.

This would suggest that one potential counselor-change strategy is client instruction as to behaviors that are appropriate and how the client can execute such behaviors. A word of caution: There are some serious secondary consequences in implementing such a strategy. In actual counselor behavior, this strategy generally takes the form of advice giving: "You should do this . . ." or "You should do it this way. . . ." Such advice giving may be maladaptive in the sense that it may actually interfere with the attainment of counseling outcome goals. If the advice is given too early, it may be inappropriate. If the client acts on the advice and it is inappropriate, his subsequent action will be inappropriate. In such a case, the counselor would be responsible for influencing the client to act in ways that are actually contrary to his best interest.

If the client rejects the advice given, he may, in the act of doing so, come to the conclusion that the person who gave the inappropriate advice is not a viable source of help. *He has rejected the counselor as a helping person.* Even if he does not, the relationship may be seriously jeopardized. Further, especially with many adolescents in school situations, what they feel they need least is another adult in their environment telling them what to do. Adolescents in school will tend to reject advice even if they ask for it, and, in so doing, they reject the advice giver as a source of help. Finally, most people who write on the goals of education see the act of helping students learn to behave "independently" as an important educational goal ("independently" here means deciding for oneself what is appropriate action and then acting on the basis of that decision). Offering advice is clearly incon-sistent with "independence" as an educational goal. Paradoxically then, advice giving as an appropriate intervention strategy for coun-selors is not advised. Advice giving is especially maladaptive when it is given too early in the counseling process; that is, when it is given before a strong relationship has been established. Special note of the advice-giving tendency is made because clients frequently ask the counselor for advice, and, in so doing, the counselor frequently is seduced into giving advice. This is especially true of counselors in the early stages of their professional training.

The techniques included in the instructional approach to coun-seling procedures have as their goal the learning by the client of new or different ways of behaving in specific circumstances. This learning is the result of the counselor instructing, teaching, telling by explain-ing, expounding, directing, or interpreting. The following tech-niques will be reviewed:

1.   Systematic desensitization

2.   Paradoxical intention (anti-suggestion)

3.   Direct instruction

4.   Bibliotherapy

5.   Thought interference

6.   Assertive training

7.   Aversion training

Systematic desensitization   An important treatment approach that has developed from the behavior management literature is called "sys-tematic desensitization." The system is generally used to reduce or eliminate undesirable and maladaptive anxiety responses and to re-place these responses with relaxation responses that are considered to be incompatible with the anxiety responses. The rationale is that anxiety responses are elicited (or triggered) by certain stimulus con-ditions. The development of this stimulus-response connection can be accounted for by principles of conditioning. Once conditioned, the individual is largely unable to control the occurrence of the anxiety responses when faced with the particular stimulus condition. The anxiety responses are noxious and interfere with the person's at-tempts to cope more effectively with the situation. Technically, a person experiencing such difficulties is said to have developed a phobia. Further, consistent with the principle of generalization, situations that are similar to the phobic situation may also elicit anxiety responses, although not as severe in intensity. People experiencing such phobias can usually rank order stimulus conditions on the basis of the intensity of the anxiety they elicit. This is a crucial observation, for the elimination of a phobia depends on utilizing this generalization principle.

Using systematic desensitization to reduce a phobia involves three basic stages: establishing a response hierarchy (or list which rank orders the stimulus conditions on the basis of the intensity of anxiety each elicits), training the person to become very deeply relaxed, and having him imagine himself in each of the situations on the hierarchy while he is in a state of deep relaxation. Short of using drugs (which frequently have undesirable side effects), the most powerful method for helping people become relaxed is the method known as deep muscle relaxation. Using this procedure, clients are trained to tense certain groups of muscles and then suddenly relax them. By carefully controlling the intensity and duration of tension, and carefully programming the sequence of muscle groups, the counselor can usually train the client to become more deeply relaxed than he has ever been. Deep relaxation is incompatible with anxiety; the two are mutually exclusive responses. If relaxation responses can be conditioned to occur under certain stimulus conditions, they will prevent or inhibit the occurrence of anxiety responses in those same situations.

Based on the principle of stimulus generalization, the counselor systematically conditions relaxation to occur instead of anxiety. After training the client to achieve a state of deep relaxation, the counselor tells the client to imagine himself in each of the situations on the hierarchy. By carefully controlling the duration of each of the images flashed, and the sequences in which they are flashed, the counselor has a powerful method of replacing anxiety responses with relaxation responses. He begins with short flashes of the entry on the hierarchy that elicits least anxiety. After progressing to longer durations of that image, he proceeds to the next image on the hierarchy and again controls the imagining of that entry. When the client no longer reports anxiety after a number of trials of that image, the counselor proceeds to the next step in the hierarchy and goes through the same process. In this fashion, he proceeds through each entry in the hierarchy, beginning with the one which elicits least anxiety, and then proceeds to the next step in the hierarchy. Thus, by the time the situations high in the hierarchy are reached, the intensity of anxiety responses to these situations has already been reduced. This procedure, along with a sample typescript, is described in detail in Appendix C.

Paradoxical intention (anti-suggestion)   This technique is based on the assumption that fear makes what is feared come true, and that positively portraying the symptoms of fear makes what is feared appear ridiculous. For example, if a client is frightened by an object or circumstance, the more he or she tries not to be frightened, the more fearful he or she will become. On the other hand, if he or she consciously attempts to be frightened and feels the symptoms of fear, he or she will feel less fearful.

Three successful case procedures are presented. All three are taken from actual counseling records:

Case 9A: Bill, age twenty-seven, was afraid of having a heart attack. Although physical examinations, including electrocardiograms, revealed no evidence of heart disease, the client was still troubled by tightness and occasional sharp pains in his chest. The goal of counseling was to eliminate the fear of a coronary by the method of paradoxical intention. The purpose of this method was to enable the client to develop a sense of detachment toward his fear by replacing the fear with a paradoxical desire: "My heart is going to beat faster, then stop, and I'll die right here."
The client was encouraged to place himself in the situations described during the goal identification stage and to help himself by the use of this technique.

Case 9B: Miss Jones had an intense fear of riding in elevators. Her employer moved his office to the top floor in an office building thereby making it necessary for the client to ride an elevator. The goal of counseling was to help Miss Jones eliminate her fear of elevators.
The counselor instructed the client to visualize entering an elevator and demonstrate her fear, in an attempt to detach the client from the fear. Such instructions as "Show some real terror now!" "Come on now, panic, and run around the room!" evoked humor and helped remove the fear from her client. Miss Jones was urged to continue practicing this technique in real situations.

Case 9C: A young woman was afraid of burglars while in the house alone. The client was basically well adjusted and had very little real grounds on which to base her fear. She was instructed to portray her fear while in the counseling situation. Humor was evoked by the counselor's instructions to "shake, stutter, perspire, etc." Through repeated attempts, she was not able to demonstrate fear. She was asked to use this technique on herself when she was left alone in the house.

Direct instruction   This procedure is used to help a client think (and, therefore, behave) in a more reasonable and rational manner.

Sometimes fears about oneself can be attacked directly, and the faulty, unreasonable logic attached to the fears can be exposed. The technique of direct instruction is based on attacking "fears about self," exposing them as nonsense, and replacing them with sound, logical thought processes. The following cases are illustrative of this procedure:

Case 9D: The client identified a fear of blushing as her main problem. This fear had bothered her considerably in the college classroom, her classroom as a teacher, in social gatherings, and in surprise situations, such as an unexpected meeting with a friend she had not seen for some time. Because of the fear of blushing and the consequent embarrassment, she had a good deal of difficulty behaving appropriately in these situations. She spoke of blushing as "awful," "terrible," and "humiliating."
The counselor helped the client change her thinking about blushing to a point where she could accept it. This was done through the use of logic, reason, teaching, and suggestions. Her fear was reduced, she behaved more effectively in situations, and the instances of blushing were drastically lessened.

Case 9E: George, a high school senior, came to the counseling center because of difficulty he was having accepting himself as a person of average intelligence and achievement. His parents were disappointed in him because he had not been admitted to any of several premedical college programs to which he had applied. The client spoke of himself as a failure and an ungrateful son. These thoughts were taking most of his time and energy.
The counselor attempted to convince the client of the irrationality of his thoughts and to reveal errors in his perception of himself. The client was shown how his thought processes were making him unhappy and neurotic. These thoughts were attacked and contradicted and a more rational philosophy of life was internalized by the client.

Bibliotherapy   This procedure is an instructional technique using textual material, such as novels, plays, stories, booklets, etc. Through identification with the characters in a story, some clients, with counselor aid, are able to gain some understanding to resolve their problems and attain their goals. The method is as follows: (a) the counselor selects some textual material that reflects the client's needs or situation, (b) the client reads and identifies with the character in the story, (c) the client projects self into the story, (d) the client reacts emotionally during the reading, (e) the client discusses with the counselor what he or she has read and how he or she reacted to what was read, and (f) the client gains new insights about self.

There are numerous ways in which this procedure may be used, depending on the identified goal, the age and sex of the client, and the available textual material.

Thought interference   This technique is based on the assumption that cognitive thought processes sometimes inhibit behavior. By "talking to oneself," a client can distort reality and make a predicament seem almost unbearable and unmanageable. By breaking up these thoughts and self-talk, the counselor can help the client to replace them with more realistic self-talk. This technique can lessen the inhibitory thought processes by restraining them. The following case is illustrative of this procedure:

Case 9F: Ellen, a twenty-three-year-old graduate student, came to the counseling center because she realized how unhappy she was with her social life. Her major concern was that she felt she was never going to get married. She felt she was going to end up "an old maid." Ellen had not had a date since high school that had not been "arranged" by her friends. Recently, rather than accept such arrangements, she made excuses that she was ill or had too much work to do. It became apparent that she anticipated the worst in every situation with men. She was afraid she would "do the wrong thing," "say something dumb," "look stupid," etc. She would end up so anxious that she would do or say whatever it was she wanted so much not to do or say.

The procedure used was thought interference. The client was instructed to close her eyes and verbalize a typical problem causing thought sequence. This sequence was then abruptly interrupted by the counselor with the command, "STOP!" Through the repetition of this procedure, and the client forcing herself to concentrate on other thoughts after the command, she learned how to stop, by self-command, to change the direction of her thinking. In real situations, this helped to decrease her anxiety, thereby permitting her to behave in a more comfortable manner.

Assertive training   In recent years helping individuals learn to respond assertively in situations where their rights are being violated has become an important counseling goal. Often people fail to respond assertively when they should because they have been conditioned to be submissive and because they anticipate some potentially bad consequences occurring as a result of responding assertively.

Learning to respond assertively includes these abilities: (1) recognize the rights one has and how they are being violated, (2) recognize one's personal inhibitions and anxieties about responding assertively, and (3) respond so as to maintain those rights while at the same time not jeopardizing one's well-being. An important part of this training includes learning the difference between assertive responding (protecting and maintaining personal rights) and aggressive responding (attacking and inflicting verbal pain).

The counseling model includes direct instruction (discussed earlier), verbal rehearsing, and role playing. Once situations have been described in which the client is reluctant to respond assertively, the

counselor helps the client identify possible irrational beliefs behind
the reluctance (e.g., "the other individual involved would think I am a
terrible individual and that would be awful"). More rational beliefs are
identified (e.g., "the other person will respect me and stop trying to
manipulate me"). Following this, client and counselor work together
to identify effective assertive responses that can be made, given the
situation and significant others involved. Rehearsal, role playing,
and reinforcement techniques are used to help the client master these
effective assertive responses. With success, inhibition about responding assertively to other situations is reduced and the tendency to
respond assertively to other situations generalizes.

Case 9G: Carl, age thirty-two, could not say "no" to anyone. Three recent
situations upset him very much. First, he had purchased three shirts from a
salesman in a men's store, even though his shirt size was not in stock. Second,
Carl, while walking through a furniture store, within a few minutes purchased
a color television, which he could not afford. Lastly, the client was demoted
from head coach at a junior high school because his superintendent thought
that that was what Carl desired; Carl did not have the courage to see the
superintendent and make known his real wish—to remain as head coach.
Using these three situations, Carl and the counselor set up these situations in
counseling and practiced making initial appropriate responses. Carl also practiced ways to remedy situations that he had gotten into. One assertive response
was decided on for each situation and was practiced until the client could
behave in counseling accordingly. Carl then proceeded, with much success, to
return the shirts, cancel the television order, and correct the superintendent's
misconceptions of what he desired.

Aversion training   This procedure involves the use of progressive
relaxation and sensitization. Rather than the goal being to reduce
anxiety, as in desensitization, the goal is to increase anxiety toward a
particular stimulus, thereby developing an aversion to the stimulus.
The first step is the use of the procedure of Progressive Relaxation.
When the client is able to relax, he is instructed to imagine a situation
where he is behaving in an undesirable manner. This scene is made as
vivid as possible by the counselor's insistence on great detail. As the
client begins to relate the undesirable manner he is about to behave in
in the scene, the counselor introduces some noxious consequences to
his behavior, such as embarrassment or nauseousness. This scene,
and the aversion at the time of the onset of the client's undesirable
behavior, is repeated several times in each counseling session and at
least twice a day by the client himself.

Case 9H: Charles, age twenty-three, was in counseling because of his compulsive eating habits. He weighed 248 pounds, had no social life, and was gener-

ally unhappy. Charles's goal was to gain control of his eating habits. He kept a record of everything he ate and drank between counseling sessions. Particular attention was given to the kind and amount of food, and when and where he ate. Having been successfully trained in Progressive Relaxation, aversion training was applied to all types of sweets, and then to between-meal eating. The following was an example of the type of aversive instruction used:

I want you to imagine you've just had dinner and you are about to eat your dessert, which is apple pie. As you are about to reach for the fork, you get a funny feeling in the pit of your stomach. You start to feel queasy, nauseous, and sick all over. As you touch the fork, you can feel the food particles inching up your throat. You're just about to vomit. As you put the fork into the pie and bring the pie to your mouth, the food comes up into your mouth. As you are about to open your mouth you vomit. *(This description of the vomiting scene will continue in vivid detail, including the smell and shocked expression of others at the table.)* At this point you turn away from the food and immediately start to feel better. You run out of the room, and as you run, you feel better and better. Charles was instructed to repeat this scene at least twice a day, between sessions. Equal time was spent in aversion training to sweets, and in positive reinforcement, as praise and pleasant imagery, when the client did not eat the food. The same procedure was used for Charles's between-meal eating habits.

Principle 2: People learn to behave in new ways by imitating the behavior, beliefs, values, and attitudes of significant others

This principle helps to account for much of the development and change of human behavior, including language development, motor skills, attitudes, values, beliefs, and emotions. The significant other, then, is described as a model who will be emulated by the learner. There are a number of factors that can influence a given person to emulate another. Clearly, the relationship to the learner is an influencing factor. The closer the relationship, the more likely is the potential model to be emulated. Another set of influencing factors has to do with the characteristics of the potential model. The counselor is more likely to be emulated if he or she is seen by the learner as a person of high status and prestige. Further, a learner is likely to emulate those actions of a person known as an expert. Novice sports enthusiasts learn to play the sport by emulating the actions of those who are considered to be experts in the field.

Yet another influencing factor has to do with the *instrumental value* of certain behavior. People who are not functioning effectively learn to do so by observing others and copying their behaviors; this is seen as instrumental to the attainment of goals and important to the learner. The principle that human behavior is purposive and goal directed is especially applicable here. A high school student, for example, who has difficulty making and maintaining friends may observe his peers, identify with those who make and maintain friends easily, and then try to emulate their interpersonal behavior.

A counselor may also help his or her client learn to function more effectively by identifying self as a model who can be emulated, and then behaving in those ways that she or he believes will be instrumental to the effective functioning of the client.

Two other dimensions worthy of further discussion are covert versus overt modeling, and direct versus vicarious modeling. In overt modeling situations, all people involved are aware that persons learn by imitating others. Such would be the case in role-play situations, used frequently in both individual and group counseling. Under covert modeling situations, the learner is not aware that his behavior is being influenced à la the imitative tendency. Such appeared to be the case in the example where the client learned unconsciously to relax by imitating the counselor.

Under direct modeling conditions, the learner emulates a model in his immediate environment. Under vicarious or indirect modeling conditions, the learner observes a second person who, himself, is imitating a third person (the model). Take, for example, the case of a child who demonstrates strong fear of water. Application of vicarious modeling, as a counseling strategy, would occur if the counselor were to make a videotape of a person who demonstrates a fear of water while watching his peers jumping in and out of the water, splashing around, and generally demonstrating the fun of such activity. The scene would then be played back to the client; what is observed would be discussed in counseling. This example also demonstrates a potential application of video technology in the counseling process, a strategy that is currently receiving much attention in counseling literature.

Some specific case studies will help to demonstrate the actual application of some of these principles in the counseling process. The case studies will describe:

1.   The use of role playing

2.   The maintenance of the counseling relationship

3.   The use of media to present models

The use of role playing   The use of this modeling technique enables the client to gain understanding of self and others in his environment, to determine how he may modify his behavior in a given environment, and to practice the modified behaviors that he desires. The proper use of the role-playing technique can lead to specific and accurate changes in the client's behavior.

The first step in the use of this procedure is the assignment of roles. This step, of course, is subsequent to the identification of the goal of counseling, problem definition, and appropriate selection of the method of aid in helping the client to arrive at his goal. In this setting, the counselor assigns self the role of the significant other while the client plays himself. The counselor may portray the client's mother, boss, spouse, or anyone else who is involved with the client at the time when the client desires to modify his behavior. Following this portrayal, the roles of each are analyzed in an attempt to gain some understanding of the dynamics that operate in the setting. After this analysis is completed, the next step is to reverse the roles, whereby the counselor portrays the client and the client plays the significant other person. The next step is to analyze these roles with an attempt to aid the client in understanding the position and feelings of the significant other. The final step is to determine what the client desires to do differently in the setting. These client behavioral changes would be practiced, via role playing and role reversal, until the client behaves in the counseling-role situation desired. When the client behaves with ease in this different role, he is instructed to try it out in a real environmental setting. Further counseling time may be necessary to modify the new role after it has been attempted.

This procedure may use people other than the counselor to play roles. Actual props are sometimes necessary, such as telephones for conversation. In general, the rule to be followed is to approach the real setting in terms of people, equipment, and situational props. The following successful cases are illustrative of this procedure:

Case 9I: Al had a long series of unsuccessful job experiences, most periods of employment lasting only a few months. Early in counseling, he stated that his major problem was his explosive temper, usually directed toward authority, and especially his on-the-job supervisors. After spending some time with the client, the counselor concurred that this was the area that was of most concern. The procedure selected to help Al to modify his behavior was that of role playing.

Al played himself while the counselor portrayed an on-the-job supervisor in a confrontation that enabled both to gain insight into Al's behavior. Discussion followed. The second step was to reverse the roles, thereby helping the client to gain some understanding of the supervisor's reaction to Al. The client then generated other ways he could behave and settled on one that was more desirable in the situation under consideration. This was practiced repeatedly over a two-week period. The new behavior became the usual behavior for the client in a confrontation situation with his superiors.

Case 9J: Joe came to counseling for help in learning to meet and talk with girls. A senior in high school, he had become aware that in social situations he experienced a good deal of difficulty interacting with members of the opposite sex. This awareness added to the client's concern, making him even more uneasy and anxious in the problem situations than he was previously. The counselor decided to use the role-playing technique. After portraying roles, reversing roles, and helping his client to feel more at ease in situations, the office secretary was asked to become a part of the counseling procedure. She portrayed herself while Joe played himself with the help of prompts by the counselor. These prompts were counselor responses that the client was encouraged to imitate. When imitated effectively, Joe was reinforced by the counselor with verbal approval. This was repeated, various environments were staged, and the prompting decreased and finally stopped. Joe was instructed to go out of his way to speak to girls. This was difficult at first, but with the counselor's continued support over a two-week period, Joe met with success and was finally able to handle these situations with ease.

Case 9K: Janet was completing the requirements for a teaching degree and was apprehensive about being interviewed for a job. She feared that she would say the wrong thing, feel nervous, and be unable to give a favorable impression of herself to the interviewer. Role-playing situations were contrived and acted out. Janet learned how to behave with a variety of interviewers—formal, friendly, casual, etc.—and how to put herself in the most favorable light for the position for which she was applying.

The maintenance of the counseling relationship   At times, the simple continuance of a good human relationship is a counseling procedure in and of itself. This relationship has been characterized by empathic understanding, warmth, genuineness, honesty, and professionalism. These characteristics, and counselor behaviors necessary for their attainment, have been discussed in Chapter 4.

The basic concept in using the relationship as a modeling procedure is effective *to the extent that the client has regard and respect for the counselor, and will, in all probability, result in the client becoming more like the counselor.* This procedure works effectively with client problems, such as the inability to converse with others in a meaningful manner, the inability to express one's feelings, the manner of approaching personal relationships in a cool or distrustful manner, and being a "phony." After such a behavior change goal is established, and the counselor selects the technique for helping the client reach his goal, the counselor then maintains and intensifies the relationship.

As the relationship intensifies, the counselor acts as the model for the client. By emulating counselor behavior, the client learns new ways of behaving toward others, including the client use of listening, attentive behaviors, and reflective response leads to affect others. The end result is that the client, while behaving in new ways, would be able to converse with others in a meaningful manner, express his feelings to others, approach personal relationships in a warm and trusting manner, and learn to be and behave like himself.

The use of media to present models   This technique encompasses the use of all audio or audiovisual media to present models to be imitated. The procedure is similar to that of bibliotherapy except that the material used is not textual by itself, but includes the use of audiovideo presenters, such as audiotapes, phonograph records, videotapes, and films. The method is as follows: (a) the counselor selects some audio or audiovisual material in which the model used reflects the client's need or situation, (b) the client listens and watches the presentation and identifies with the model, (c) the client discusses with the counselor what he has seen, and (d) the client tries the new, learned behavior with the counselor (role playing) and, finally, in the real life situation.

The basic principle that people learn by imitating others is well documented in research literature. However, counseling research has only begun to explore the parameters and the potential application of these notions to the counseling process. While it is doubtful that application of such basic principles as these will ever be considered a panacea to counseling, it is important to recognize that the counselor who identifies himself as a model likely to be emulated, whether he is aware of it or not, can systematically utilize this principle to enhance his counseling effectiveness.

Any counselor identifying himself as a model must also accept the responsibility, which includes an awareness on his part of his behaviors, attitudes, values, and beliefs that the client may emulate. He must come to grips with the issue of whether it is in the client's best interest to acquire these new behaviors, and to think through whether he has a right to influence the client, often without the client's awareness.

**Principle 3: The reinforcement contingencies
in a person's environment
influence the way he behaves
in that environment.
Changing the reinforcement contingencies
can be expected to influence
a change in behavior**

This is, of course, the operating credo of the Behavior Modification approach to counseling. Systematic application of this principle in the counseling situation demands thorough comprehension of all the basic concepts and laws of learning described by this system. To articulate this system in comprehensive detail would be beyond the scope of this book. Briefly, systematic application of this system requires understanding of the following concepts: reinforcement, punishment, extinction, discrimination, generalization, target behavior, shaping, successive approximation, and schedules of reinforcement.

Application of operant conditioning principles is clearly consistent with the basic assumption that human behavior is purposive and goal directed. The applier of such principles must begin with a clear description of the new behaviors to be acquired. He or she must then determine what environmental events will serve as effective reinforcers for the client; that is, what goals are important for the client to attain. Following this, the counselor must determine how he or she can control the occurrence of these reinforcers so as to shape the desired behaviors. He or she must also consider the additional effects of systematically applying the principles that will be described later in this chapter.

It is necessary to discuss several types of environmental consequences. Those consequences that achieve a desired "input" for the client (approval, candy, money, successful completion of an important task) may be described as "positive reinforcers." Those consequences that achieve a non-desired input (verbal chastisement, disapproval, physical pain) are described as "punishment." Behaviors that result in positively reinforcing consequences will increase in likelihood or frequency. But behaviors that result in punitive consequences generally do not decrease in likelihood or frequency; their occurrence is only temporarily suppressed.

Sometimes the counselor can control the environment so that behaviors result in no intended external consequences. If that occurs consistently, the behavior can generally be expected to decrease in likelihood or frequency. That process is referred to as *extinction*. At other times, people will behave in ways so as to avoid unpleasant or disastrous consequences. If their behavior does result in the avoidance of such consequences, it can be expected to increase in frequency or likelihood when similar situations occur again. This is the process of *avoidance conditioning.*

In order to use reinforcement techniques in counseling, the counselor must be aware of (1) the operant, and (2) appropriate rewards. The *operant* is the specific client behavior that the counselor will reinforce. For the strongest learning effect on the client, the client must freely exhibit the operant to be reinforced. Ideally, the counselor should wait patiently for the operant. However, the counselor can use *successive approximations;* that is, begin rewarding client behavior that is close to the desired behavior, then, in a step-by-step process, lead the client to the appropriate behavior. Another approach would be the counselor's use of interpretive response leads to get the client to behave as desired. In any event, it is important that the client exhibit the desired behavior on his own. Once he does, the counselor can reward the client for this behavior.

In the context of a counseling situation, most counselors systematically include such principles in their intervention strategy and base their approach on the application of positive reinforcement principles. They would ask themselves, "What kinds of environmental events would serve as effective positive reinforcers for this particular client?" and, "How may I then systematically control those positively reinforcing events?" For very young children, tangible and consumable reinforcers seem very effective (candy, little toys, trinkets). For older people, some sort of positive social input seems to have a powerful reinforcing effect (genuine attention, approval, recognition, etc.). For many people, successful completion of a challenging task seems to have a powerful reinforcing effect.

Most often two or more of these basic operant conditioning principles are applied simultaneously. The counselor views the client as currently using inappropriate or undesirable behaviors in certain situations. In those situations, certain other behaviors would be more appropriate, effective, or desirable. Thus, the counselor has two related tasks: first, eliminating the inappropriate behavior from the person's behavioral repertoire using some sort of extinction-based process and, second, simultaneously establishing the new and more desirable behaviors in the person's repertoire, using some sort of positive reinforcement-based process (see Case 9H under Aversion Training).

With some clients, the difficulty is not so much that they are generally behaving inappropriately, but that they are using certain behaviors that are appropriate in certain situations but inappropriate in others. Helping people learn to distinguish between those occasions or situations in which certain actions are appropriate and those in which the same actions are not is the process of *discrimination training.* Using such a strategy, the counselor's task is to help the client learn the conditions under which a given action is appropriate. Usually such a strategy is based on helping the person identify the ways in which the two or more situations involved differ from each other. Once the differences between situations have been learned, the task then is to help the person learn to behave appropriately.

The following reinforcement counseling techniques will be reviewed in order to demonstrate the methods of this procedure:

1.   Operant conditioning

2.   Successive approximation of goal

3.   Positive attention

4.   Extinction through non-reinforcement

5.   Discrimination training

Operant conditioning   This technique is characterized by the direct rewarding of specific client behavior. Specific behavior is directly related to the goal of counseling as established by the client with the aid of the counselor. The following case is illustrative of the use of this technique:

Case 9L: Dwayne, a college senior, was having difficulty making friends. It became obvious to the counselor that the client "turned others off" by the manner in which he spoke of himself. Continually using negative self-references and "running himself down," Dwayne could understand why others didn't like him ("I'm just not much to know"), but desired to change in order to give others an opportunity to get to like him.

The client spent some time in relating his home life while growing up, and, with the aid of the counselor, gained some understanding for his self-deprecation. Gradually, the counselor began to reinforce Dwayne's positive self-references. The counselor did this by showing attention, holding eye contact, and verbally expressing his pleasure when the client said good things about himself. These attentive vocal and nonvocal counselor behaviors were not used when Dwayne verbalized negative things about himself. Over the course of seven sessions, Dwayne made more and more positive references about himself, and found that this carried out into his daily contacts. The client was pleased with his success, related to the counselor that others were more pleased with him, and, in general, stated that the "felt a good deal better about myself, and so did others."

Successive approximation of goal   This technique employs the use of the step-by-step method of arriving at a desired goal. After the goal has been established and the input of the client in terms of the goal has been measured, a course of action using sequential steps to the goal is developed by the counselor with the aid of the client. The following case was successful and illustrates the method for successive approximation of goal:

Case 9M: Lisa, ten years of age, had a great fear of water and would not play in the family pool. By using successive approximations, the counselor helped

Lisa to enjoy the pool. Beginning with a familiarity of the pool area by playing near the pool, through successive approximations—feet in water, splashing feet, hands in water, sitting on pool steps, etc., to complete submersion—the counselor successfully helped Lisa to accomplish her goal by using the counselor as friend and play partner as the reinforcer.

Positive attention   This simple technique is based on the reinforcement potential of positive attention, while ignoring all unwanted behaviors. The following case demonstrates the successful use of this procedure by a classroom teacher under the consultative direction of a counselor:

Case 9N: Phil was an eleven-year-old boy who was considered an "acting-out child" in the classroom. He would wander around the room, disrupt group activities, and become angry when corrected or disciplined. Phil's test results showed he had average intelligence, but he was doing poorly in his school subjects. Phil stated to the counselor that he wished he didn't have to act the way he did, but didn't know of any other way to behave. He admitted that he enjoyed the attention his disruptive behavior brought him. The counselor, consulting with the teacher, and with his help, used Phil's need for attention to help Phil change his manner of behaving. The teacher gave Phil positive attention whenever he was working at his desk quietly or whenever he was behaving in a socially acceptable manner in a group activity. This helped Phil to satisfy his need for attention while successfully modifying his behavior.

Extinction through non-reinforcement   A behavior that at one time was rewarding can be modified by changing the reward structure so that it is no longer rewarding to behave in that manner. In other words, a behavior that is not reinforced will be extinguished and replaced by a more rewarding behavior.

Case 9O: Bobby, age five, was brought to the counseling center because of poor speech development. He spoke very little and used only single words and phrases; mostly, he made his wants known through gestures and grunts. A physician felt that there was no organic basis for this problem. Bobby's development in other areas had been normal. The goal of counseling was to change Bobby's nonverbal behavior into verbal behavior.
Observations of the family interaction and interviews led to the assumption that Bobby's nonverbal behavior was being reinforced. Bobby had, in effect, three mothers caring for him and anticipating his every need—his mother and two sisters, ages thirteen and fifteen. He had no need to speak. A gesture brought him what he wanted.
All the family members were instructed to become "blind" to Bobby's gestures. They were to indicate that they did not know what he wanted and that he would have to tell them. When the nonverbal behavior failed to attain reinforcement, it began to extinguish, and Bobby gradually began to use speech to request what he wanted. The successful attainment of goals occurred, which in turn reinforced his speech behavior.

Discrimination training   Behavior does not simply "occur." People respond to situations, and appropriate behavior depends in part on the particular situation. Sometimes people generalize behavior as being appropriate in one situation, but not in another situation. Often behaviors are over-generalized. The more similar two situations are, the more likely there will be generalization. As the following case demonstrates, the intended impact of discrimination training is to help the client distinguish between two situations, so that the behavior in one situation will not be used to generalize another situation in which it would be inappropriate. The basis of the strategy is to help the client identify the differences between the two situations.

Case 9P: Eleanor, in her mid-forties, had been divorced and had remarried. Her first husband treated her cruelly, to the point where she learned to respond in his presence with considerable fear and anxiety. She also generalized this fear response to other situations. Even discussing her husband, long after the divorce, evoked strong fear. The woman had enrolled in a course attended by about fifteen students. The instructor required considerable interaction in the classroom between the students and himself. The woman responded with strong fear of the instructor, and since the course required classroom interaction, she was clearly experiencing considerable difficulty. Upon discussion, it became clear that she was generalizing the fear responses she had learned with her husband to the instructor. Many of the apparent physical features of the instructor and her husband appeared similar to her. The counselor then asked the woman to describe some ways in which the two men were dissimilar; as she talked, she found more and more ways in which they were different from each other. She later met with the instructor and continued to focus on these differences. During a follow-up session, she reported that the differences between the two men were quite apparent, especially with respect to their behavior toward her, and that she no longer was responding with strong fear. The entire discrimination learning process took approximately ten to fifteen minutes.

Principles and strategies based on awareness as a process goal

Principle 4: Some people learn to function more effectively by becoming aware of certain characteristics about themselves or their environments

Awareness is a major concept in the counseling process. An important point is that for certain clients (those who are quick to grasp abstractions, are non-defensive, and able to relate abstractions to appropriate behavior) facilitating awareness may be a powerful way to help achieve certain kinds of outcome goals. While many theorists have agreed that awareness is an important process goal, they seem to disagree about the specific kinds of phenomena they want their clients to become aware of.

The essential issue can be expressed by raising a series of inter-related questions: Awareness of what will lead to what kinds of changes with what kinds of clients? Given a specific client with certain characteristics and a particular goal, what kinds of awareness will help the client achieve his outcome goal? If a client is helped to achieve awareness of specific information or ideas, what impact will occur? While research in human behavior is a long way from attaining defini-tive answers to these vital questions, the assumption may be made that awareness of some sort is a valuable process goal for clients with a variety of outcome goals. It will be useful to distinguish between awareness of self-related characteristics and awareness of environ-mental characteristics.

It is from this point that counseling becomes most judgmental, complex, and least amenable to structure. For any given client, with any specific goal, we cannot be certain which (if any) kinds of aware-ness will be of maximum favorable impact. Thus, the approach will be to help the counselor consider some of the specific kinds of awareness he may wish the client to acquire, and some of the potential impacts. In a sense, the approach will be to generate some interesting alterna-tives. The alternatives (or combination of alternatives) to be im-plemented depend upon the goals and characteristics of the client and the talents of the counselor.

For some clients, especially those desiring to make career and/or educational decisions, awareness of specific skills, talents, aptitudes, and interests will be essential. For some, awareness of demand char-acteristics of the environment will be especially impactful. For others, awareness of values and beliefs will have important instrumental value. For clients having interpersonal difficulties, awareness of how one's behavior affects significant others would appear essential (i.e., aware of the interpersonal consequences of one's actions). Similarly, awareness of the impact of the behavior of others would appear to be of real value to a client having these problems.

We may borrow from the basic notions of Chapter 3 to generate some important client awarenesses. In that chapter, we indicated an essential assumption: that human behavior is purposive and goal directed. From that assumption, we can make some important corollary statements. Effective functioning is directly influenced by the clarity, accuracy, and specificity with which an individual identifies his goals. The more clearly, accurately, and specifically a person identifies his goals, the more effectively he or she is likely to function. One reason individuals fail to function as effectively as they might otherwise is that they have not identified clearly the goals they are trying to attain. Thus, becoming aware of the really important goals they are striving for may be seen as a major desirable process goal for many clients. Counselor responses, such as the following, are especially helpful in facilitating this dimension of awareness:

> ——If you had the best of all possible situations, what would you like to accomplish most?

> ——In contrast to the way things are now, how would you most like them to be? Are you sure?

> ——How will both of us know when counseling has been successful? What criteria should we use to determine such success?

Given a client who is aware that his or her behavior is maladaptive, but is confused as to why it persists, a counselor might wish to respond:

> ——If you are behaving this (undesirable) way even though you do not want to, perhaps it is because there is a purpose to your behavior. That is, your actions are probably attaining some desirable goals for you. Can you think how your actions might be paying off for you?

Clearly, the intended goal of these counselor responses is to help the client become more aware of the intended goals of his or her actions.

Another assumption is that associated with any given action is a set of consequences. As a corollary, it may also be said that effective functioning depends upon an individual's ability to accurately anticipate the consequences (immediate and delayed; observable and nonobservable) of his or her actions. The more accurately he or she can anticipate consequences, the more effectively he or she is likely to function. Thus, helping a client become aware of the actual consequences of his or her previous actions and the potential consequences of his or her future actions represents additional potential awareness-based process goals. To achieve this impact, the counselor may wish to consider some form of the following response:

———Given the situation you described, and the particular people who were involved, what do you think happened as a consequence of your actions?

Assuming a reasonably accurate description of consequences, the counselor might then offer a values clarification response:

———Were you glad about those consequences?

Assuming the client failed to indicate some important consequences, the counselor might follow up by saying:

———What other consequences might also have occurred?

———What things might happen as a consequence if you were to do the things you say you might do?

———Would you feel glad or upset about those consequences?

———Given that you did not like what happened in the situation you are describing, what consequences would you have preferred?

The intended impacts of these counselor responses are two: (1) to help the client become more fully aware of important consequences, and (2) to become more fully aware of how he or she values those consequences. The valuing of consequences is a process equally as important as the anticipation of the consequences.

The interrelationship among three important constructs should be clearly identified: desired goals, actions, and consequences. People are said to be functioning effectively when the actual consequences of their actions are in agreement with their desired goals. However, people frequently behave in such ways that the actual consequences of their actions are incongruent and incompatible with their desired goals. The adolescent male who wants acceptance and regard from his peers, but who relates to them with constant bullying tactics, is a good example. It is likely that his peers will reject him as a consequence of such bullying actions. Another example is of the student who is caught cheating. His goal was to do well on the exam; he attained his goal. But the additional consequences that occurred were strongly negative.

Helping people become aware of the interrelationships among desired goals, actions, and actual consequences is a major set of process goals. An essential part of this process is to help the client search for, become aware of, and implement new alternatives that will more effectively achieve desired goals and/or result in less negative consequences. Counselor responses, such as those indicated above, help facilitate this awareness-based process. Here are some additional potential responses:

———Given that we have looked at the consequences of your actions, do you think you really achieved your desired goal?

———From what you say, it would seem that what actually occurred was opposite to what you really wanted. Can you think of some different ways you could have handled the situation so that you might have attained what you really wanted?

———Given what you want, and the way you say you intend to get what you want, what additional consequences might occur if you were to go ahead with your plan? How would you feel if those additional consequences were to occur? Can you think of some other possible plans where you could get what you want without the negative consequences?

Another level of awareness refers to awareness of emotions. This process may be described by borrowing from the basic S-R (stimulus-response) paradigm, as well as from concepts of emotions. Looking at emotions first, it may be said that for any given individual, specific emotional responses are more likely to occur in certain kinds of situations. Further, the intensity of any given emotion may depend on a specific situation. Thus, helping a client become aware of the dominant emotions he tends to experience, the intensity of given kinds of emotions he tends to experience, and the situation in which these are likely to occur may be an especially impactful awareness-based process goal. Take, for example, the following client response (adolescent male, high school, second interview): "It's because I'm black. People don't come right out and say it, but I know deep down they look down on me and treat me as if I were inferior. I really resent that." A valuable process goal might be to help the client become aware of the strong resentment, anger, bitterness, and hostility he feels, and the situations in which he feels that way. Later on, another counseling process goal may be to help him learn to cope with his feelings and the situations identified. An impactful counselor response might be: "I guess those feelings of anger and resentment are things you feel often and very strongly. Can you tell me about some specific times you felt especially bitter and resentful?"

We may also begin with the other element in the paradigm to provide a slightly different approach to the facilitation of emotion awareness. Certain situations elicit given emotions. Further, the intensity of those emotions depends in a large part on the situations. Thus, helping a client become aware of certain important situations and the kinds and intensity of emotions elicited by those situations is another potential awareness-based process goal. An example might be of an adolescent girl who discusses her relations with authority figures and communicates her difficulty in these relationships, but gives no more specific information than that. The counselor response may be: "It seems that whenever you are with people who have power and control over you, some very strong feelings occur and you have difficulty controlling them. Could you tell me specifically the kinds of feelings you have in these situations?" Such response can help the client gain this kind of awareness. Once the feelings are identified, the counselor can help the client become aware of the way those feelings affect her ability to cope with and relate to such people. The client's awareness will offer important clues to desirable outcome goals and important notions to the counselor as how to be of valuable help to the client.

Clearly, the two emotion-awareness approaches are not incompatible, and both are frequently considered desirable for many clients who are capable of awareness. Note that in both cases the counselor's response followed the same basic format. He first identified or reflected what he heard, and then responded with a CTRL (Counselor Tacting Response Lead) whose purpose was to help the client (and self) become aware of the relationship between situations and intense feelings.

An area of counseling where awareness becomes especially essential is in the decision-making process. The following section describes the decision-making process and relates awareness facilitation to that process.

Principle 5: Some people learn to function more effectively by acquiring an effective method for decision making

As developed in Chapter 2, a major counseling goal is that of helping people make important life decisions.

Choices regarding current and future educational plans, occupation, and marriage and the family are major decision areas for which people regularly seek the help of counselors.

Some decisions are made on impulse, with no thought or consideration of the consequences. A woman who sees a dress in a store window and exclaims, "I must have that dress! The price doesn't matter. Whether my husband will like it doesn't matter!" might be a good example. Another person might order a meal in a restaurant ("I feel like having steak tonight"). Other decisions are automatic— almost a reflex action. Little thought is involved in stopping at a red traffic light. Other decisions, especially those made by people who seek the help of counselors, require much more thought and consideration. There is a methodology or process by which such decisions are arrived at, and implied in that methodology are some important process goals for helping clients make important decisions.

The methodology of the decision-making process is that of: identifying the problem, determining goals, describing existing conditions related to the problem, generating all potential alternatives, predicting the likelihood of all possible consequences (immediate and delayed, observable and nonobservable), value judging the desirability of all possible consequences of each alternative, selecting, and implementing the selected alternative and evaluating actual consequences. According to basic decision methodology, the alternative selected should be the one that will have the greatest likelihood of achieving desired goals, that will result in the least negative consequences, and that will be consistent (and not inconsistent) with basic values.

Each element in this methodology becomes a basic and necessary process goal for the fullest involvement in helping a client whose goal is to make a decision. Said another way, each element becomes a specific task that the counselor must undertake for counseling to be of maximum utility for the client. Thus, the counselor must be sure that he or she has helped the client to:

1.　　accurately identify the problem

2.　　become aware of the basic goals related to the decision that the client wants to accomplish

3.　　describe, account for, and become aware of those existing conditions that are related to the decision

4.　　generate and become aware of all potential alternatives that will attain the identified goals

5.   predict and become aware of the potential consequences that might occur for each alternative if it were implemented, and the likelihood of those consequences

6.   become aware of his or her basic values related to evaluating the desirability or undesirability of the consequences he or she predicts

7.   develop a set of criteria for evaluating each alternative so that the criteria developed are a synthesis or an abstraction of: the goals identified, the conditions described, the consequences predicted, and the values identified

Further, the counselor must help the client evaluate each alternative in light of the criteria developed above. Once this process is accomplished, the client will have hopefully narrowed the potential range of available alternatives. However, counseling is not yet completed. The counselor must help the client identify the steps he must take and tasks he must accomplish to implement the alternative or alternatives selected.

It is important to analyze further some of these basic tasks. We begin with the interrelated tasks of identifying the problem and establishing the goals. Whereas a statement of a problem is usually an indication of some dissatisfying state of affairs, statements of goals are indications of conditions that will exist in the future if the current problem is resolved. The high school senior may enter with a problem, such as "I can't decide which colleges to apply to, and I need some help deciding." His problem is that he cannot decide. His goal is to attend the college that is "best" for him. In a sense, counseling may be seen as the process of deciding really what is meant by "best," and a major part of the task is that of developing criteria to determine the "best" college.

To accomplish this goal, client and counselor together will have to develop criteria to evaluate alternatives, to identify potential alternatives, and to eliminate those options that fail to satisfy the criteria developed.

Goal identification, however, goes much deeper. Attending college is only a process goal for attaining other goals, and, therefore, it is important that the client acquire some awareness of the goals beyond the goal of attending college. Such goals might include: entering into a career field for which a college education is necessary, a desire to learn and study, conformity to social norms, attainment of prestige and stature, capitulating to parental pressure, satisfying an achievement motivation, and a chance to meet new people. Thus, helping a client become aware of desired goals is not a simple or superficial task. For some clients, clarification of goals may become a difficult experience.

Since "creativity" may be operationally defined as the tendency to generate new alternatives to solve a problem, it is clear that creativity is an integral part of the decision-making process. Helping an individual select from several alternatives, that is, to become creative, is a major counseling task. Choosing a college or a career is frequently referred to as the process of exploration. Exploration in decision making is the process of generating alternatives, projecting oneself into each alternative, and asking oneself what consequences would occur if the given alternative were, in fact, selected. From here, the process is one of evaluating the consequences and value judging their desirability. A major part of counseling for decision making is that of helping clients in this exploration process.

"Brainstorming" may also be understood as a facet of the "generating alternatives" process. In brainstorming sessions, no alternative is evaluated until all have first been generated. The rationale is that when alternatives are evaluated too quickly certain unappealing alternatives might be rejected too quickly. The implications for decision-making counseling are clear.

Later in this discussion, we will relate the "alternative generating" step in the counseling process of information systems, as well as its implications for effective counseling.

"Describing existing conditions" refers to two interrelated assessment or evaluation processes: assessment of self and assessment of environment. The process of helping a client assess self is one of helping him or her become aware of and to take into account those factors and characteristics about self that are related to the decision problem. The process is one of facilitating self-exploration, the goal of which is clearly to help the client achieve greater self-awareness. The dimensions of assessment discussed in Chapter 8 may also be seen as dimensions of client awareness. Thus, self-awareness might include such things as: awareness of one's level of general intellectual development; awareness of one's level of development regarding specific skills, aptitudes, and talents; awareness of various activities (interests) one prefers to engage in; and awareness of one's dominant interpersonal characteristics.

People acquire self-awareness by comparing self with self (idiographic), and by comparing self with others (nomothetic). The counselor who helps a client ask himself "At which activity am I more skillful—researching and reviewing published literature or writing creatively?" is helping the client make an *idiographic* comparison of his talents. Also, a client asking himself "Which do I prefer more—playing an outdoor sport or sitting at home reading?" is comparatively assessing his interests. These are the kinds of comparisons the items on the *Strong–Campbell Interest Inventory* (1974) and the *Kuder Preference Record* (1954) ask test takers to make. The rationale is that by engaging in such self-comparisons, an individual will become aware of activities he prefers most and least, and this awareness will then become a major influencing factor in the process of choosing.

The counselor may facilitate such self-awareness as a natural part of his discussion with his client or he may administer tests as those described above to help initiate the self-comparison–self-awareness process. The purpose in using such tests is to help the client identify what he or she has discovered about self as soon as possible after the test has been taken, and then to help the client explore how those discoveries affect beliefs about self. The following simulated dialogue may help to clarify this process.

Counselor 1:	Well, Ted, you came in for help in choosing a career, and we decided to help you make a sensible choice by getting you to learn more about the kinds of activities you prefer most and the kinds you prefer least. So we decided that the *Kuder Preference Record* [1954] would help you toward this goal. You took it, and then scored it yourself. Can you tell me some of the things you might have learned about yourself as you were responding to the items?
Client 1:	Gee, I'm not really sure where to begin. Could you help me get started?
Counselor 2:	Well, perhaps there were certain items that you remember especially well. Perhaps some that you couldn't answer easily and had to stop and think about.
Client 2:	Well . . . . Yeah, come to think about it, I guess there were a couple. Like one where the three choices were to work in an automobile plant, be in a circus, or work in crop fields. I had a lot of trouble with that one because I liked all three. I like being outdoors, I like performing in front

of people, and I also like building things and putting things together. I had some trouble with that one.

Counselor 3:   Um . . . hm. The problem with that item was that all the alternatives seemed appealing. Can you remember which you rated as preferring most and which you rated as preferring least?

Client 3:   Um . . . I think I put down working in a circus as most, and in an automobile shop as least.

Counselor 4:   Um . . . hm. Can you tell me the thinking you went through to come to that decision?

Client 4:   [pause] Well, I figured in a circus you would meet a lot of people. You would do a lot of traveling, and see new places and all.

Counselor 5:   I guess that would mean that traveling and meeting new people are two activities you value very highly.

Client 5:   Yeah . . . that's for sure.

Counselor 6:   Well, how might that be related to your thinking about a career?

Client 6:   Well, I sure would want a career where I would be meeting lots of new people. But . . . actually as I think about it, I probably would get tired traveling after awhile. I don't think I would want to keep traveling forever.

Several things should be clear from this dialogue. First, once the counselor had finished his introductory remarks, his responses were very short—two or three sentences. But at each choice point situation, his goal was to facilitate greater self-awareness. Each response he made was clearly to facilitate that process. He did not offer advice; he did not interpret. All his responses were to help the client introspect about himself. Second, the client came for help in career choice, so a major part of the counselor's responsibility was to relate the introspection process to the decision at hand. This he clearly did at Counselor 6. From here, the counselor helped the client go through the same process with other items on the inventory and eventually with the scales the inventory yielded.

When a client asks himself, "How do my skills as an automobile mechanic compare to those of significant others?" or "Do others prefer clerical work as much as I do?" he is involved in making *nomothetic* comparisons. His answers to these questions are clearly related to choices regarding future career and education. A person who wants to be an insurance salesman, for example, will want to predict as accurately as possible whether he has the necessary skills and talents to compete successfully with others in the field. Thus, he will want to know what skills and talents are related to effective performance in the field, the level of such skills related to success, whether it is a highly competitive business, and the level of the skills held by those identified as being successful.

Thus, part of the process goal identified as "describing existing conditions" is really the process of self-assessment, self-exploration, and self-awareness. An essential part of the task is gathering information about self. The two basic information sources are recollection of behavior in past experiences and scores on various kinds of test instruments.

"Describing existing conditions" also refers to the process of identifying and becoming aware of those environmental factors that are important to take into account in reaching a decision. This is really a two-step process: first, identifying important environmental characteristics for consideration and, second, identifying the desirable "level" of each characteristic. To the high school senior who wants to attend college, the size of the student body may be an important characteristic of colleges to consider. However, even if the student has done this, he has only accomplished the first step: identifying an important characteristic. The second step is equally important: determining what college size is desirable.

In essence, the client is developing a set of criteria to use in exploring and evaluating potential alternatives. He will consider those alternatives which satisfy his criteria and reject those that do not. If he generates no alternatives that meet his criteria, then he must reevaluate the criteria to determine which he is willing to sacrifice. This phase of decision making is basically an elimination process. Those alternatives that do not meet given criteria are eliminated. Since each new criterion eliminates options, clients may easily develop criteria for which no alternatives qualify. When this happens, the client must decide which criteria are least important. As he disposes of a given criterion, more alternatives become viable. The process of evaluating and reevaluating criteria is part of the process of value clarification. Basically, the client is asking, "Of all the criteria I have specified, which is least important for me to consider?" and "Which criteria do I feel I can most easily give up and still be satisfied with my choice?"

Basically, this is the process that computer-assisted information systems take the client through. They suggest characteristics and ask the client if the given characteristic is important (and, if so, what "level"). As the client indicates each characteristic, the computer scans its total repertoire of alternatives and indicates how many options still qualify. With each characteristic, more options are eliminated. When a certain maximim remains, the client may inquire about the remaining alternatives. The information system then indicates those alternatives that satisfy all criteria, and gives basic information about each alternative.

Below are listed some of the most important college-related characteristics students may wish to consider in choosing a college:

——Region

——Major fields of study

——Type of school

——Cost

——Student body characteristics (size, average entrance scores, etc.)

——Accreditation

——Enrollment size

——Source of control

——Prerequisites

——Application deadline

——Financial aid possibilities

——Special programs and services available

——Campus life

——Athletic programs

——Prestige value

The process of helping a client develop criteria to evaluate alternative careers is basically the same. The dimensions to take into account will, of course, differ. Below are some of the career-related characteristics a counselor may wish to help the client consider:

1. Financial rewards

2. Nonfinancial rewards (e.g., the reward of helping others, as in medicine, counseling, teaching)

3. Opportunity for advancement and promotion

4. Skills and talents necessary to do well in various given career fields

5. Demand characteristics (what is expected of an individual working in a given career field)

6. Future stability of the various fields considered

7. Job security

8. Job stress

9. Kinds of relationships that significant others demand

10. Effect of career choice on outside job situations (e.g., effect on one's family of working in a given field)

11. Values demanded for good performance and its relationship to one's own core values (e.g., if one values integrity, can he do a good job and not feel quilty as a key member in, say, an advertising agency)

While further analysis of this process is beyond the scope of this text, it is worth noting that simulation procedures are being used more and more to help clients project themselves into various career fields and evaluate the potential in that field. The specific kinds of stress inherent in a given career field are decision-relevant factors frequently overlooked by both clients and counselors. Medicine, teaching, selling on a commission basis, truck driving, construction work, and engineering, each has its unique source of stress. Yet, people in the process of choosing are rarely aware of the specific kinds of stress associated with these career fields. Rarely, too, are clients helped to become aware of how they would respond to such stresses. Full counseling with clients in the process of choosing includes helping them become aware of such stresses and how they would respond to them. Video and film simulations would appear to have potential in helping clients acquire such awareness. For example, a female client interested in working as a hairdresser might be exposed to a video vignette in which a customer irately indicates to a beautician on the screen that she did a terrible job. It is clear, however, that the beautician worked hard and tried to do a conscientious job. Following this vignette, the counselor might ask the client some of the following questions:

——Suppose you were the beautician in that scene. How would you feel about what that customer said?

——How would you want to react to her?

——How do you think you might in fact react to her?

——Do you think this kind of thing might happen to you as a beautician? How often?

——How might your answers to yourself on these questions influence your choice about being a beautician?

We have indicated that predicting the consequences of implementing each alternative generated earlier is a major step in decision making and in the process of decision counseling. We have indicated that this is a major part of the process of exploring alternatives. This step is related to one of the basic assumptions in Chapter 3: associated with any given action are a series of consequences.

Granted that certain consequences are delayed and others are nonobservable, this step is perhaps one of the most difficult in the decision-making process. We cannot possibly predict all the consequences of every given action. Further, prediction at the time of decision is always a matter of estimating the likelihood of a given consequence occurring. For any given consequence of any given alternative, we cannot accurately predict the likelihood of that consequence occurring. Thus, two factors that constrain human effectiveness are: our inability to anticipate accurately all the consequences that may occur as a result of a given action, and our inability to anticipate accurately the likelihood of a given consequence. (It is from this rationale that Dewey once defined "intelligence" as the ability to anticipate accurately the consequences of one's actions.)

However, these notions suggest some ideas for effective counseling. They suggest that part of decision counseling is the process of helping a client consider potential consequences that he or she may not have considered. Another part is that of helping the client to more accurately estimate the likelihood of various consequences, given an alternative for consideration. The counselor, then, should be an individual capable of helping his client more accurately predict all relevant consequences and their likelihood. To help a client become more fully aware of consequences and their likelihood means that the counselor himself must be aware of such consequences.

In decision counseling, this very difficult process may begin with a few simple counselor responses, such as: "Up to now we have looked at some alternatives and have taken into account some criteria to evaluate these alternatives. From this, we have narrowed the field down to three alternatives. Let's try to think through what might happen to you if you were to select each alternative."

Selection is a process of choosing the alternative associated with the least negative consequence. Negative consequences can be reduced, but not always eliminated. If a client decides that the prestige of a college is of high value, then a consequence of choosing such a college will very likely be that he or she (or the family) will be forced to pay a considerable sum for tuition or to assume the burden of a financial loan. If money is tight, it may be necessary to choose a less expensive college. As a consequence, he will probably attend a less prestigious school. Thus, part of decision making is a matter of being aware of both positive and negative consequences and being prepared to cope with the negative consequences when they occur. Counseling, therefore, includes helping a client to anticipate and cope with some potentially negative consequences concerning his choice.

In this total process, the counselor will have helped the client become aware of: the important goals related to the decision, the factors about self and environment of the existing conditions, the alternatives available, the potential consequences and their likelihood, and important personal values related to the decision. From this, the counselor will have helped the client become aware of criteria so that he or she can evaluate the alternatives identified. If the counselor is skillful and diligent, he will have helped the client to become aware of each of the steps necessary to arrive at a decision so that the client may, in the future, learn the process and implement it himself at the next important decision situation.

From the basic methodology of the decision-making process, we may develop the following checklist of process goals that will help the client with decisions:

1.   Have I helped the client identify the problem?

2.   Have I helped the client become aware of goals related to the decision?

3.   Have I helped the client generate potential alternatives available?

4.   Are there information systems available that would provide information about available alternatives? If so, have I helped the client learn to use such systems to his or her benefit?

5.   Have I helped the client develop criteria to evaluate alternatives?

6.   Have I helped the client to identify those characteristics about self that are related to the decision?

7.   If test information is available, have I helped the client to understand accurately what conclusions he or she can validly draw about self and the predictions he or she may make from this information?

8.   Have I helped the client predict and become aware of the potential consequences that might occur for each alternative, if it were implemented?

9.   Have I helped the client become aware of basic values related to evaluating the desirability or undesirability of the predicted consequences?

In this process, information and information systems may be seen as helping the client perform four vital functions: identifying available alternatives, generating criteria to evaluate, anticipating potential consequences of implementing each alternative, and assessing the likelihood that each alternative can be effectively implemented. As indicated earlier, many people needing help in making decisions are not aware of the potential alternatives open to them. High school seniors who want to attend a college generally have a very limited idea of the more than 2,500 colleges that exist. People who want new careers are often not aware of potential and appealing careers available to them.

A major role of information systems is to provide data about existing alternatives. A number of information systems are available to high school seniors wanting to choose a college. Each system is a storehouse of information, constructed in such a way that, once a student has developed his criteria for choosing, the system can quickly indicate to him the alternatives that satisfy these criteria. As the counselor and student develop criteria, the student becomes more aware of certain self-related characteristics. With the utilization of the information system, the student is bound to come across new alternatives of which he was not previously aware.

In the college choice problem, many students may not think of enrollment size as a characteristic to take into account in developing criteria. Not only do information systems suggest this characteristic, but, once an alternative is selected, the system indicates that as a consequence. For example, supposing that Humangrowth U. has an enrollment of 5,000 undergraduate students, and Gaudydorm U. has an enrollment of 10,500 students, the information system will indicate to the high school senior that he will be one of 10,500 at Gaudydorm, whereas, if he chooses Humangrowth, he will be one of 5,000 students. Similarly, by indicating entrance scores on various standardized tests, information systems will indicate that a given score will fall into a given range at a given college. Supposing that a student's score on the SAT verbal is 550 and the mean score at Humangrowth is 650, while at Gaudydorm the mean is 500, then this information will let the student know that, even if he is accepted at both places, a consequence of selecting Humangrowth would be that his score on the SAT would be well below average at that school. In contrast, a consequence of choosing Gaudydorm would be that his score would be slightly above average. Thus, the information will help him predict a consequence. The counselor's role, of course, is to help him understand the potential implications of those consequences. In this case, the counselor would want to help the client understand any possible relationship between SAT scores and college grade-point averages. He would also want to help the client ask himself whether he would function more effectively as an above-average member of a group of college students or as a below-average member.

Similarly, information helps people more accurately assess the likelihood of given consequences occurring as a result of an implemented choice. Expectancy tables are generally used to aid in such predictions. Suppose an Appliance Repairing Aptitude test is developed and validated. After giving the test to all people entering this field, it was found that 95 percent of those scoring fifty or above remained in the field after one year, whereas only 40 percent of those scoring forty-nine or below remained longer than that period of time. This information would clearly help a potential entrant to predict the likelihood of his remaining in the field after one year, if he chose this career field.

The purpose of this section, then, is to help the counselor relate these ideas on the value of information systems to effective counseling. The counselor's role is not that of a walking compendium of decision-relevant information for every client. Rather, part of his or her role should be that of a resource person, one who knows where and how to get information easily, and how to help clients use the information in the process of making wise decisions. The vital part of the counselor's role is to help the client become aware of the valid conclusions, inferences, and predictions he or she can draw about self from such information, and relate the new awareness to the decision at hand. In this process, the counselor must keep in mind that facilitating such self-awareness is a process goal to attain the outcome goal of making a wise decision.

Principle 6: Some people learn to function more effectively by acquiring a more favorable sense of self-worth

As developed in Chapter 3, the basic views people acquire about self have a powerful influence on the effectiveness with which they relate to others, the goals they set for their personal futures, and their ability to make wise decisions. People who like and respect themselves are more likely to relate well with others, to develop deep versus superficial relationships, to set attainable goals, to have well-developed ideas for achieving the goals they set, and to make decisions that are in the best interests of both self and others. Their daily actions are less likely to be maladaptive or counterproductive. Thus, helping clients acquire a favorable sense of self-worth is often an important counseling goal. There are several basic strategies available for changing self-concept, each based on a different set of theoretical propositions regarding that construct. The approach here will be to examine briefly the theoretical propositions and the implications these hold for potential counseling strategies.

The phenomenological approach   This position holds that a person's sense of self-worth is influenced by the kind of regard he or she receives from significant others and by important confirming or disconfirming life events. A person whose peers continually doubt his or her worth, who regard him or her as less than adequate, competent, or acceptable, is likely to develop a pervasive sense of self-doubt and a view toward self as an inadequate, inferior, and unacceptable person. In contrast, a person in contact with significant others who regard him as a person of worth, deserving of respect, and capable of effective living, will develop a favorable sense of self-esteem. Thus, the basic approach of the phenomenological orientation is to provide the client with an intensive set of experiences with an individual whose attitudes are sharply different from the attitudes of previous significant others. The basic assumptions about a client held by counselors of this orientation are that he or she is a person of worth, whose worth is unconditional, who is entitled to be looked upon with respect, and who has the innate capacity for favorable growth. These assumptions are communicated to the client by the work and energy the counselor invests in supplying high levels of the core conditions. Being in the presence of another who offers these conditions leads to the development of greater respect for self. The credo of this orientation is that "the offering of caring from another leads to caring for self."

Self-concept as a set of attitudes about self   A different approach to changing self-concept is to define self-concept as a set of attitudes a person holds about self. With this definition, principles of attitude change may be applied to changing attitudes toward self.

One set of principles comes from the theory of cognitive dissonance. This theory holds that if an individual has two ideas or pieces of information in awareness that are inconsistent with each other there will be an inherent tendency to reduce the discrepancy. Thus, the work of the counselor is to help the client become aware of underlying attitudes toward self and subsequently to confront the client with ideas and information that are inconsistent with those basic attitudes. If the client holds the attitude that he or she is incapable of success, then providing the client with success experiences is one way to create such dissonance. A risk with this approach is that the client may try to maintain the original view of self by discounting or rationalizing away the discrepant information.

A related strategy counselors sometimes use is to put the client in the role of trying to prove that the counselor should accept as truth the beliefs the client is holding about self. For example:

> ———You know, you keep talking about yourself as a useless person. That's what you believe about yourself. But my beliefs about you are different from your beliefs about yourself. Could you convince me that your way of seeing yourself is the way I should see you?

An adaptation of this approach is based on the idea that part of helping a client acquire new beliefs about self may include the process of "unhooking" his or her beliefs from those of significant others. For instance:

> ———From what you have said, it does seem that your mother thinks of you as less than acceptable. But what I want to know is how you view yourself. . . . Who says you must view yourself the way your mother sees you?

A related idea is based on defining self-concept as a set of theoretical statements or conclusions a person has developed about self. ("I conclude about myself that I am unacceptable to my peers.") To be valid, theoretical statements and conclusions must be consistent with facts. According to the reasoning of logic, when facts and conclusions are inconsistent, it is the conclusions that must be changed.

References

Kuder, G. F. *Kuder Preference Record—Personal.* Chicago: Science Research Associates, 1954.

Strong, E. K., & Campbell, D. P. *Strong-Campbell Interest Inventory.* Stanford, Calif.: Stanford University Press, 1974.

10. The process of marriage counseling

In many ways the goals of marriage counseling are similar to the goals of individual counseling, that is, to help those involved in the process learn new ways of engaging in more rewarding behavior. More rewarding behavior is, of course, a subjective decision in individual counseling. It is more so especially when looking at the relationship between two people who are seeking assistance for some difficulties that they are experiencing in their relationship. However, there are also some important differences in the foci and processes of individual and marriage counseling.

Whereas in individual counseling, the client or person being helped is the individual client, in the marriage counseling process, as in the marriage relationship itself, the client is the relationship that exists between two persons. Although the counseling process in marriage involves two persons and their behavior, the focus and intent is

Material originally presented in: T. P. Delaney & D. J. Delaney, *A communication approach to conjoint marital therapy* (St. Bonaventure, N. Y.: St. Bonaventure University, 1974).

on both the individuals in the relationship and on the relationship itself. On occasion, there may be some evidence of intrapersonal difficulty in one or both of the marriage partners, and, as a result, individual counseling may be necessary for the distressed individual concurrent with marriage counseling which focuses on the relationship between the individuals.

In many respects, marriage counseling can be viewed as a form of crisis intervention. It would appear that in most cases some precipitating event or circumstance occurs in the environment of the couple that brings them to seek assistance. These precipitating events may be directly related to the marriage, or underlying difficulties that exist in the marriage, or pressures that are felt as the result of the deterioration of the relationship. Most precipitating events fall into one or more of the following conditions:

——the intrusion of a third party into the relationship; that is, the development of an affectionate relationship with some other individual by one or both of the partners

——an experiencing of the lack of sexual satisfaction on the part of one or both partners in the relationship

——changes in the structure of the family that upset the routine within the unit such as difficulties with a child in child-rearing practices or the separation of a child from the family through his own actions as leaving for school or for marriage

——illness in the family, especially terminal illness of a child

——interventions into the relationship by in-laws, or the strength of allegiances that one partner has for his or her own family and family ties

——strong differences in the belief systems of the couple and resulting conflicts in establishing styles of living

——fears of the aging process and death

——changing roles as the result of social influences

——work, business readjustment, and retirement

——wife beginning or stopping work

——involvement in violations of the law

——financial pressures

——pregnancy

——unrealistic expectations of marriage and living together

While these precipitating events are reasonably identifiable, the real difficulties that occur in the relationship are often hidden. The real difficulty may be the couple's inability to articulate the difficulties, or their inability to focus on the relationship when it is involved with their own individual perceptions and personal needs. At the same time, analyses of the precipitating event may be used to facilitate a closer look at the interpersonal differences, to help the individuals explore the relationship in greater depth, and subsequently to uncover some of the hidden needs in the relationship that are not being met.

Process goals

The process goals of marriage counseling include exploration of the following questions:

——How can we make the difficulties that we are experiencing more exact, accurate, and clear?

——Once the causes of these difficulties are known, what alternatives do we have concerning the relationship, and what can we realistically do with these alternatives?

——How can we decide which alternatives to choose?

——When we do decide what we want to do with the marital relationship, what kinds of procedures can we employ to help us achieve the desired goal?

——How do we evaluate the procedures that we have used? When do we know that we have achieved our goal in the relationship?

To help add some structure to this process, the stages can be identified as follows:

1.   Open communication

2.   Exploration of alternatives

3.   Decision making and goal identification, including counselor determination of counseling strategies

4.   The implementation of the helping strategies

5.   Evaluation, termination, and follow-up

Each stage will be analyzed in the order given above.

Open communication

This process goal, which identifies the counselor's activities during the first stage of marriage counseling, involves helping the couple to develop a system of effective communication. That is, each spouse must learn to communicate very clear and accurate messages, so that they can be received as intended. As is true in individual counseling, most marriage counseling clients find it difficult to share openly with the counselor. In marriage counseling, the problem of defensive and guarded communication is compounded because each of the partners has developed his or her own pattern of defensive communication with the other. Sharing feelings, beliefs and perceptions about the problems in the relationship risks attack and criticism from the partner as well as ownership of responsibility for the problem. It is threatening to both partners and each has his or her own defensive way of coping with the threat: one may attack directly; the other may dodge and defend by subtle attack. Nonetheless, if marriage counseling is to be effective, open communication must be facilitated and defensiveness must be reduced. Each partner must learn to listen actively and non-defensively to the feelings, perceptions, and needs of the other partner. Applying these skills to a relationship where there has been turmoil and frustration can be arduous and painful.

There are a number of possible approaches to breaking down the built-up barriers of communication. Most are based on the application of principles of constructive confrontation. They range from mild to intense forms of confrontation. The following interaction between Bob and Joan will be used to demonstrate several different confrontation approaches:

Joan:	Bob has been having a lot of pressure at work lately. Often when he comes home he criticizes me about something and yells at the kids. It seems to be getting worse and I'm at the point when I am really afraid of Bob when he comes home.
Bob:	[*shouting*] I *do not* shout at the kids and when I do criticize you, you deserve it! I really get bugged when I come home and supper won't be ready for an hour. If you understood how tired I am when I get home you would have supper ready.

A standoff. Each partner thinks his or her feelings are justified. Both are spending much energy accusing the other and protecting self. Neither can spring loose enough to develop effective approaches to solving their problems. Both must learn to tune in more actively to the other's needs; both must learn the skills of effective conflict resolution.

Let's look at some approaches the counselor might use to help the partners communicate more openly and take on more responsibility for dealing with the problem.

Mild Confrontation: OK, let's try to understand what is happening at this moment. Joan, you are feeling very threatened. Bob, I sense you are feeling very angry.

Moderate Confrontation: I am sensing intense feelings from both of you right now. Joan, you are feeling very anxious. Bob, you are feeling very angry. Would this be a fair example of how your arguments develop and get out of hand?

Moderate Confrontation: Joan, right now you are feeling very anxious. Bob, you are feeling very angry. As I see it, both of you are focusing on self, but not on the other. Tuning in more actively to the needs and feelings of the other will be an important skill to work on for both of you.

Intense Confrontation: Bob, Joan just shared with us that she is often afraid to be with you, especially when you come home from work. By shouting at Joan you seem to be saying that her fears are stupid and unjustified.

Intense Confrontation: Bob, I hear you shouting and feeling angry, as though you perceive yourself as being unfairly accused. Yet underneath the anger, I am sensing that you are feeling a good deal of pain from what Joan shared.

Confrontations such as these are risks that can lead to more open communication between the partners and the counselor. As developed in Chapter 6, the level of intensity depends on the counselor's assessment of the client's level of readiness to encounter and work with the idea in the confrontation. The problem presented affirms that healthy marriage relationships require active listening, open communication, and in-depth understanding of the feelings, perceptions, and motivations of both self and partner. All these are necessary for the effective use of conflict resolution skills. Developing these skills are frequently major process goals for marriage counseling.

Occasionally, when communication is blocked (one partner dominates and/or intimidates the other), counselors will meet with each of the partners individually. In these individual meetings, the issues explored usually include:

———What feelings and perceptions are you experiencing about the things we have been discussing?

———Are we discussing the issues we should be talking about together? If not, what are your perceptions of what we should be discussing?

———Are you willing to share with your spouse the things you have shared with me?

Sometimes counselors must use individual meetings as a last resort. However, this procedure has risks. While one is talking, the other partner is probably wondering what is being said about him or her. The counselor runs the danger of being perceived as taking sides and possibly manipulating one partner behind the other's back. The procedure of meeting with one partner without the other partner being present should be used with careful discretion and only after the ground rules of what the counselor will and will not do are carefully communicated to both parties.

Over time marriage partners build up *short cut* communications and code words. In marriage counseling, the counselor's active listening skill requires the ability to tune in to these messages and to recognize their significance both for the partners and for the relationship itself. The following are examples:

Wife: You never seem to come home on time anymore. After work you usually wind up in a bar somewhere drinking with your cronies.

Husband: I wish that you would stop calling me a drunk. I resent that and it is simply not true.

Wife: I didn't call you a drunk, I was simply saying that . . . .

The wife expresses anger about her husband's drinking. Yet the husband hears the wife calling him a drunk. The husband's inferential leap (short cut) occurred because this may be a painful area for him, or because this has historical precedence, that is, it is repeated over and over again in the marriage relationship. A mild level clarification-seeking confrontation may help: to the husband: "Your wife talked about your drinking a lot after work with your friends. You seemed to hear her calling you a drunk."

Another example of the short cut, code-word process is the following:

Husband:	It seems that we always wind up doing what you want to do. Even sexual intercourse is that way. Whenever I make advances toward you, I never know whether or not you will accept them or whether you will put me down in some way.
Wife:	I am not selfish, nor frigid! If either of us has a problem in the area of sex, I think it is you.

The husband did not use the pejorative words "selfish" or "frigid" in his statement and, yet, that is what the wife is reacting to. Here the wife's inferential leap suggests that she is anticipating where the husband's statement is leading and is attempting to preempt the line of discussion. Notice the wife's effort to defend against attack by counter-attacking. Sex is clearly a problem in this marriage. Rather than owning one's contributions to the problem, each partner blames the other. No movement will occur until each owns some personal responsibility for the problem and works on his or her personal contribution. The counselor must move each partner to the point of saying: "I am making some contributions to the problem. I am committed to making this marriage work and thus will work to improve upon the contributions I am making to the problem. I will acknowledge, encourage, and support the work my partner is making to change, and can expect support from my partner for my efforts." When both partners have reached this point, it is possible to establish a parallel contract.

To facilitate open communication, the counselor's role is to intervene in these communicative processes and to help each person to think about what he or she wants to say, to say the things accurately, and at the same time to check, by way of feedback from the other, whether or not the communication is accurate. At the same time, the receiver, while providing feedback to the sender concerning the appropriateness and adequacy of what was sent, does have an opportunity to respond in his or her own manner. If the counselor looks for short cuts to communication, identifies these, demonstrates what is going on, sets the task to send and receive messages clearly and accurately, and provides a rationale for this, then he or she is helping the spouses to communicate more openly.

To facilitate more accurate message sending and receiving, marriage counselors often use an active listening exercise as an intervention procedure. There are two rules in this structured process: first, before person two can react to the statements of person one, person two must repeat, with accuracy, what person one has said; second, person two's reaction that follows must be in the form of an "I message." Using the examples above, the process may go as follows:

Wife:	You never seem to come home on time anymore. After work you usually wind up in a bar somewhere drinking with your cronies.
Husband:	You're saying that I seem to prefer to drink with my buddies than to come home. Is that right?
Wife:	Close enough.
Husband:	Maybe if things were better at home I would feel differently.
Husband:	It seems that we always wind up doing what you want to do. Even sexual intercourse is that way. Whenever I make advances toward you, I never know whether or not you will accept them or whether you will put me down in some way.
Wife:	You never know how I'm going to react to you, especially when it comes to sex. Is this what you're saying?
Husband:	Right.
Wife:	I probably would be more receptive if your approach were different.

In both cases, the spouse repeated what the initiator said before commenting. In both, the initiator offered affirmation that the listener had heard correctly, and in both, the responder's subsequent message was predominantly "I" focused rather than "you" focused. Both couples are still experiencing intense hostility. But they are changing their ways of communicating with each other, especially in conflict situations.

As the couples learn to communicate this way, the counselor is actively listening with a diagnostic orientation. His or her orientation is to try to understand the roots of the conflict—the wants of each partner that are not being met and the ways in which each copes with frustration. Later on, the counselor can reflect the roots of the conflict and subsequently help the couple apply their newly acquired active listening skills to resolving such conflicts.

Exploration of alternatives

Later stages of marriage counseling are unlikely to happen until at least minimum levels of open communication have been achieved (level three of Carkhuff's Self-Disclosure Scale discussed in Chapter 5). For many couples, this may take several sessions. Assuming that this level has been achieved, counseling can move to the second stage—exploring alternatives. During this stage, the critical process goal is to explore the primary alternatives to the present marital situation. This includes the process of identifying and analyzing the available possibilities:

> ——*Separation:* Who will leave? How will he or she leave and where will he or she go?
> ——*Divorce:* How is this achieved? What is the role of the attorneys and what is the role of the spouses in the divorce process? How are settlements made and on what data are decisions based concerning settlements? What is the responsibility of each spouse to children in the divorce or separation? How are these responsibilities actualized?
> ——*Improving the relationship:* What are the parameters within which each partner is willing to explore and to change? What are the limitations and expectancies that each spouse has for the other, including the degrees of reality concerning all these alternatives?

Following this procedure, the counselor may wish to meet individually with each spouse and to explore the possibilities and alternatives for the relationship, adding some, narrowing others, and discarding some. Situations arise where the only alternative for the relationship discussed while the counselor is with both spouses is the improvement of the relationship. When the counselor meets individually with one of the partners, that person may define another alternative, such as divorce, and an exploration may indicate why this was not raised while the other spouse was present. Sometimes the reasons for this are the feelings on the part of one that the other would not know how to handle the suggestion of a divorce, that he or she would not be able to accept it, or that he or she may become violent and physically abusive when they leave the counseling office. On other occasions, the perceived religious constraints of one may block the other from raising this possibility. The process at this time is intended to establish the parameters within which the partners have freedom to move. Alternatives to the marriage, or rationale for the alternatives and limitations may exist for any number of reasons and these should be explored fully.

Alternatives can be broken down into three major areas: (1) improving the marital relationship, (2) maintaining the existing relationship, and (3) terminating the relationship either by separation or divorce. These options may be open to some couples, but not to others. They may be open to one individual partner in a marriage relationship, but not to the other partner for social, economic, religious, and/or personal reasons. It is appropriate for the counselor to help both partners understand that some agreement should be made concerning the limits and degrees of freedom that they have in exploring the direction or redirection of their relationship.

Decision making and goal identification

Based on the successful completion of the first two process goals (establishing a system of open communication and establishing the parameters within which the marital relationship can be defined), the spouses are able to assess their desires and commitments for the future of the marriage relationship. It is appropriate for the counselor to help the couple understand that the help they receive must be based on their making a decision for themselves. The counselor can help them think through their decision, but cannot lead them to a "best" decision. The counselor should work with the couple, going back over areas that they have explored previously, trying to help them to have realistic understandings of what is happening in the relationship and what is happening in the marriage counseling process. Where they have been, where they are at this point, and the kinds of interventions that can be employed to help them once they have decided what it is they want to do with their relationship are important in facilitating achievement of the process goal. If there are difficulties in achieving this process goal, it may be that more work is necessary on developing even better systems for communicating or that more time and energy is necessary to reexplore and redefine the alternatives that are open to them and how they see the possibilities for the relationship.

Implementation of helping strategies

Following the making of a mutual decision concerning the future of the marriage relationship, the counselor is in a position to employ certain strategies that will help the couple move toward the realization of the goal that they have established as a result of their decision. The three areas to be considered again are: (1) maintenance of the relationship, (2) divorce or separation (termination of the relationship), and (3) improving the relationship.

1.   *Maintenance of the relationship:* On occasion couples decide to maintain a marriage even though it is a poor one. These reasons include financial considerations, religious convictions against divorce, personality characteristics, and certain social pressures and forces. While one might conclude that a decision to maintain a relationship based on any of these reasons is generally a poor one, under some very difficult circumstances this may be the least unattractive alternative. In these cases, the counselor can help the couple to continue to communicate with each other, to help them be open and honest about their feelings, and to try to accept the feedback necessary for at least a minimal level relationship. The counselor may also explore with the couple certain areas that may lead to some improvement that will help them cope with the stress and tension that exist in the marriage. These areas will be identified below.

2.   *Divorce/separation:* On occasion couples decide, as a result of marriage counseling as well as other factors involved in the relationship, to terminate their marriage. This decision does not, however, terminate the process of marriage counseling. Divorce is generally a traumatic experience that triggers intense feelings. Some partners experience strong feelings of guilt for having broken a moral code they value as important. Others experience feelings of failure and inadequacy. Still others experience hurt and rejection. A highly dependent partner may

well experience anxiety about his or her ability to be self-reliant in the future. The impact of such a decision on children, relatives, and friends is always a difficult issue to work through. Reflection, active listening, clarification, and acceptance can help participants work through these feelings. The counselor can also help the participants develop ways to cope with reactions from children, relatives, and friends. Additionally, the counselor can help the participants develop realistic expectations about divorce procedures.

3.   *Improving the marriage relationship:* The very act of making a decision to improve a marriage relationship in itself contributes to the improvement of that relationship. Both participants would have had to do some intensive personal searching to have arrived at that decision. Such a decision is a reaffirmation of the importance of the relationship and usually in itself is an expression of caring. Sometimes, just having to make the decision is sufficient to improve the relationship.

Major areas for improving the marriage relationship include: (1) sexual relationships, (2) relationships between the couple and their in-laws, (3) child-rearing practices, (4) differences in religion, and (5) financial planning. Each of these areas will be considered.

1.   *Sexual relationship:*
Although each marriage partnership works out its own unique patterns of sexual expression, an active sexual relationship that is enjoyable to both participants is generally considered a key factor in a healthy marriage. In most marriage counseling situations, the sexual relationship of the partners is an important issue for discussion. Usually, it is difficult for a couple to discuss their sexual practices with anyone, the counselor included. This means that the counselor must work hard to make it comfortable for the couple to talk openly about sexual concerns.

Whether the counselor is able to do this or not depends upon his or her personal feelings about human sexuality. The counselor who is embarrassed to talk openly about sexual matters and who finds specific sexual practices shocking or disgusting will be unable to stimulate work-talk in this area. In contrast, the counselor who recognizes that sex is a natural and important part of adult life and that there are many ways for sexual expression, will find it less difficult to help the couple talk freely about their sexuality. Learning to help others overcome embarrassment and inhibitions is thus more a matter of clarifying one's own beliefs and emotions about human sexuality than a matter of learning specific techniques.

In sexual relationship counseling, the counselor's task is to help the couple clarify their needs in their sexual relationship, to see how well these needs are being met, and to determine whether or not some modifications in their practices ought to be considered. The counselor can help each partner to see what is happening in this area, to understand the dynamics, and to help each to understand the needs and wants of the other. He can encourage the couple to try different approaches to sex so as to add some variety to their sexual practices.

Very often counselors find that a couple in marriage counseling does not talk openly to each other about their sexual relationship. Counselors should encourage them to do so, should help each partner to identify the things that please him or her most, to help the partners to understand some of the pleasures they receive from sexual acts, and to encourage the couple to vary their practices and discuss them openly while focusing on ways to improve their enjoyment. On occasion, counselors do find that there are some serious problems or difficulties in this area that require more in-depth help. There may be problems of impotency or sexual frigidity; however, counseling in this area requires in-depth training on the part of the counselor and the possession of credentials to conduct sex therapy. If the counselor has these credentials, he may proceed into strategies directed toward intervening in the difficulties, or he may decide to refer the couple to someone who has these competencies and skills. Even if no sexual difficulties have been presented during the course of marriage counseling, it is still the counselor's responsibility to explore these areas with the couple in order to improve the relationship in their marriage.

2.   *Relationship between the couple and their in-laws:*
Serious difficulties in marriage relationships are sometimes the result of the controlling influences of in-laws who project themselves into the couple's relationship. Not only parental in-laws, but sibling in-laws as well, may impose powerful stresses on a marriage relationship. Counselors in marriage counseling should help the couple to explore these areas and to help them understand each other's feelings as they relate to their own parents and the parents of the spouse. Sometimes very simple practices that have developed over time might cause concern to one of the spouses. This may be spending more time with the parents of one of the spouses than with the parents of the other. This may cause some concern to the son or the daughter of the parents who are not receiving much attention from the couple. These

habits in the relationship develop over time and quite often individuals find it difficult to talk about them, to identify them, and to think about them in terms of a renegotiation of in-law relationships. Again, counselors have the responsibility to explore these problems with the couple. If there are difficulties, a counseling goal becomes that of helping the couple to find workable solutions.

3.   *Child-rearing practices:*

This is another dimension of the marital relationship that counselors should explore with the couple. Again, no difficulties may be found in these areas, but it is worthwhile to explore. If there are no particular concerns, the counselor should at least encourage the parents to spend time discussing their approaches to child rearing and to try to develop some consistent patterns. If, on the other hand, some difficulties or problems in child rearing are presented by the couple, counselors should be prepared to explore these fully, and, if they have the competencies, to enter into interventions and strategies that would help the spouses to alleviate the problems that exist between them and their children. In other words, if the spouses have developed approaches to child rearing that are consistent and logical, and are following practices of others who have successfully raised children, then the parents should be encouraged simply to talk more about these with each other and to continue with their practices. Counselors should also have competencies in this area in order to help those spouses who have difficulties in agreeing on the raising of their children or difficulties in determining the approaches they should take in specific matters of child rearing.

4.   *Differences in religion:*

This dimension is a very sensitive area for many couples. Counselors should approach the discussion of differences in religion openly and matter-of-factly. The focus here, for the counselor, should be that these differences can be made compatible no matter how great they may seem, if a couple sincerely decides to improve their relationship. The importance of this compatibility can be seen on occasion when a spouse has a strong religious belief in one area and feels that these beliefs, in a great part, provide some order, direction, and determination for his or her very being. When these strong attachments to religion are not shared by the other spouse, difficulties often arise in other areas, such as child rearing and sexual practices. The counselor's focus is on helping the couple to examine these areas openly, to express their feelings, and to try to understand the position of the other. On occasion, counselors may find it necessary to refer clients to clergy for further development of their understandings of religion and for clarification of various religions. It is important to note here that the counselor should know the person to whom he is referring the clients, that the referral source should be a person who has a broad view, not only of his own religion, but of religions in general, and an understanding of how religion fits into the scheme of a person's life and lifestyle.

5.   *Financial planning:*
Couples get into difficulties in financial matters as a result of poor planning, overspending, improper use of credit cards, poor credit references, lack of understanding of interest rates, etc. The counselor should try to stress planning in an open discussion of how monies ought to be spent in the relationship, as well as recommending shared responsibilities in decision making and spending. If there are money difficulties, the counselor should be in a position to provide the couple with a referral agent to whom they can bring more serious matters of financial difficulties. A referral agent for help in this area may be a financial counselor at a local credit bureau.

Evaluation, termination, and follow-up

The process goals of evaluation, termination, and follow-up are similar to the process goals found in individual counseling. The counselor assesses the effectiveness of his or her interventions in helping a couple to decide what they want to do with a relationship they share, and to implement this decision. The process is terminated when the goals of this process have been achieved. A follow-up is conducted to determine if the counselor may be of further assistance, as well as to determine his or her effectiveness in helping.

11. Termination and follow-up

This chapter deals with the termination and follow-up of the counseling process and the use of each counseling procedure and technique. The process began in the initial session where the counselor stimulated open communication in an atmosphere in which the client felt at ease in saying the things he wanted to say. The second step was the establishment of a facilitative relationship characterized by empathic understanding, warmth, genuineness, and professionalism. This stage was followed by the client's identification of that area in which the counselor could be of some assistance, and the counselor's determination of how she could best help the client. This help, or the use of the most appropriate counseling procedures, was discussed in Chapter 9.

Termination and follow-up
of the counseling strategy

When the counselor ceases to employ a counseling procedure, it can be said that the use of that procedure is terminated. The counselor may terminate procedures because they have been successful or unsuccessful in helping the client reach his goal. In order to evaluate its success, the counselor "follows up" or seeks evaluation from the client or significant others in the client's life, such as parent, teacher, or spouse. Based on this evaluation, the counselor may (1) decide to use another procedure, if the first proved unsuccessful; (2) if successful, help the client to reformulate another specific goal for continuing counseling that can start at the goal identification stage of the counseling process; or (3) if successful, and no other goal seems important or appropriate at the time, to terminate the counseling process.

Termination and follow-up
of the counseling process

When the counselor and client no longer see each other for the purpose of counseling, the counseling process is terminated. It is the counselor's responsibility to evaluate the success that counseling has had for the client. This evaluation is made through "following up" the client to determine if the goal reached as a result of counseling has stabilized over time. If it hasn't, such contact may lead to further counseling. This follow-up procedure is an integral, though removed, part of the complete process.

Counselor terminating behavior

The goals of the terminating session are to: (1) reinforce the client's behavior changes in the direction of the goal as stated by the client; (2) make sure the client has no other pressing concerns; and (3) help the client realize that he may seek the counselor's aid at any time in the future, as the "door is always open."

Termination as part of
the counseling process

There are important emotional factors involved for both the client and the counselor in the termination stage. The counselor must be especially attuned to these emotions and be prepared to respond to them. To a large degree, the kinds of emotions that are likely to occur depend upon where the counseling process has gone and how successful the counseling has been in achieving the outcome goals established in stage three, the identification of goals. The following approaches are the basic kinds of situations and the particular emotions associated with these situations.

Premature termination chosen by the counselor

At times, external events in the counseling situation may require that counseling be terminated before successful goal attainment has occurred. This happens frequently in school situations: the end of the academic year may have occurred, the client may be moving to a new school, or the counselor may be leaving. These occurrences may not represent a serious difficulty if a close relationship has not been established. But once a strong relationship has been established, premature termination may generate intense client feelings. This may occur where client and counselor have learned to trust each other deeply, to the point where the client has talked about many private and potentially embarrassing things: his sense of pervasive self-doubt, things about which he feels guilty, or things that could get him into trouble if significant others knew about them.

Clearly, the news of termination of counseling will have a strong emotional impact on the client. The client may feel betrayed by the counselor and angry toward him. The impact of counseling to this point may have been strong in the sense that the counselor has "opened up" the client, but has not as yet helped him learn to accept and cope with his new awareness. The client most likely would feel frightened. He may well ask himself whether the counseling has been more harmful than helpful. It is possible that the client will blame the counselor for this difficult situation. After all, it is the counselor who is responsible for not only causing the painful awareness, but for prematurely terminating the relationship. Under such conditions, it would be a rare person who would not consider himself betrayed.

Any of these feelings, or combination, may be expected, and they are likely to be intense. They will not "go away." Counselor and client must deal with them together. The counselor may feel guilty about the impact he or she has had on the client and this may interfere with his or her ability to help the client deal effectively with these feelings. Since the feelings the client has toward the counselor are intense and negative, they may be threatening to the counselor. As a consequence, the counselor may prefer to avoid looking at the client's feelings.

Clearly, this avoidance strategy would be the least appropriate and a most maladaptive alternative for the client's best interest. The client's feelings must be dealt with and the counselor must be the one to initiate it. For the counselor to do so will require a strong feeling of personal security. An insecure counselor could not possibly help the client discuss negative feelings toward her or him.

The process of dealing with client feelings toward a counselor is basically the same as the process of dealing with client feelings at any stage of the counseling process. They must be dealt with openly and candidly by both parties and they must be accepted by the counselor in a non-evaluative and non-defensive manner. It will help considerably for the counselor to communicate his or her own feelings about the situation to the client. A counselor response such as "I don't like what has happened and I, too, wish this weren't the case. I understand your feelings very well, and, although it hurts, I am glad you told me how you feel," may well offer strong support to the client. It may help, too, for the counselor to express his or her feelings about losing the relationship with the client: "I want you to know that I, too, feel hurt by this. Our relationship has meant a lot to me, and I, too, feel very bad that it must end soon. I feel bad that I have had to be the one to end it before it should be ended."

If the counselor had known before counseling began that he or she would be leaving, it would have been preferable to have avoided the awareness-oriented strategy, or else had communicated to the client in advance that their time together would have to be limited. Thus, the news of the counselor's leaving would not have been a surprise and both would have been prepared. The discussion here, however, assumes that the counselor did not know in advance that early termination would be necessary.

Under such conditions, an appropriate strategy might be to explore the possibility that another counselor can continue with the client. In choosing such a strategy, the counselor must be especially sensitive to the client's feelings of anger and betrayal. To such a proposal from the counselor, the client may respond with strong resistance. He may respond by saying, "Why go through it all again. I trusted you and had a strong relationship with you. I really don't believe I could accomplish that with someone else. It's too painful to have a deep relationship like we had and then lose it. I don't want to go through it again with someone else. Besides, what if she were to leave me too? That would be just another betrayal."

This is frequently the client's initial reaction. However, in time, some clients reconsider and choose to continue with a new counselor. If the counselor is to make a referral, he or she must be prepared to assure the client that the new counselor will also be competent, and this means the counselor must see the referral source as a competent professional.

If the client chooses not to continue with a new counselor, the counselor must accept that decision. An exception to accepting the client's decision might be if the counselor sincerely believes that the client's future functioning would be severely impaired by leaving the client at the time of termination. However, since counselors value the concept of being aware of the consequences of alternatives, the counselor has an obligation to help the client understand the potential consequences of his or her choice. This is not the same as persuasion. It is one thing to help a person be aware of the consequences of the choice he or she has made, and another thing to persuade the client to prefer another alternative.

Premature termination due to external involvements of the counselor has been considered because it has some important implications for other stages of the counseling process. The crux of the problem is the client's intense negative feelings toward the counselor. The situation is just one clear example of a client who experiences strong negative feelings toward the counselor. Other experiences might include: a confrontation by the counselor; influencing the client to consider things he would rather avoid looking at; a time when the client believes nothing valuable is happening. These issues were discussed at length in Chapter 6. The basic point to be made is that whenever something happens in the counseling process that influences the client's feelings toward the counselor, dealing openly with the new feelings has very high priority as an immediate process goal. This principle holds whether the new feelings are negative or positive. Frequently, the counselor must take the initiative to open the issue. When the feelings of the client are negative, the counselor must accept them without hostility or defensiveness. The feelings are the client's and he has a right to them.

The first of two basic strategies to be used in this situation is to
1. help the client explore his feelings and come to some conclusion as to whether they are appropriate. A second is to explore the conditions of
2. the counseling process (including, especially, the counselor's behavior) that influenced the feelings, asking whether it is possible to

change the conditions or not. One must be careful here, for often the client's expression of anger toward the counselor may be a manipulative ploy to control the counselor's actions. A crucial issue to consider is whether it is good or not good for a particular client to be able to manipulate the counselor. For some clients having certain difficulties, being able to manipulate the counselor may have immediate favorable impact.

Premature termination chosen by the client

Another especially critical situation in the counseling process occurs when the client communicates to the counselor that he has rejected the counselor as a viable source of help. This may occur at any stage of counseling. A client, especially a silent client, will communicate this from the very beginning of counseling. Another client may communicate rejection of the counselor later. One may communicate rejection simply by not returning for later sessions. Another might tell the counselor that he feels counseling is not valuable and worthwhile to him and he sees no point in continuing. Sometimes such a statement by a client will be quite appropriate. Counseling is not being of benefit. At other times, especially when counseling is awareness-based, such a response may suggest that the client is fearful about the impact counseling may have on him.

A major first step under such conditions is for the counselor to identify his or her own feelings about being rejected by the client. Fear and anger directed toward the client are likely counselor emotional responses under such conditions. Counselor-trainees are especially likely to respond with anxiety, for being rejected by the client is evaluated as reflecting counselor ineffectiveness. The counselor's goal is to be successful with his or her client. Being told that counseling is not being helpful may represent a serious block to goal attainment, a frustrating situation in which both anxiety and anger are likely responses.

Unfortunately, such emotional responses often interfere with effective counseling. Again, the general principle holds: when stress occurs in the relationship between the client and counselor, it is generally more adaptive to deal openly with the stress than to avoid dealing with it; responding to the stress in the relationship is far more likely to result in favorable consequences than will the avoidance of the stress.

Take as an example an adolescent female who has been seen three times for counseling. At the beginning of the fourth session, she says, "I've been thinking it over and I've pretty well decided that counseling is not doing me any good. Nothing has changed and it doesn't look like anything will. You're a nice person and I don't want to make you feel bad, but counseling has really been a waste of time for me."

Such a client response is likely to make the counselor feel anxious, angry, and, possibly, guilty. The client has challenged the counselor's competency and security. Any counselor not aware of the emotional impact of this client's response would be unlikely to respond effectively at this point.

Borrowing from the basic principle, an effective counselor strategy would appear to be to discuss what is involved in the client's decision. A response such as the following can be facilitative: "You've certainly made it clear that you don't see counseling as being worthwhile for you. First, I want you to know that although what you have told me upsets me, nonetheless, I am glad you did tell me this. Could you tell me how you came to this conclusion?"

Client:	As I said, nothing seems to be changing. Nothing new has happened. We seem to be going "round and round" in circles and never getting anywhere. . . . I don't feel we're getting anywhere with my problem.
Counselor:	I guess this counseling experience has been quite frustrating for you and that you are giving up hope that anything valuable could happen. . . . Could you tell me what you think should be happening here for counseling to be worthwhile for you?
Client:	Well, like we seem to be trying to understand me—my attitudes toward myself, my parents, teachers, and school, and all like that. Well, you know, that's been interesting and all, but it hasn't helped me with my anxiousness when I take tests. Like I took another test just last week. I knew the stuff, but I froze up and failed it just like the others.

Note that at this point the counselor chose to deal with the issue openly. She responded first to her own feelings and then commenced to explore the issue of what should be, but was not, happening. Alternative counselor responses to the client's opening lead might have been, "Well, I guess it's your privilege to decide against further counseling. I wish it could have worked out more favorably for you." Or, "You said counseling has been a real waste of time for you, and that nothing has changed. But I really wonder if that is so? Do you really feel that nothing has changed?" From this case, try to think through the impact each of these response leads would have for the counseling process.

Critical situations like the one given above force the counselor to make serious and important decisions. The counselor must decide whether the client's criticisms that nothing valuable or instrumental to the attainment of outcome goals are valid, or whether they are statements of resistance. If the counselor decides the criticisms are valid, he or she must reassess and reevaluate the approach to counseling.

In intensive counseling, the counselor must always evaluate and reevaluate the appropriateness and efficacy of the intervention strategy. Where it is not being effective, he or she must be willing to change. In the above example, the goal of counseling was to reduce test anxiety. That goal had been determined in earlier counseling sessions. From the client's remarks, it was clear that the counselor's strategy was based on facilitating awareness. The feedback the counselor received from the client was that this strategy was not paying off. The counselor must decide, then, whether persisting with that strategy would eventually pay off, or whether implementing a new strategy would be more likely to achieve the goal of reducing test anxiety. Using systematic desensitization is a very different strategy, which, for this counseling goal, would appear to have a higher likelihood of success.

Termination as a consequence of successful counseling

In the goal-setting stage, the client and counselor determine counseling goals and establish criteria for determining when these goals could be considered attained. In the termination stage, they must consider the criteria, assess the changes that have occurred, and, on this basis, evaluate whether counseling has been successful. If it has been successful, the client's behavior outside of the counselor's office must have changed and the new behaviors must be evaluated as more desirable than the old behaviors. Even in similar cases where counseling has been successful, some important emotions may occur, which must be dealt with.

One of the bases of the kind of intensive counseling described here is the relationship between client and counselor. For counseling to be of maximum impact, the relationship must be uncommonly close and intense. When counseling goals have been attained, it is time for the intense relationship to be terminated. As anyone who has experienced the separation of a loved one can attest, terminating an intense relationship is not easy for anyone involved. The last few moments of the relationship can frequently be the most difficult.

There is a natural tendency to feel a sense of loss, a void, a feeling of loneliness when an intense relationship is to be terminated. Once again, the counselor cannot deal with these feelings by avoiding them. He or she must handle the termination process so that the client feels he or she can be independent of the counselor.

Probably the easiest approach is to review and summarize what has taken place—the stages of counseling and the kinds of changes that have occurred. Once accomplished, it is highly appropriate for the counselor to communicate the impact the counseling experience has had on him or her and the feelings generated toward the client. This makes it easier for the client to share his or her feelings, and, if appropriate, express gratitude. Once this has occurred, formal termination is usually easier.

Frequently, clients feel unsure about whether they are ready to terminate. They have seen things change through counseling, but they have felt that when things went badly they could turn to the counselor for help and support. When termination occurs, the counselor will no longer be available. If the counselor senses such insecurity, it must be discussed before termination can be completed. Of course, it would be wise to anticipate this difficulty and work it through in several sessions prior to termination, but such is not always possible. An appropriate counselor response lead to enter into this area might be, "We certainly have achieved some important changes since we have been together. In fact, it looks as though we have pretty well achieved what we set out to accomplish. Sometimes people who have changed in some respect wonder whether they are really ready to handle situations especially difficult and new situations that they may encounter. I wonder if you might feel that way."

If the client answers no and the counselor accepts this answer as valid, things are fine. If the client says yes, then the insecurity must be explored. If there are situations that both the client and counselor would agree would be difficult for the client to handle, then termination would be premature. If the client says, "I am not sure," and on further discussion he experiences the normal anxiety of entering into a new situation, then the counselor can help the client reassure himself by recalling the previous "new situations" that he has handled so effectively.

An important dimension which emerges from this discussion is that of client dependency on the counselor. Counselors generally believe that it is good and desirable for their clients to be self-reliant—not dependent on others to attain goals that are important to them. However, the issue is considerably more complex. The mere fact that clients seek a counselor's help suggests that in some way client dependence on the counselor is an inherent and unavoidable part of the counseling process. By coming to the counselor for help, the client implies dependency on the counselor for help to deal with whatever concerns he or she wishes to discuss. When goals of counseling are established, it is clear that the client is dependent on the counselor for help in attaining these goals. By continuing in counseling, the client implies that he believes he has a better chance of attaining his counseling-related goals with the counselor's help than without it—clearly a statement of implicit dependency.

There are some important responsibilities associated with being a person on whom another is dependent. One ethical responsibility is that the counselor may not use the client's dependence for his or her own benefit. This is an especially important principle for counselors who enjoy having others dependent upon them (as "mother" or "father" figures).

A second responsibility is to determine the "limits of dependency." It is one thing for a client to be dependent on a counselor for help in attaining goals of counseling; it is another for the client to be dependent on the counselor as a primary source of human caring and interest. Clearly, if perpetuated, the latter would not be in the best interest of either client or counselor. Nor is it in the best interest of the client to seek approval and support from the counselor for every action he undertakes. Eventually, the client must decide on what actions are best, without the counselor's approval. This goal must be attained before counseling can be effectively terminated.

A third area of responsibility is that after the stated goals of counseling are attained, the counselor must help the client become self-reliant in using the new behaviors. The counseling relationship, however intense, is always temporary. When it is terminated, it is generally best for all parties involved to terminate it as fully as possible. This means that at the end of the counseling relationship, the client must be able to function on his own without being dependent upon the counselor for further help.

Criteria for determining success

Borrowing from the content of Chapters 2 and 8, in order to evaluate whether counseling has been successful or not, criteria for success must be established. If counseling has been successful, then some observable change must have occurred. Thus, establishing criteria for success includes identifying the new behaviors that are to occur and the conditions or situations in which such behaviors are to take place. Below are adequately stated goal statements for determining counseling success for each of five clients.

The first client came to the counselor and indicated that when she takes tests she freezes, becomes "uptight," and usually "blows" the tests. The second client reported he just could not seem to make friends. The third client was referred to the counselor by one of his teachers. The teacher indicated that this client starts trouble by causing fights and other disruptions. The fourth client, an adult, came on her own and described herself as a "wishy-washy" person who was afraid to say anything, at any time, and anywhere. The fifth client stated that he had a poor self-image and no self-confidence.

During the goal-setting stage, criteria for determining counseling success were established for each of the five clients. They are stated as follows:

Client 1:   Counseling will be successful when the client takes tests and reports that whatever anxiety is experienced is controllable and does not interfere with her effective performance on the tests.

Client 2:   Counseling will be successful when the client interacts with his peers on the playground and after school, and reports that the group has accepted him as an equal.

Client 3:	Counseling will be successful when three consecutive weeks have passed with not one fighting incident reported by the client or a member of the school faculty.
Client 4:	Counseling will be successful when the client demonstrates that she can assert her position strongly and forcefully on debatable issues, and will be able to demonstrate this when a position contrary to hers is taken by a significant other.
Client 5:	Counseling will be successful when the client stops saying to himself that he is worthless and incompetent even when his performance does not meet his own standards of acceptability.

Note that in all cases the new, more desirable behavior and the situations in which that desirable behavior should occur are clearly specified. For each client counseling would be successful when the respective criteria are considered attained. During the termination stage, client and counselor mutually consider the criteria established during the goal-setting stage and evaluate whether these goals have been attained. The primary purpose of the termination stage, then, is to determine whether counseling has been successful. Another essential goal is that of working through the emotional investment associated with the intensity of close relationship maintained throughout the counseling process.

Case study 5: Doreen—a termination session

This client was a thirty-six-year-old married woman who sought counseling because of several difficulties she was having with handling her own emotions and her relationship with her husband and her three stepchildren. The goals set up in counseling focused on her intrapersonal difficulties. When upset, Doreen would have severe headaches and lock herself in her room for days at a time. The following is a typescript of the eighth and final session of counseling. This typescript demonstrates the termination procedure as discussed in this chapter.

Client 1:	You can ask me how I am—I'm fine, I'm smart.
Counselor 1:	How are you?
Client 2:	I'm fine. I can control myself.
Counselor 2:	I'm glad.
Client 3:	I have problems but they're not way big as they used to be. I lost my temper only one time.
Counselor 3:	In two weeks . . . ?
Client 4:	Yeah. . . .
Counselor 4:	Wonderful.
Client 5:	Yes. I mean—like usual I couldn't find anything to break so I picked up my house slipper and threw it against the wall. My husband, he won't give me a chance to break anything. [*laughing*] He gets all scared. I was picking things up and throwing them and then he gets all shook up; he started picking things up and throwing them. And I said, "Gee, I'm glad I'm helping you." And we both laughed 'cause it was so funny. But it made me feel . . . you know. . . . But he still doesn't understand it . . . but I want to, uh . . . I mean it makes me feel better if. . . .
Counselor 5:	[*interrupting*] Right! To get it out. Sure.
Client 6:	He gets all shook up, because he doesn't see me like that, you know. . . . Well, he's never, I. . . . It's just been lately I've been doing that. . . .
Counselor 6:	That's good. And you're feeling better for it. Headaches? Any headaches?
Client 7:	Well, just that . . . like, I say that one time. . . . But now, maybe I have a headache and I don't even know. It's uh . . . one of the twins . . . he and I are so good friends it's pitiful. And he wants to be with me all the time; he's in the kitchen with me and . . . last night, I was so shocked, I was laying in bed watching TV, 'cause my

husband wanted another show and I
wanted another one. So I stayed in my
room . . . and Billy just walked in and lay
on the bed with me. I mean, I didn't say
one word; but . . . and then he was really
enjoying it. And I was shocked. I mean,
you know. . . . Then he said, you know, "I
wish I could stay up later," and I didn't say
anything. So he said, "Well goodnight,
Mommy." I mean, but, we're friends.
We're having a real big problem with the
other one. Well, I don't know if my husband should; but now when I tell my husband, gee, he did this today again. What
am I going to do? He says, "Well, you
know, he's . . . what he's doing, you cannot blame him for it, because he's sick . . .
or something." Well, I . . . I don't know.
But now Steve's stealing in school and, I
mean, my children are all embarrassed.
. . . They've had money missing in school
and I know it's Steve, because he's
brought the money home and. . . . He's
been buying milk when we haven't given
him any money to buy milk. And . . . so . . .
I don't know. And then, Bill comes home
and says, "Mommy, I'm so ashamed because Steve took some money." But since
Bill had done it before. Remember, I told
you . . . that happened? They went and got
Bill and questioned him. This lady saw the
boy, and she said it was Bill. But she didn't
know we had twins. So, Bill is so hurt. You
know, he said, "You know teachers scold
me because. . . ." And he told her that, "No,
it's my brother. Not me." And then my
other son got embarrassed because he
said everybody's talking about Billy stole
some money because Bill's name is Bill,
and Billy's name is Willy. [*laughing*] I
mean, the whole family's all messed up in
school because of that.

Counselor 7:   But, you're doing a lot. . . .

Client 8:   Oh, yes. Yes. But like I said I . . . worry about the children so. . . . But, it's not as bad as it used to be. I mean . . . uh, I keep thinking well, Steve's going to get hell, but . . . I mean, he won't talk. I . . . I can be mean to him; he won't buy that. I can be real nice to him. . . . He'll just say, "I don't know, I don't know." And twice already, I asked him, I says, "Steve, please tell me how much you took so I can pay back the money. Mommy and Daddy are so embarrassed, but we want to pay the kids back that you. . . ." He said, "I told you I don't know!" And he just walks away, you know. So I told my husband, "You know, I give up. I mean, what am I gonna do?" But it . . . bothers me. I mean, uh . . . and he keeps saying, "I wish . . . I can't wait till we go to Grandma's." So, she's the only one, you know. . . . 'Cause when we see her, first thing he does is cry. Then he tells her his troubles. And us. . . . Bill's not enjoying counseling too much. He says, "Well . . . ." One week . . . the other week he came home happy. I said, "Oh! You know you had a nice time?" He said, "Yeah, we didn't have anything to talk about, so we played." So then this Monday came, he said, "Oh, we're going. . . ." He's happy at going. He came home, y'know, so I said, "What's happened, Bill?" He said, "Nothing"; he went upstairs. So when he came down to my room, I said, "Bill, what happened Monday with the counselor?" He said, "Oh, we talked for ten minutes. . . ." I told him, "Tell him anything you want to." He said, "Yeah, but only ten minutes we talked, and I don't know what to talk about, so we just sat there." And he said he just sat for the rest of the time. And he came home mad. Oh, he was mad. [laugh-

ing] He said, "I don't like this kind." But, Steve, he comes home, like nothing happened, or . . . like he just went for a ride and came home. I worry because I keep wishing I knew what was going on in his mind. If he would just say, "OK, I stole the money." 'Cause we didn't beat him up or anything. We just want to make everything right and help him. And he goes to school and he takes his clothes off. I mean, he unbuttons all his shirt and. . . . He's acting cuckoo in school, the kids come home and tell me, so my husband said, "Gee, we don't know. . . ." I mean, do you think I should tell the teacher . . . uh . . . that he's going to counseling, or . . . ?

Counselor 8: Why don't you wait and see what happens in counseling.

Client 9: I mean, the teacher called me, and she said, "Any help she can give." You know, and . . . but, I don't want her to do something else . . . and, you know, would be different from his counselor. Then we'd really kind of mix him up. But as far as me, I'm just fine. I mean, um.

Counselor 9: I'm glad.

Client 10: I did yesterday what I wouldn't do in my whole life. I mean, uh . . . oh, I don't know. In a way I think I hurt somebody's feelings without being rude, or something like that. Well, my daughter had brought some pizza home for a class, for me to hold . . . in our freezer. And I keep telling her, "Y'know I gotta go shopping. So, we have no room. It's just a small little thing; but . . . you kids are going to have a party. OK, I help you." So three Saturdays went by and nobody picked those pizzas up and . . . I been putting my meat someplace else. . . . So I told Sharen, "Do something about it." She says, "Oh, the kids said just hold it." So what I did was I wrote a little note to the teacher and I sent Willy with the pizzas. The boy just picked up the pizzas and found a place for them. But I told the teacher I was sorry. I didn't want to do this and hurt the kids. But if I keep it any longer, I think they'll only take advantage of it. And it made me feel real good. And when Sharen came home, I said, "Ooo, anybody mad at me?" And she said, "Oh, no. No, nothing. . . ." So, well, I never did that before. I would hold it and hold it. But I thought I'll try this once. I mean, you know . . . well . . . so it made me feel real good . . . I don't know, it's just like I been coming to school. Something . . . to a class . . . I mean I learn, uh . . . you know, to . . . well . . . anyway, it's helped.

Counselor 10: Is there anything else I can help you with?

Client 11: No. I don't think so. Because like I said, because myself . . . I feel fine. It's just that I'm worried about the children. But I can't come here for them.

Counselor 11: That's right.

Client 12: Gee, I said it, that's their problem, huh? [*laughs*]

Counselor 12: That's right. [*laughs*]

Client 13: Oh boy. [*laughs*]

Counselor 13: Yep. [*laughs*]

Client 14: I mean, I want to help, but. . . .

Counselor 14: Are . . . uh . . . any of the counselors seeing your husband?

Client 15: Only one. Only Steve's, but my husband, see, writes down, y'know all week what Steve does . . . anything unusual, and then tells her. I don't know if it helps, but . . . like you said, you know when he does something good . . . uh . . . praise him and all that?

Counselor 15: Yes.

Client 16: Doesn't do anything good. I mean all he does is go to bed on time. Which we tell him is good and all that kind. But that's all he does. The rest of the time he's rude. He's like a big bully and no respect. And he . . . he won't put his clothes in the wash yet. [*laughs*] And he'll go to school with the same clothes and . . . so my husband said, "Well, if it makes you. . . ." Well, twice I've gone I'll go get his clothes, but . . . after that I thought, well, heck, that's too bad and I'm getting tired of, you know. So then, now, the kids are . . . I don't know, whether the kids are trying to help me, or what. But when Steve sits next to them, they'll all move.

Counselor 16:   Um, hmm.

Client 17:   And they did that to him, oh, one night. Everybody moved. So, I said, "What's a matter?" and they said, "Oh, Steve's pajamas smell." So when I went . . . that night, I was surprised, the pajamas were in that basket, the laundry basket. So I said, "See, the kids are catching on then." And now the children, any time they're mad, they just ignore each other. Y'know, they even ignore me or my husband [*laughs*] but that's all right with us. But my husband. I . . . I don't know, I think maybe if my husband did, you know, come like this, he'd understand more. Things seem to bother him a lot now. I mean, when I tell him, "Well, that doesn't bother me," he says, "Well, it should. It bothers me!" [*laughs*]

Counselor 17:   [*laughs*]

Client 18:   I mean, I'm surprised that I . . . lots of things that I don't feel; it's bothering him.

Counselor 18:   Uh, huh.

Client 19:   So I told him in the car, "Why don't you go to counseling? Why don't you try?" He said, "Oh, I don't need it." So, but everything seems . . . I notice now . . . everything's bothering him.

Counselor 19:	Yeah.
Client 20:	I mean, uh, he feels hurt when the kids don't do something or say something. You know now he's feeling hurt because of my oldest daughter. She doesn't kiss him goodnight. And he had a long talk. And she told him she had reason, but she didn't want to tell him. So he's feeling hurt. So I told him, "You know, it doesn't bother me the kids don't kiss me goodnight, as long as I know they love me and they respect me and. . . ." But he said it bothers him. He said because well, affection means something. But like I said, I'm Oriental . . . and, you know we don't have that kind, so it doesn't bother me.
Counselor 20:	Right.
Client 21:	I mean, uh . . . but it's really bothering him. And he told me, he said, "Well, Billy kisses you goodnight." I said, "Well, for a while he did because he thought he had to, since I got married to you."
Counselor 21:	Oh, yeah.
Client 22:	So Billy kisses me goodnight. Well, to me it is OK, but yet, you know, uh . . . it didn't bother me if he did or didn't. And he stopped. I think he was kind of ashamed. You know how boys are when they get to be twelve. And I understand, but my husband doesn't.
Counselor 22:	How are you handling the kinds of . . . hate feelings that you have, Doreen?
Client 23:	Well, that's the only part Steve's doing; I hate him. But I don't want to hurt him. But he, because I hate him, I think of my mother-in-law and I hate her more. I mean, my husband and I argued about my mother-in-law two nights now. He told me, us. . . . Well, I told him . . . the way Steve is . . . and just imagine what's going

	to happen when we go there. I don't want to go.
Counselor 23:	Oh, yeah.
Client 24:	So my husband. . . .
Counselor 24:	[*interrupting*] That's pretty soon, isn't it?
Client 25:	Yeah, after school. I mean, on vacation. So I told him, "I don't want to go, because, well, I don't know." I told him. I learn so much and now I can control myself and maybe I'll just tell her, you know, "Be quiet," or tell her to mind her business, or something. My husband doesn't want me to.
Counselor 25:	Yeah.
Client 26:	He said, "Oh well, can't you just take it for thirty-six hours?" I said, "Well, I don't know . . . the way I feel right now . . . I think I can tell her." And he's getting scared. So he said, "Well, can't you do this for hu . . . mani . . . tarian purpose?" What's that mean?
Counselor 26:	[*laughs*] Just, uh . . . in terms of one human to another, you know.
Client 27:	Oh. That's what he told me. I said, "I don't know, whatever that means, I don't know." He said, that's what he said, "Can I do it for humanitarian purpose?"
Counselor 27:	You do whatever it is you'd like to do that'll make you feel better.
Client 28:	Well, what I was thinking. I don't want to go, yet I'll go, but . . . if I see Steve doing . . . you know, running to her and start crying and saying, "You know, Grandma, Mommy did. . . ." I want to tell her. Or I want to go up and say, "Steve, will you please leave her alone and get away." I never been able to say that, but uh. . . . But that's what he does. It's happened every time. As soon as he sees Grandma, he, he starts crying.
Counselor 28:	And unloads all his problems, troubles.

Client 29:	And she believes him, she does. And my husband and I haven't told her anything about the boys going to counseling, or me, or anything, you know; my husband don't want me to. . . . So I told my husband, "If it gets worse, I'm going to tell her. Everything that's happening here." And all the letters I write, I kinda lie a little bit. Tell 'em how good the children are and all that, but . . . I guess that's for humanitarian purpose. No, but. . . . It's too bad. Steve seems to be getting worse than better. But I was just thinking. Well, it's just like me. For a while I was getting terrible. I mean a real upset and so maybe it's his turn to kinda mess it up a little bit. I'm hoping, you know.
Counselor 29:	Yeah, I'm sure he's struggling; trying to find himself, you know. And this is uh . . . coming out in all kinds of ways.
Client 30:	Well, I hope the counselor is having, you know, success with Steve. Because he don't talk. He just don't talk. I mean at home they blah, blah. But when we go out to people, he don't talk. Only Grandma, is the only time. And I tried to tell Bill, "Tell him. Tell the man." He said, "Well, what am I going to tell him?" I said, "Tell the man if you like school or if you don't like your teachers." He said, "Oh, I'm not. . . ." I said, "No, tell him anything. If you're mad at me, or if you're mad at daddy, or you know. . . . You tell him." But Bill doesn't understand. But, he says he doesn't like to talk. He said, "I don't like to talk. So we just sit." But he'll . . . he'll answer questions. But, they won't just talk.
Counselor 30:	Yeah. . . . [*pause*]
Client 31:	But other than that. . . .
Counselor 31:	It seems to me that uh. . . .

Client 32:	Oh. And I met a boy from Purdue. He, my husband's cousin, came to visit and he brought a boy from Purdue. And we were talking. And then he brought uh . . . he's taking psychology.
Counselor 32:	Oh, yeah.
Client 33:	So then, uh. . . . And I just told him. "Oh! I know a psychologist!" He says, "You do?" He said, "Who?" and I said, "Oh, a Dr. _____," and he said, "Hey! I read some of his . . . !" I said, "He's the one!" "You know him?" I said, "Oh yeah." My husband, he looked at me. . . . [*both laugh*] So this boy was telling me about, he went and got analyzed. You know.
Counselor 33:	Oh, yeah.
Client 34:	He had his problems, too, and I looked at him and I said, "I'll bet you I know what your problem is," and he says, "Oh." And then he went and got his handbag with all his junk. But he said he feels good, going and talking like that. So he's taking a course. And he said he read a lot of yours; they got at his school. All these papers and stuff.
Counselor 34:	I figured it does. [*laughs*]
Client 35:	Well, that's good. Boy, I wish my husband would come.
Counselor 35:	Well, if he . . . if he would ever like to . . . uh . . . all he has to do is call.
Client 36:	Well, he won't. I mean, uh . . . maybe I can help him at home. [*laughs*]
Counselor 36:	Yeah. Well. [*both talk together*]
Client 37:	He always tells me I'm smart-alecky, because . . . just because, you know, I think I know uh. . . .
Counselor 37:	Well, you do.
Client 38:	Well, that's good. That means I don't have to see you anymore. [*laughs*]
Counselor 38:	Nope [*laughs*] and that's good, huh? [*both laugh*]

Client 39:	But for the first time I have to tell someone it's so good not to be able to fear anymore.
Counselor 39:	I'm glad. [*laughs*] I really am.
Client 40:	[*laughs*] I hope I never see you again. [*both laugh*]
Counselor 40:	Wonderful!
Client 41:	Boy! That makes me feel good.
Counselor 41:	Yeah.
Client 42:	Now I can go out and lick the world. [*laughs*]
Counselor 42:	You can. You're one person that can. I mean that. [*serious*]
Client 43:	I don't know. It's just that I've learned to tell myself everytime I do something, or I get upset. I tell myself, "Oh, you're doing it." And my husband reminds me all the time, too, that I'm upsetting myself. 'Cause sometimes I get mad and I say, "Oh, just because of Steve." And he says, "No, just because of you." Which is true. Well, that's good then. I'll go home and let you go home. [*laughs*]
Counselor 43:	Well . . . yeah, if anything were to happen, although I don't think it will, if it would, just give me a call.
Client 44:	Oh. Thank you. [*laughs*]
Counselor 44:	I'm always here. And it's been very nice talking to you and I've enjoyed it very much.
Client 45:	Like I said it's like coming to school. I found out a lot about myself. I'm not ugly. I'm not mean. I'm not [*laughs*] . . . I'm terrific.
Counselor 45:	That's right. You sure are.
Client 46:	Thank you. Bye, bye.
Counselor 46:	Goodbye.
Client 47:	I hope I never have to see you again.

Appendix A. An outline for case write-ups

The effective counselor must pay continuous attention to four sets of variables. <u>The first set of variables relate to attributes and characteristics of the client.</u> Some critical questions here are: <u>Who is this person I am trying to help? How does he or she view self? Others? What are his or her views about a personal future? How do I perceive this person as an affective being? What critical events of the past have contributed to present-day behavior and outlooks?</u>

<u>A second set of variables counselors must confront relate to their behavior and underlying attitudes and feelings toward their clients.</u> Falling into this category are questions such as: <u>What feelings do I experience toward this client,</u> and <u>How do the feelings I experience influence my tendency to block or facilitate open communication?</u> Other critical questions a counselor must confront are: <u>Who in my past does this client remind me of? Am I transferring feelings from that past person to his client?</u>

[handwritten marginalia: "1. — who she — vulnerable — swayed by / Mom / Father but / Parenting / 2. Warmth Respect Openness Confidence / No one past"]

3.   A third set of factors relate to an assessment of the state of the relationship in the present: How deep is the level of trust? How safe does each feel with the other? If things are not developing in a satisfactory manner, what can be done to improve the situation?

4   A fourth set of factors involve the application of principles of human behavior in offering help to this client. Here the essential questions for the practitioner are: What principles of human behavior help me to understand this client? What theories of counseling offer me ideas as to how I can effectively help this client?

The effective counselor thinks about all these questions during the counseling session as well as during the period after the session in which he or she critiques the session. The outline that follows is offered to help counselors organize their thoughts about the counseling session during the critiquing activity. The outline can be especially useful for developing case write-ups as a part of a counseling practicum experience.

Initial concerns

Why did the client approach you (or why did you approach the client)? What were the important concerns and circumstances that brought the two of you together? If third parties are involved (such as a teacher or parent), what were the observations and concerns of the third party? (This section will be especially important during your first contact with a client. If you see the client in subsequent sessions, after the first session, this section should be devoted to a discussion on how you plan to follow up after the initial session.)

Overview and analysis of the session

What did you talk about? What were the dominant issues and themes for this session? What specific process and outcome goals were you trying to achieve? What results were you hoping would occur: New insights and awarenesses? Change of certain perceptions? To confront the client with some important observations? What made these goals important?

Observations and diagnostic assessment of the client and life space circumstances

What observations and impressions do you have about your client and his or her life space? Would you describe your client as: Open? Closed? Comfortable? Threatened? Aware of personal feelings or closed to them? Hostile? Resistant?

Who are the significant others in the client's life and what kind of relationship exists with each of them? What factors or circumstances in the client's life space relate to the client's concerns and will help you to understand him or her? What hypotheses and speculations do you have about your client and what is the basis for them?

Observations about self

What observations did you make about yourself during this session? What did you do that you liked? Disliked? Every counselor experiences anxieties about what to say, how to follow through, whether he or she accurately understood feelings, whether a critical point in the session was handled effectively, etc. It is especially useful to focus on events such as these and analyze them in your critique.

Plans for next session

How do you hope to follow up in subsequent sessions? What issues and concerns do you think are worthwhile to explore? What process goals will you try to accomplish?

Help!

Specifically what kind of help would you like, either from your practicum supervisor or from fellow students, about this client, this session, and your helping efforts?

Appendix B.   Helping effectiveness scale

Although subjective measures, such as consumer satisfaction measures, have a low status in the repertoire of evaluation tools, the information gathered from these methods may be useful at times. In counseling this is true, especially when these measures are used with measures of behavior change. The Helping Effectiveness Scale is presented as a consumer satisfaction measure of help received by persons from professional helpers.

Helping effectiveness scale

Directions

The task is to determine how you feel about the help you have received. For the purpose of this scale the word "helper" is used

D. J. Delaney, S. H. Silverman & P. B. McDermott, *Development and evaluation of the Illinois Helping Effectiveness Scale* (Urbana: University of Illinois, 1973).

for helpers, counselor, counselors, etc. You are asked to rate each of the following statements on a five-point scale on your answer sheet as follows:

1. I *strongly disagree* with the statement

2. I *disagree* with the statement

3. I'm *not sure* whether I disagree or agree with the statement

4. I *agree* with the statement

5. I *strongly agree* with the statement

For example: Item A—The helper was friendly. If you were to *agree* with this statement, you would answer in space No. 4 on your answer sheet. If you were to *strongly disagree,* you would answer in space No. 1 on your answer sheet. A similar procedure is used for *strongly agree* (space No. 5), *disagree* (space No. 2), and *not sure* (space No. 3).

Please work quickly and answer each statement with the first feeling about the statement that comes to your mind. Remember also that there should be only a few items about which you are not sure, whether you agree or disagree.

1. I feel free to come back

2. My helper talked in terms that I could understand

3. My helper listened to me

4. The helper is a very "human" person

5. The helper was very patient

6. I felt secure in my relationship with the helper

7. I was open, honest, and genuine with the helper

8. The helper was a warm, sincere individual

9. My helper was friendly

10. I understood what my helper said

11. The helper's tone of voice encouraged me

12. The helper creates a feeling of "warmth" in the relationship

13. The help was quite worthwhile

14. The helper's remarks made things clearer for me

15.   The things we did seemed worthwhile

16.   Overall, the experience was good

17.   The helper gave the impression of "feeling at ease"

18.   Generally, the helper was well-organized

19.   I felt a sense of satisfaction

20.   The helper understood my feelings completely

21.   The helper had a casual and relaxed manner of opening the interview

22.   The sessions seemed worthwhile

23.   The content was good

24.   The types of questions asked were good

25.   The helper answered my questions to my satisfaction

26.   The helper exhibited professional dignity and bearing in our relationship

27.   The helper increased my general knowledge

28.   Homework assignments were helpful

29.   Homework assignments were helpful in understanding the issues

30.   Things done were easy to follow

31.   I felt the helper would have jumped on me if I said the "wrong" thing

32.   I felt like a misguided delinquent around the helper

33.   I felt frustrated with the helper

34.   The helper's language was confused

35.   The helper was uncertain of himself

36.   The helper frightened me

37.   The helper behaved as if the interview(s) was a routine, mechanical process

38.   The helper pushed me into saying things that weren't really true

39.   The helper was artificial in his behavior

40.   I distrusted the helper

41.   I was tricked into relating confidences I did not wish to disclose

42. The helper insists on always being "right"

43. The helper has a condescending attitude

44. The helper gives the impression of being intellectually aloof from me

45. I often had the feeling that the helper talked too much

46. The helper was awkward in his behavior

Appendix C. Specific procedures for relaxation training and exemplary typescript

In Chapter 9, systematic desensitization was described as one of several counseling strategies based on providing careful verbal instructions to the client. In this appendix, specific procedures for providing training in progressive relaxation are described in detail. Also presented is an actual typescript of its application with a client who had debilitating fear of riding airplanes.

Procedures for progressive relaxation training

Training for progressive relaxation begins by explaining to the client that this is the most important procedure in the treatment and, therefore, must be mastered if counseling is to have any chance of being successful. The following is the method:

The client should be seated in an overstuffed chair. Legs should be extended, head resting on the back of the chair, and arms resting on the arms of the chair. No part of the body should require the use of muscles for support. The room should be quiet and the lights dimmed. The subject should then be put through relaxation exercises. The instructions are:

Hold the arms of the chair quite tightly. I want you to observe certain things that are a result of your holding this chair tightly. First of all, there are certain sensations. To begin with, you have sensations in your hands; you may experience other sensations. With your right hand, point out to me all the places where you get any kind of feeling that seems to be the result of holding the chair tightly. Now let go of the chair and notice the different feelings entering the relaxing muscles. We are now going to go through most of your body. As you tense and relax each of these muscles, focusing on the sensations, you will begin to learn the difference between a state of tension and a state of complete relaxation. As you learn this, you will become deeply relaxed, more deeply relaxed than you have ever been before.

Now, I want you to make a fist with your right hand, tensing the muscles of your right hand and forearm; tense them until they tremble. Feel the muscles pull across your fingers and the lower part of your forearm (hold the fist tightly for five to seven seconds). Now, just release your fist and relax. Pay attention to the muscles of your right hand and forearm as they relax. Note how those muscles feel as relaxation flows through them. (Relaxation period should last from ten to twenty seconds.)

Again tense the muscles of your right hand and forearm. Pay attention to the muscles involved. Notice how the muscles pull across the top of the hand in the fingers and in the upper and lower parts of the forearm. Now, let the hand go limp. Feel how relaxation flows over the hand and forearm. Your hand and forearm are becoming deeply relaxed, more deeply relaxed than ever before. Each time we do this, you'll relax even more until your arm and hand are completely relaxed with no tension at all, warm and relaxed.

(Instruct the client to raise a finger if his right hand and forearm are completely relaxed; this usually takes from two to four tries.) Using the same procedure, have the subject tense his right biceps, leaving his hand and forearm on the chair. Proceed in the same manner as above, in a hypnotic monotone, using the right (or left) hand as a reference point. For example, move on when the client reports his right (or left) biceps feels as completely relaxed as his right (or left) hand and forearm.

The following statements can be used to put the client into a relaxed state:

1.   You are feeling sensations of numbness or tingling.

2.   You are experiencing the effortless, pleasant feelings of relaxation.

3.   Release the muscles and feel how relaxation flows in.

4.   Feel the sensations of warmth and relaxation.

5.   Just let yourself sink deeper and heavier into the chair . . . heavier . . . and deeper.

6.   A pleasant feeling of warmth and heaviness is entering your body as you become more and more deeply relaxed . . . more comfortably relaxed.

7.   Growing deeper and still deeper, somehow getting even heavier . . . and more relaxed.

8.   Each time you exhale, you are getting more relaxed . more and more relaxed, deeply relaxed.

9.   You are letting your muscles go further and further into relaxation; they are becoming more loose . . . loose and heavy, and relaxed.

10.   Your breathing is becoming easier and more rhythmical, no energy is being used.

11.   Your body is feeling very heavy and calm.

12.   Just breathe right out, relaxing and enjoying the soothing relief; all the muscles of your body are becoming more relaxed every time you exhale. Go on breathing normally, easily, freely, completely relaxed.

13.   Continue relaxing for awhile, enjoying the calm, pleasant sensation of deep, total relaxation; your hands and arms are limp, your shoulders resting naturally, your face and neck muscles relaxed and serene.

14.   Breathe deeply, in and out, in and out.

15.   The tensions are vanishing from your forehead.

16.   You are letting the muscles of your _____
relax; continue relaxing until they are as relaxed as the muscles
of your _____ .

17.   You can feel how it is to be completely relaxed.

18.   You can tell the difference between a state of tenseness
and a state of complete relaxation.

Having relaxed the right (or dominant) hand, forearm, and biceps, the
counselor should proceed to other gross-muscle groups in the same
manner.

1.   For the right (or left) hand and forearm: You can feel the
muscles and skin of your left hand pulling over the knuckles.

2.   For the right (or left) biceps, proceed as in step 1.

3.   For the muscles of forehead and top of face: Frown
hard, tensing the muscles of forehead and top of the face. Relax.
You can feel the tensions vanishing from your forehead.

4.   Squinch your eyes tightly and wrinkle up your nose.
Tighter, tighter; you can notice the tension around your eyes
and nose; now, relax; you are letting all the muscles around your
eyes and nose completely relax and the relaxation spreads over
your entire face. You can observe the difference between tension
and complete relaxation as you let your muscles become completely and deeply relaxed.

5.   Draw the corners of your mouth back, feeling the jaw
and cheek muscles pull, and noticing the tension in your cheek
and jaw muscles.

6.   Push your head forward pressing your chin against
your chest, feeling the muscles in your neck pull.

7.   Pull your shoulders back, feeling the muscles become
tighter in your chest and back.

8.   Pull your stomach in and try to push it against your
backbone. Feel the muscles tighten.

9.   Push your stomach out making the muscles tighter, as
if you expect someone to punch you in the stomach.

10.   Tighten the muscles of your right upper leg; feel one
muscle on top and two muscles on the bottom of the upper leg
tighten.

11.   Push your toes forward arching your right foot, keeping your heel on the floor. You can feel the muscles tighten in the under portion of your right calf. Feel the pressure as if something were pushing up under the arch.

12.   Keeping your heel on the floor, pull your foot back, feeling the muscles in the upper portion of your calf pull tightly.

13.   Now your left upper leg.

14.   Now your left under-portion of the calf.

15.   Now your left upper-portion of the calf.

For most muscle groups, it will only be necessary to tense and relax the muscles twice. However, for certain stubborn muscle groups, it may be necessary to go through the tension-release process three or four times in order to reach an optimal state of relaxation. Many clients find the tension-release cycle more effective when they inhale deeply and hold their breath while tensing muscles and then exhale while releasing the muscles. When a muscle group does not respond after four trials, move on and return to it later. It must be remembered that some clients might develop muscle cramps from prolonged tensing of the muscles. If this occurs, cut a few seconds off the tensing period and instruct the client not to tense the muscles quite so hard.

Clients will be brought back to "normal" by means of the numerical method of trance termination: "I am going to count from one to four. On the count of one, start moving your legs; two, your fingers and hands; three, your head; and four, open your eyes and sit up. One, move your legs; two, now your fingers and hands; three, move your head around; four, open your eyes and sit up." The counselor should not allow the client to leave the chair until it appears that he or she has returned to a relatively normal state. All clients will be asked if they feel alert before they leave.

All clients will be asked to try to practice twice a day for not more than fifteen minutes each time. These practice sessions should be at least three hours apart. The practice sessions should be held when the client is alone. It should be suggested to each client that his second practice session could be accomplished while lying in bed at night just before going to sleep.

By the third session, if the client has been practicing relatively well, relaxation can be induced by a modified-relaxation-period method as follows:

1.   Stretch out both arms, making a tighter and tighter fist. Now relax.

2.   Face (same as original method).

3.   Neck (same as original method).

4.   Chest (same as original method).

5.   Stomach (same as original method).

6.   Stretch out both legs, pointing your toes outward, and tense up all the muscles in your legs; make the muscles tighter and tighter. Now relax.

Desensitization proper

This technique, or procedure, is used together with training in progressive relaxation to help a client overcome a fear or phobia, such as height, water, closed spaces, elevators, darkness, etc. The client is first trained in progressive relaxation, and then, with an established hierarchy of anxiety-producing stimuli, is systematically desensitized to these stimuli.

The hierarchy may be a series of statements that will help the client recall an experience, photos or other pictures that may help recall, or the actual stimuli, if this is feasible. The following explanations may be given the client:

1.   Procedure: The specific technique we will be using is called desensitization. This method of treatment is based on the picturing of situations in your mind while you are completely relaxed. You will find yourself more relaxed than you have ever been before. In case you are wondering if my objective is hypnosis, be assured it is not. At no time during this treatment will you be hypnotized. You will simply be in a state of very deep relaxation, which you should find very comfortable. Relaxation alone can be used to reduce tension. However, the ability to relax completely will take time for you to acquire. Therefore, it will be necessary for you to practice the technique of relaxation between our sessions.

2.   Construction of anxiety hierarchy: There are probably certain situations in which you will find yourself becoming more tense than others. I have here a set of cards, each of which has a

situation described on it. I would like you to arrange these cards so that the situation in which you feel most comfortable comes first, followed by those situations in which you feel less and less comfortable. The last card in your arrangement should contain the situation in which you feel the most uncomfortable.

The client's imagery should be tested as soon as he has been relaxed in the second session as follows:

I would like to test your ability to visualize objects. With your eyes closed, try to visualize yourself lying in bed in your room just before going to sleep. Can you see it? Try to describe what you are now imagining in your mind. OK, erase that image and continue relaxing.

The subject's visualization should at least be as clear as a vivid memory. With practice, images should become clearer. The client should be made to realize that he or she should visualize the situations as if he or she were there, not simply watching self.

Next, the client should be told that he or she is going to begin working on the items on the tension scale and that he or she will be asked to picture these items in his or her mind, with the easiest situation on the tension scale first. He or she should also be told that if at any time a feeling of uneasiness or tension develops, it should be signaled by raising the right forefinger. If either the client signals anxiety or the counselor notices that the client is tensing up, the client should be instructed to immediately erase the image from his or her mind and to continue relaxing. The client should then be asked in which muscles he or she felt tension. The counselor should then instruct the client to tense and relax these muscles and to continue to relax until he or she is back to a pre-anxiety state of complete relaxation. The counselor should then go back one step in the hierarchy. If no anxiety has been evoked by the presentation of this item, the counselor returns to the previous anxiety-evoking item, having the client visualize it now for only three to five seconds. If no anxiety is felt during this brief presentation, the counselor proceeds to work through that item, and then introduces the next item on the hierarchy. Any time anxiety is felt, the same procedure should be followed. However, whenever anxiety to the same item is signaled more than once in a single session, the client should be asked if there was less tension present the second time. In addition, sometimes the steps in the anxiety hierarchy may be too great. When this is the case, interpolation of new items between steps may be necessary.

The general procedure should be as follows: Each item should be presented three consecutive times unless anxiety is present. Each item should be visualized for five seconds. If no anxiety has been signaled, thirty to forty-five seconds should be allowed to elapse before the item is presented a second time, for ten seconds; if no anxiety has been signaled, twenty seconds should be allowed to elapse before the item is presented a third time, for fifteen seconds. As each item is completed in this manner, attention is placed on the next item in the hierarchy.

The first item in the hierarchy should be made very easy so that the client can gain experience with the procedure. For example, the client becomes experienced when he or she can picture scenes while deeply relaxed, and then be able to switch them off when no anxiety is present.

The counselor must possess good clinical sensitivity, if the treatment is to be successful, for he or she must know when to go back, when to construct new items, and when to move up the hierarchy.

At the beginning of each session, the subject should be reminded about the importance of visualizing the scenes as vividly as possible. Reminders to signal anxiety should also be stressed. Every session should begin with the next to the last item that has been successfully completed in a previous session. Every session should be ended with the presentation of an item that has not evoked any anxiety. Most clients should be able to go through the entire hierarchy in five sessions.

The following is a demonstration of the use of systematic desensitization in the treatment of a phobia reaction—flying as a passenger in an airplane. This is a segment from the fourth session in the use of this strategy, the seventh session in the counseling process.

Counselor: You're completely relaxed, at ease. There's no tension anywhere in your body. Your arms and legs, completely sinking down into the couch. Now, I would like to test your ability to visualize objects with your eyes closed; try to visualize yourself in a pleasant situation. Visualize the situation as if you were there, not simply watching yourself. Do

you have a mental picture? All right, try
to describe to me what you are now imagining in your mind.

Client: [*Client describes a scene at home with her
husband. Due to her state of relaxation her
voice is too faint to be picked up on the tape.*]

Counselor: All right, fine, erase that scene from your
mind. Now, we are going to begin work-
ing on the items in your tension scale. I'm
going to request that you picture certain
situations in your mind. If at any time you
begin to feel uneasy or tense, I would like
you to signal by raising your right
forefinger about an inch.

Now I want you to imagine that you are in
your home. It's very cool and comfortable
and you are seated near the telephone.
[*pause*] All right, stop imagining this
scene. Now, if that scene didn't worry
you, if you felt nothing, don't do anything. If that scene disturbed you, raise
your right finger. All right, just keep on
relaxing.

Now, I want you to imagine that you're
seated at the telephone and you're talking
to an airline's clerk and you're making a
reservation for an airplane trip. [*pause*]
Now, stop imagining that. Now, if imagining that disturbed you even a very small
bit, I want you to raise your right index
finger. If it didn't worry you, do nothing.
Now once again, I want you to imagine
that you're seated at the telephone, you're
talking to the airline's clerk, you're making reservations for an air trip. [*pause*] All
right, stop imagining that. If you felt any
disturbance, raise your right index finger; all right, just keep on relaxing. Concentrate on your muscles. Sink deeply
into the couch, very, very relaxed.

Now, I want you to imagine yourself in

front of the airline's office. You enter, you walk to the counter, then you purchase a ticket. [*pause*] Now, stop imagining that. Now, if imagining that disturbed you even a small bit, I want you to raise your right index finger. If you felt nothing, do nothing. Fine, concentrate on your muscles. Sink deeply into your calm, relaxed state.

Now, I want you to imagine that you're in an automobile. You're approaching the air terminal, the car stops in front of the terminal, you get out, and you walk into the terminal. [*pause*] All right, erase that image from your mind. If the image that you saw disturbed you, raise your right index finger. Fine, just keep on relaxing. Once more, imagine that you're in an automobile. You're approaching the air terminal, you stop in front, get out, you walk into the terminal. [*pause*] All right, erase that from your mind. If you felt any disturbance, raise your right index finger.

Imagine, once more, you're in an automobile. You look out and you see the air terminal. The car stops in front, you get out, and you walk into the building. [*pause*] All right, now stop imagining that. Just relax. Concentrate on your muscles. If you felt any disturbance, raise your right index finger. Very well.

Now, I would like you to imagine that you are following a redcap, who is carrying your luggage. You walk up to the check-in counter, you check in your luggage. [*pause*] Now, stop imagining that. Now, if imagining that disturbed you even the smallest amount, I want you to raise your right index finger. If it didn't, do nothing. Now, once again, I want you to imagine that you are following a redcap who's carrying your luggage. You walk up to the counter, your luggage is weighed in, you talk with the clerk, she examines your ticket. [*pause*] All right, stop imagining that. If you felt any disturbance, any tension, I would like you to raise your right index finger. All right, continue relaxing. You're experiencing a state of complete relaxation, there's no tension in your body. You feel very calm, very relaxed. All right, imagine that you're sitting in the terminal; you're waiting. You look out of the window and you see planes departing. [*pause*] Now, stop imagining that. If you felt disturbed, even a small amount, I want you to raise your right index finger. If it didn't worry you, do nothing.

Once again, you're sitting in the waiting room, you're waiting for a plane. You look out of the window and you see planes departing. [*pause*] Now, erase that image from your mind. Continue relaxing. If you felt any disturbance, any tension, raise your right index finger. All right, just keep on relaxing. Concentrate on your muscles.

Now, I want you to picture that you're walking through the terminal towards the boarding gate. You arrive at the gate. You have your ticket checked. [*pause*] Now, stop imagining that. If that image disturbed you, even a small bit, I want you to raise your right index finger. Just relax. In what muscles did you feel tension?

Client:	My head.
Counselor:	All right, squinch up the muscles of your forehead and your eyes.
Client:	I mean inside of my brain.
Counselor:	Oh, sorry.
Client:	I'm relaxed now.

Counselor: Relax all of the muscles of your body. Feel the relaxation flow through. Your arms and legs are limp, very relaxed. Sink right down into the couch.

Now, once again, I want you to imagine that you're walking through the terminal towards the boarding gate. You arrive at the gate, take out your ticket, and have your ticket checked. [*pause*] Now, stop imagining that. If imagining that disturbed you, raise your right index finger. Concentrate on your muscles, just keep on relaxing.

Now, once again, you get up from the seat, and you walk through the terminal towards the boarding gate. You arrive at the gate, there's a cluster of people standing around, you wait your turn. Then you have your ticket checked. [*pause*] Now, stop imagining that. If you felt any disturbance at all, even the smallest amount, I want you to raise your right index finger. All right, relax. There's no tension in your body, you're completely relaxed.

Imagine that you're in the waiting room, you're sitting there, you're reading the newspaper, you glance out of the window, and you see planes. [*pause*] All right, stop imagining that. If that scene disturbed you even a small amount, I want you to raise your right index finger. Very good, continue to relax. Concentrate on your muscles.

Again, I would like you to imagine that you're sitting in the waiting room. You look out of the window and you see planes. There are many planes, they're landing, they're taxiing towards the building. You look into the distance and you see another plane coming in. [*pause*] All right, stop imagining that. If you felt any tension imagining that scene, raise your right

index finger. Fine, keep on relaxing. Sink
right down into the couch. You're completely at ease, no tension anywhere in
your body.

All right, now imagine that you're sitting
in the waiting room. You get up, you walk
down the corridor towards the boarding
gate. [*pause*] Now, stop imagining that. If
you felt any disturbance at all, even a
small bit, I want you to raise your right
index finger. All right, relax. Concentrate
on your muscles. There's no tension in
your body, the muscles of your legs and
your arms are limp, relaxed. Completely
at ease.

Index